The Providential Life & Heritage of Henry Obookiah

OBOOKIAH,

A NATIVE OF OWHYHEE.

The Providential Life & Heritage of Henry Obookiah

WHY DID MISSIONARIES COME TO HAWAI'I FROM NEW ENGLAND AND TAHITI?

CHRISTOPHER L. COOK

PA'A STUDIOS
WAIMEA, KAUA'I, HAWAI'I

Copyright © Christopher L. Cook, 2015
First published in 2015 by Pa'a Studios - Christopher L. Cook
Post Office Box 761 Waimea, Hawai'i 96796

First Edition - The Providential Life & Heritage of Henry Obookiah

ISBN -13:978-0692440964 (Christopher L. Cook)
ISBN -10:0692440968

Printed in the United States of America
Text set in Garamond Premier Pro. Titles set in American Scribe from Three Islands Press.

Hawaiian language Bible scriptures taken from 1839 edition of Hawaiian Bible
Ka Palapala Hemolele A Iehova Ko Kakou Akua.

English language Bible scriptures taken from the *King James Bible.*

Text of *Memoirs of Henry Obookiah* and frontispiece engraving of Obookiah taken from
New Haven, Nathan Whiting edition published 1819.

Edward Welles Dwight portrait courtesy Norman Rockwell Museum Archives,
Dwight Collection; painted by J.P. Rosseter in 1809, water color on paper.

Caleb Brintnall portrait by Thomas Prichard Rossiter c. 1840-1845, courtesy Dodds Family.

Maps from collection of Christopher L. Cook.

All photographs except where noted by Christopher L. Cook.

Author photo by Leland A. Cook.

✳ *To my devoted wife,*
Evelyn Eileen Simpson Cook

And to

Deborah Liʻikapeka Lee and the ʻŌpūkahaʻia ʻOhana
Psalm 112:6, "A Righteous Man is Remembered Forever."

The descendants of Captain Caleb Brintnall and his family,
especially James Dodds and Peter Brintnall Cooper

HEBREWS 11:13-16

These all died in faith, not having received the promises, but having seen them afar off, and were persuaded of them, and embraced them, and confessed that they were strangers and pilgrims on the earth.

For they that say such things declare plainly that they seek a country.

And truly, if they had been mindful of that country from whence they came out, they might have had opportunity to have returned.

But now they desire a better country, that is, an heavenly; wherefore God is not ashamed to be called their God: for he hath prepared for them a city.

A make aku la kela poe a pau, iloko o ka manaoio, aole hoi i loaa ia lakou na mea i oleloia mai, aka i ko lakou ike ana ia mau mea i kahi loihi, ua paulele ilaila me ka olioli, a ua hai aku ia lakou iho, he poe kanaka e, he poe malihini ma ka honua.

A o ka poe i hai aku pela, ua hoike maopopo lakou i ko lakou imi ana i wahi e noho ai.

No ka mea, ina i manao lakou i kela aina a lakou i haalele ai, ua hiki no ia lakou ke hoi aku ilaila.

Aka, ua makemake lakou i [aina] maikai aku, oia o ko ka lani. No ia mea, aole ke Akua i hilahila ia lakou ke kapaia oia he Akua no lakou, no ka mea ua hoomakaukau oia i kulanakauhale no lakou.

ISAIAH 49:1

Listen, O isles, unto me; and hearken, ye people, from far;

E haliu mai oukou iau, e na aina, E hoolohe hoi oukou, e na lahui-kanaka, ma kahi mamao aku; .

1 KINGS 9:27

And Hiram sent in the navy his servants, shipmen that had knowledge of the sea, with the servants of Solomon.

And they came to Ophir, and fetched from thence gold, four hundred and twenty talents, and brought it to king Solomon.

Hoouna ae la hoi o Hirama i kona poe kauwa, na mea holomoku i ike i ke kai, me na kauwa a Solomona.

Holo ae la lakou i Opera, a lawe mai lakou mai laila mai, i ke gula eha haneri me ka iwakalua talena, a lawe hoi ia i ke Lii ia Solomona.

Events of seemingly small importance in the view of those witnessing them, assume enlarged proportions when viewed through the medium of the historic past. Many events in the early history of the Hawaiian Islands most forcibly and remarkably illustrate this assertion.

The Rev. Samuel Damon, Honolulu - 1870

CONTENTS

FOREWORD

All of us who live in Hawai'i, especially those of us who have an interest in our history, should be deeply indebted to Chris Cook for his detailed and inspirational volume *The Providential Life & Heritage of Henry Obookiah*. Through extensive research and personal interviews with descendants of some of those involved with Hawai'i's Christian history, Chris has put together a masterful volume that is not only historically accurate but also spiritually inspiring. One can see the invisible hand of Divine Providence throughout its pages as Henry's story unfolds.

From Henry's narrow escape from the edge of a spear aimed at him, to his untimely death at the Foreign Mission School, to the landing of the brig *Thaddeus* in Kona Bay, Chris paints a masterpiece of words that transports the reader back to those formative days. He points out that the subsequent Hawaiian revival, which changed the course of our history, had its genesis in the life and legacy of this humble Native Hawaiian youth.

Out of all that I have read on Hawaiian history, and especially it's religious heritage, *The Providential Life & Heritage of Henry Obookiah* stands alone. Be blessed. You are in for an adventure.

Aloha,
Danny Lehmann
Director, Youth With A Mission, Hawai'i

PREFACE

The Providential Life & Heritage of Henry Obookiah brings together an expansion and exploration of the slim little book first published in 1818 in New Haven that changed Hawai'i forever–*Memoirs of Henry Obookiah: A Native of Owhyhee.*

In writing this book I have undertaken careful and persistent primary research in Hawai'i and New England. This labor has brought to light new episodes in the life of Henry Obookiah (Ōpūkaha'ia as he was known in Hawai'i), and fresh insights into events that determined his fate, and the fate of Hawai'i once Christianity arrived in the Islands.

Decades of research, study, travel, photography, and writing in Hawai'i and New England, and beyond have gone into the creation of *The Providential Life & Heritage of Henry Obookiah.* I have been seeking a fuller picture of the life of an extraordinary Native Hawaiian scholar and Christian, Henry Obookiah. I also document how Henry's life led to the sending of the pioneer company of the Sandwich Islands Mission to Hawai'i.

Obookiah lived for about thirty years, his exact birth date is unknown. During his short life the path of this adventurous Native Hawaiian youth swept across a wide range of the world. Improbably, Obookiah, a youth from rural Ka'ū, served as the key link in the chain of events that led to the sending of missionaries to the Islands by the American Board of Commissioners for Foreign Missions. Remove Henry Obookiah's scholarly work in preserving the Hawaiian language, delete the love he drew out of staunch New England Christians, silence his Macedonian cry to the Second Great Awakening church in America, and Hawai'i today would be a lesser place.

The coming of the Gospel to Hawai'i was an epic event in the global history of Christianity. From the Native Hawaiian perspective, their ancient religion embodied an amalgam of the religions of their homelands located in the Pacific Islands and Southeast Asia; their ancient belief system reached its farthest eastern spread prior to AD 1000 when the first settlers landed on the beaches of Hawai'i. In 1820, exactly two hundred years following the arrival of the Mayflower Pilgrims in New England, the Christian Gospel of the Reformation was spread to Hawai'i by American Protestant missionaries. In the aftermath of the collapse of the ancient Hawaiian religion in 1819, Native Hawaiian rulers embraced Christianity, in part due to input from Tahitian Christians who arrived in Hawai'i prior to the New England Missionaries.

The legacy of the Sandwich Islands Mission is the subject of shelves of informative books, in accounts told both from Native Hawaiian and Western perspectives. This account of the coming of Christianity to Hawai'i is by no means definitive and ends in the mid-1820s. There are many viewpoints that can be taken, especially on the impact of the Sandwich Islands Mission in Hawai'i–this is just one account. Many more pieces of Henry Obookiah's life story are still to be found, and I am sure will come to light in time. I hope this book inspires additional research.

The reader is urged to read thoroughly the history of the Hawaiian Islands, of events both prior to the arrival of the Sandwich Islands Mission and beyond their coming, to better understand the incredible achievements of Hawai'i's peoples, and of the problems they have faced, especially the travails faced by Native Hawaiians.

The more one learns about Hawai'i, especially when exploring accounts of notable Native Hawaiians, one realizes how much more there is–and always will be–to learn.

HISTORICAL PERSONAGES

Ali'i Nui (paramount chiefs)

KAMEHAMEHA I (c. 1758-1819) Warrior king Kamehameha the Great united independent island kingdoms through great military and political skills, creating the Kingdom of Hawai'i, named for his home island. Died at the 'Ahu'ena Heiau at Kona in 1819. Led Hawai'i in early decades of western-contact. Last *ali'i nui* of ancient religious-political *kapu* system.

KA'AHUMANU (c. 1768-1832) The "Favorite Wife" of Kamehameha, and the daughter of Maui ali'i nui, guardian of Liholiho, Kamehameha II. Ruled as *kuhina nui*, premier, of the Kingdom of Hawai'i. Became a Christian in 1825.

KAMEHAMEHA II - LIHOLIHO (1797-1824) Kamehameha's son and heir, borne by his sacred wife Keōpūolani. Led in overthrow of the centuries-old kapu system, died during a royal tour to London.

KEŌPŪOLANI (1778-1823) The "Sacred" wife of Kamehameha due to the high rank of her *mana* as determined by her bloodlines. Mother of Liholiho (Kamehameha II) and Kauikeaouli (Kamehameha III). First ali'i nui to be baptized.

KALANIMOKU (1768-1827) Chief advisor to Kamehameha, a powerful general known as "iron cable of Hawai'i." Took part in breaking and abandoning the kapu system in 1819, became a Christian. Led warriors in a Christian prayer prior to a battle on Kaua'i in 1824, proposed written laws based upon the Ten Commandants.

Kāhuna (priests)

PĀ'AO - Legendary *kahuna nui* (high priest) from South Pacific established first human sacrifice *heiau* (temple), at Wahaulu on windward coast of Hawai'i Island circa twelfth-century. Brought spiritual and behavioral laws that evolved into kapu system.

HEWAHEWA (b. about 1774-d. 1837/1838) Last Kahuna nui (high priest) of Kingdom of Hawai'i under Kamehameha and Liholiho. Accompanied Kamehameha in warfare. Direct descendant of South Pacific priest Pā'ao. Encouraged Liholiho to overthrow ancient kapu system. Prophesied arrival of Sandwich Islands Mission, later lived in Valley of the Kāhuna at Waimea on North Shore of O'ahu.

PAHUA (b. mid-to-late eighteenth-century d. mid-nineteenth-century) A kahuna (priest) of the god Lono at the Hikiau Heiau at Kealakekua Bay. Maternal uncle and mentor-teacher of Ōpūkaha'ia.

Foreign Mission School

'ŌPŪKAHA'IA - HENRY OBOOKIAH (1787/1792-1818) Born at Ka'ū, Hawai'i Island in either 1787 or 1792; 1792 is the traditional birth date, but interviews of kūpuna from Hawai'i Island undertaken in the mid-1860s claimed 'Ōpūkaha'ia was born in 1787. As a ten-year-old his parents were killed by warriors of Kamehameha following the battle of Kaipalaoa in Hilo. Trained to a be a kahuna under his uncle Pahua at Kealakekua Bay. Served as a sailor on voyage to New York in 1808-09 aboard sealing ship *Triumph*, Captain Caleb Brintnall. Took on name Obookiah aboard ship. In New Haven taken in by Yale students and began western education. Adopted by family of missionary pioneer Samuel J. Mills of Torringford, Connecticut. Baptized in Torringford. Attended academies in Massachusetts and Connecticut. Studied to become missionary to his home islands. Foreign Mission School in Cornwall, Connecticut opened in 1817 in part to support his mission. Died of typhus fever in February 1818. Memorial volume, *Memoirs of Henry Obookiah*, secured his place as an evangelical celebrity, model "heathen" student, and American folk hero. Credited as seed of American Board of Commissioners for Foreign Missions' mission to Hawai'i sent in 1819. In 1993 his remains were moved from Cornwall to a memorial gravesite at Kahikolu Church overlooking Kealakekua Bay.

HOPU - THOMAS HOPOO (1793- mid-nineteenth-century) Born in North Kohala, Hawai'i Island, sailed with Ōpūkaha'ia aboard the *Triumph*, working as cabin boy. Served aboard privateers in the War of 1812. In 1815 began formal study in New England and became a practicing Christian. Attended Foreign Mission School at Cornwall, 1817-1819. Sailed aboard brig *Thaddeus* as member of first company of the Sandwich Islands Mission.

HUMEHUME - GEORGE PRINCE TAMOREE (c. 1798-1826) Son of Kaumuali'i, ali'i nui ruler of Kaua'i and Ni'ihau islands. Sent to New England at age four to be educated. Abandoned, worked as a young teen on farms and in laboring. Enlisted as a Marine during the War of 1812. Attended Foreign Mission School in Cornwall, Connecticut. Returned to Hawai'i aboard brig *Thaddeus* with the first Sandwich Islands Mission company. In 1824 led an attack on the fort at Waimea, Kaua'i, resulting in his banishment to Honolulu and early death from influenza.

EDWIN WELLES DWIGHT (1789-1841) son of a Stockbridge, Massachusetts Congregational pastor, Dwight was a member of the Brethren foreign mission society at Williams College. In 1809 he found Henry Obookiah weeping on the steps of Yale for lack of a western education. Dwight became a mentor of Obookiah at Yale; reunited with Obookiah when serving as principal of the Foreign Mission School; edited and wrote narrative of *Memoirs of Henry Obookiah*, a small, about 100-page book sold as a fund-raiser for the school that became a best-seller in the United States.

Sandwich Islands Missionaries

REV. HIRAM BINGHAM (1789-1869) son of a Vermont farmer, Bingham graduated from Middlebury College and Theological Seminary at Andover. Member of the Brethren foreign mission organization. Ordained in Goshen, Connecticut in 1819 as the coleader of the first company of the Sandwich Islands Mission sent to Hawai'i by the American Board of Commissioners for Foreign Missions. Bingham and his wife Sybil Moseley Bingham served at the mission station in Honolulu for twenty-one years. Played key role in creating Hawaiian language Bible.

REV. ASA THURSTON (1787-1868) Born in Fitchburg, Massachusetts, graduated from Yale College and Theological Seminary at Andover. Ordained in Goshen, Connecticut to colead with Hiram Bingham the first company of the Sandwich Islands Mission. Thurston and his wife Lucy Goodale Thurston founded the mission station in Kailua on Hawai'i Island. He served the mission for over forty years, worked translating the Bible into the Hawaiian language.

London Missionary Society

REV. WILLIAM ELLIS (1794-1872) Born in London. Bible translator, printer and publisher, cultural chronicler at Tahitian station of London Missionary Society.

Sailed to Hawai'i in 1822 where he introduced Tahitian hymns. First western missionary to preach a sermon in the Hawaiian language. Chronicled Native Hawaiian culture of 1820s.

New England

CAPTAIN CALEB BRINTNALL (1774-1850) Most successful of New Haven's seal fur trade captains during America's China Trade era. Invited Ōpūkaha'ia to sail aboard his three-masted ship the *Triumph* in 1808, providing a home for him in New Haven in 1809 following their China trade voyage. Returned to Hawai'i in 1816 as captain of the *Zephyr*, serving as an "Admiral of the Sandwich Islands" for Kamehameha, patrolling off Kaua'i during Russian American Company incident.

SAMUEL J. MILLS JR. (1783-1818) Born in Torringford, Connecticut. Visionary pioneer of Protestant foreign missions from the United States. At Williams College led landmark Haystack Meeting and founded Brethren student missions society. Discovered Obookiah at Yale, brought him to Torringford where his family adopted Henry. Mills oversaw the education of Obookiah and became a brother to him. Foreign and domestic missions organizing genius: played key role in formation of American Board of Commissioners for Foreign Missions and American Bible Society. He planned to lead the Sandwich Islands Mission with Obookiah, but died aboard ship off the coast of West Africa on a scouting mission for the American Colonization Society, possibly of consumption.

REV. SAMUEL J. MILLS (1743-1833)- Colorful pastor of the Congregational Church of Torringford (1769-1833). Father of Samuel Mills Jr. Widely and fondly known as Father Mills, he served as a father figure for Obookiah whom he brought into his home as a son. Known for his unwittingly humorous style of preaching.

REV. LYMAN BEECHER (1775-1863) Leading Congregational minister in New England during the Second Great Awakening. Preached the funeral sermon for Obookiah. A descendant of a pioneer New Haven family, Beecher served as pastor of the Congregational Church in Litchfield, Connecticut. His daughter, Harriet Beecher Stowe, wrote the anti-slavery novel *Uncle Tom's Cabin* and his son Henry Ward Beecher became one of America's best-known preachers following the Civil War.

PROLOGUE

IN THE SPRING OF 1796 Kamehameha–the statuesque, powerful warrior king, an *ali'i nui*, marked by oracles as born to rule the Hawaiian Islands–stared blankly out in the direction of the island of Kaua'i. Dressed in Hawaiian tapa garments and wearing a royal red and yellow feathered helmet, he stood on a cream-colored sandy beach in Waianae, a coastal village set along the sunny leeward coast of O'ahu.

Blanketing the beach to his left and right were the survivors of his ill-fated double-hulled *peleleu* canoe invasion fleet of over 10,000 warriors launched the previous day to conquer Kaua'i. Hundreds of the sleek, narrow koa wood vessels lay haphazardly in the sand. Sinnet rope lashings used to connect the hulls hung ripped into shreds. Haggard men, beaten by the sea, exchanged accounts of their escape from the clutches of the treacherous Ka'ie'ie Waho Channel, from the powerful wind of Kulepe that twists and turns over the sea. That day they mourned the loss of dozens of drowned fellow warriors; no victory druming greeted their return.

Towering behind Kamehameha, 4,000-foot Mount Ka'ala blocked the first wisps of early morning trade winds. The tall remnant of this volcanic crater protected the coast, casting a wind-shadow. Offshore a glassy, indigo-blue ocean surface spread for miles, pocked only by piles of sea birds circling round schools of pelagic fish and war canoes staggering back from mid-channel.

The day prior Kamehameha's lust to possess Kaua'i's verdant lands seemed ready to be sated; he desired to drink the water of Wailua, bathe in the streams of Mount Nāmalōkama, to surf the round, rolling perfect waves of Makaīwa. He blessed his assault with sacrifices and prayers made at Waianae to Kūkā'ilimoku, Kamehameha's personal war god. But about twenty miles into the channel crossing the largest canoe-borne invasion force ever assembled in Hawai'i sailed into a maelstrom. Ripping cross currents, high winds and towering swells rose suddenly. The Ka'ie'ie Waho Channel presented a huge battlement wall to the invaders, seemingly stirred up against Kamehameha by invisible forces that shielded Kaua'i.

The portent behind this defeat–the greatest of his long career of victories–vexed Kamehameha. Named the "Lonely One" for his inward searching nature,

Kamehameha sensed a turn underway in the spirit of Hawai'i, his defeat by unseen powers a guide as well as a loss.

Flowing in Kamehameha's bloodlines were the ancient Polynesian roots of Hawai'i. Kamehameha possessed the spirit of the brave men, women and children who a millennium back stepped off voyaging canoes sent from South Pacific homelands, their journey across vast unknown seas north of the humid equatorial waters over. And of those settlers' ancestors, a wandering canoe tribe irresistibly drawn out of a South China Sea village a thousand years before the birth of Christ.

Kamehameha's power came from a later wave of migration from the South Pacific, one of conquest, landing about AD 1200. His royal ancestor Pili, a paramount Tahitian chief, was installed as ruler by the legendary high priest and navigator Pā'ao. Pā'ao invaded Hawai'i Island, then the most populous of all the islands in Hawai'i, as leader of an army of towering Tahitian warriors. Pā'ao overshadowed Hawai'i with a strict system of behavioral laws and regulations known as the kapu system and enforced through the threat of death. Pā'ao built the heiau known as Waha'ula on the lava flow-strewn Puna coast of Hawai'i Island. To connect with their ancestral gods, workers raised stone walls atop the flat, wide-open basalt rock altars erected by the first settlers. The walls obscured the rites of the secretive priesthood and the upright ancestral stones brought centuries earlier aboard the first wave of voyaging canoes.

It is said that in the star-filled night of Kamehameha's birth in 1758, Halley's Comet streaked in the sky above his birthplace on the isolated coast of North Kohala on Hawai'i Island. From his auspicious birth onward Kamehameha lived through a time of great change. He flourished, innately adept at waging war and winning political games, and built up his empire island-by-island, from Hawai'i to O'ahu. His savvy mercantile skills tapped the purses of western traders who began sailing to Hawai'i for provisioning, wooding and watering. The traders were directed, and lured, through reading the journals of Royal Navy Captain James Cook of England. Cook discovered Hawai'i for the West in 1778, first landing off Waimea, Kauai.

Back onshore at Waianae in 1796, the "Lonely One" again drew within himself for direction. He regrouped his forces, putting off the conquest of Kaua'i and Ni'ihau for another time, now content with his conquering of O'ahu at the Battle of Nu'uanu fought months earlier.

In the summer season of 1796 a messenger sent to Kamehameha (still on O'ahu) spread alarming news: an army gathered in Ka'ū on the arid south tip of Hawai'i Island was pushing north, rampaging through Puna and nearing Waiakea Bay in the coastal village of Hilo. Leading the attack into Kamehameha's territory was Nāmekehā, the vengeful brother of Keoua, an ali'i warrior prince assassinated five years earlier at the dedication of Kamehameha's monumental Pu'ukohola Heiau at Kawaihae.

In the ranks of Nāmekehā's army marched Ke'au, a *makaʻāinana* (commoner class) soldier. Ke'au dwelt in the coastal village of Nīnole in Ka'ū with his wife Kamoho'ula, a woman of royal blood, a cousin to Kamehameha. They were parents of two sons: 'Ōpūkaha'ia (a name meaning either a caesarian-section birth, or a warrior whose stomach was slashed open), about ten years old, and an infant boy.

In mid-summer 1796, Kamehameha ordered his army to board his restored peleleu war canoe fleet to sail and paddle south at flank speed for Kaipalaoa (a significant heiau and canoe landing located along the north bank of the Waiakea River at Hilo).

CHAPTER ONE
'ŌPŪKAHA'IA'S LIFE IS SPARED

History of Five Sandwich Islanders

'Ōpūkaha'ia fleeing from a warrior with his baby brother on his back following the murder of his parents as imagined by an English engraver. The style of the drawing recalls plates accompanying Captain Cook's journals, which the artist apparently referenced. His warrior is incorrectly pictured wearing a feathered cape.

Island of Hawai'i, late summer 1796

A NATIVE HAWAIIAN BOY ABOUT TEN YEARS OLD–a curious, innocent boy named 'Ōpūkaha'ia whose life, and death, would change Hawai'i forever–ran carrying his infant brother on his back. Barefoot, his calloused feet leapt at every stride as he crossed a verdant landscape, *mauka*, inland, of the wave-swept windward coast of Hawai'i Island. Pursuing him, rapidly catching up, a man easily twice his size sought to kill them. Windows of sunlight illuminated pockets of the dark, vine-entangled forest.

At a glance, this appeared to be a father-son game. But the pace of the chase was too quick, the boys' shrieks too terrifying.

A gruesome sight lay near the mouth of a black basalt lava tube cave, about fifty paces back. There tall warriors dispatched by Kamehameha (the warrior chief who conquered and consolidated the Hawaiian Islands in the 1790s) wielding shark tooth-lined clubs, *leiomanō*, worked at dismembering the bodies of 'Ōpūkaha'ia's parents. The shock of seeing his father, Ke'au, a planter-fisherman, and Kamoho'ula, his beloved mother, kin to Kamehameha, being brutally slaughtered traumatized 'Ōpūkaha'ia. The boy fled from the death scene, controlled by a primordial fear.

Now close enough to see the sweat pouring down the children's backs, the pursuer slung his short spear–a sharp, hardwood *pāhoa* dagger–into the infant's back. The blow stumbled 'Ōpūkaha'ia. Falling forward, he clutched the limp, bleeding body of his brother.

The tattooed fighter picked 'Ōpūkaha'ia off the red-dirt forest floor and forced him to return to the cave, to stand beside the bloody remains of his parents. The winded warrior sought an order from his commander, the leader of this mission of vengeance. Life or a quick death for ʻŌpūkahaʻia hung on the response.

ʻŌpūkahaʻia trembled. He was a humble child from a rural village, a lowly pawn in the climb to power of the most powerful warrior-king in all Hawaiʻi.

"Too young to fight back, but old enough to take care of himself," the gray-haired chief standing to the side of the warrior might have thought. Whatever his motive, he spared the life of ʻŌpūkahaʻia by signalling for a lowering of the pāhoa.

Out of Kaʻū

As a child, ʻŌpūkahaʻia played along pocket beaches cut into the black-as-ebony lava outcrops that line the coast in Kaʻū. His family dwelt in the sea front village of Nīnole, near the arid grasslands found at the south tip of Hawaiʻi Island.

Life as led in Kaʻū was far from the idyllic, languid, easy-going picture of a Hawaiian village held in the minds of those from outside Hawaiʻi. Sources of drinking water was scarce on the coast forcing Nīnole's tough and ingenuous, hardworking people to plant gardens a long walk mauka, inland. There streams flowed in the foothills behind Nīnole, far from the village's Kaʻieʻie Heiau on the coast.

To collect drinking water divers dove into the Pacific off rocky lava outcrops clutching hollow gourds. It took strength to overcome the buoyancy of the gourds which they filled with freshwater flowing from underground springs that lay a few fathoms beneath salty ocean water. Remarkable strength of breath allowed the free divers to stay below for minutes.

Though life could be hard in Kaʻū, especially when a famine hit, ʻŌpūkahaʻia grew up nourished within his family circle, protected and loved by his extended family, his *ʻohana*. Members of an *ʻohana* relied on, and loved, each other. (The word *ʻohana* comes from the intertwining taro plant root system that underlies and ties together the picturesque, large plants that grow in rock-walled taro *loʻi* ponds.)

This peaceful existence was disturbed throughout the eighteenth-century when seasons of inter-island warfare disrupted the harmony of life in Nīnole.

In the spring of 1796 the warrior chief Nāmakehā of Kaʻū, employing a desperate battle strategy in a last-ditch effort to remove Kamehameha's control, moved his army north into the windward Puna and Hilo districts. Nāmakehā took advantage of Kamehameha's army being occupied on Oʻahu with the invasion of Kauaʻi.

nearKamehameha made a speedy response, sailing his army south aboard his peleleu fleet of war canoes, landing at Kaipalaoa on the north side of the mouth of the Waiakea River, near today's downtown Hilo. At Kaipalaoa Kamehameha's veteran, battle-tested forces, backed up by his artillery, decimated the rebellious Kaʻū army. To emphasize what would happen to any chief who dared to challenge his rule, Kamehameha ordered his men to slaughter surviving Kaʻū warriors and their camp followers. The Kaʻū survivors fled fast and far, some leaving behind generations of family ties to settle in safety in the Kona District located on the leeward side of the island.

In the grassy clearings at Kaipalaoa, Kamehameha had extinguished every ember of rebellion. The nineteenth-century historian William Alexander wrote, "Nāmakehā was hunted down, and offered in sacrifice in the heiau at Piihonua,

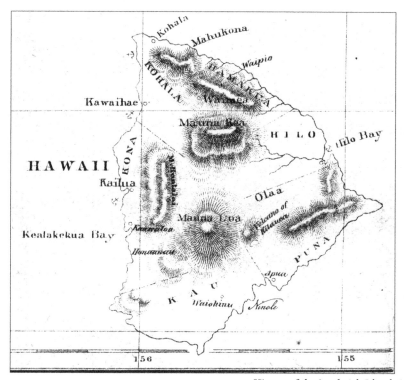

History of the Sandwich Islands Mission
A missionary map of significant Hawai'i Island places in the mid-nineteenth century.

Hilo. This was the last of Kamehameha's wars. All opposition to his authority was now at an end."

Though it cost many lives, and orphaned 'Ōpūkaha'ia–sending his young life on a new, sometimes despondent, path–Kamehameha's victory at Kaipalaoa, along with battles fought across the Hawaiian Islands, initiated a lasting peace to the kingdom he created. Coming to an end was a century marked by warfare within, and between, islands. The many positive aspects of Hawaiian life then again brought harmony to the *maka'āinana,* the commoners: love shown as *aloha*; great hospitality, *ho'okipa*; stewardship of their lands, taking responsibility for their *kuleana*, their homestead and duties; being *pono*, on the up and up, righteous; taking care of things, *mālama*; living as an *'ohana*, a family, both personal and extended; working hard, *hana*; being patient, *ho'omanawanui*; expressing thanks, *mahalo*.

From his compound at Kaipalaoa, months later Kamehameha issued his landmark *Ke Kānāwai Māmalahoe* edict (The Law of the Splintered Paddle). "Let every elderly person, woman and child lie by the roadside in safety," the law stated. The roots of this edict traced back a decade to a day when Kamehameha found himself reconnoitering along the coast in Puna. His patrol was spotted by two local fishermen who ran away to warn villagers of the danger of being taken away. Kamehameha's men gave chase, but he caught his foot in a lava field crevice,

During his childhood, 'Ōpūkaha'ia was fed fish and shellfish gathered along the coast at Nīnole (foreground) and taro, sweet potatoes and other vegetables grown in mauka valleys where freshwater streams flowed.

snared like a squid in a Hawaiian fishing lure. Local men retaliated, attacking, clubbing Kamehameha in the head so hard a hardwood koa canoe paddle splintered. A dazed Kamehameha overheard the fishermen discussing the sparing of his life; the men saw life under the god Kane as sacred. Recalling this merciful act, Kamehameha's moral judgment told him that it was *pono* (righteous) for all of Hawai'i's people to have the freedom of movement and safety from attack.

'Ōpūkaha'ia's family was drawn into the Battle of Kaipalaoa by a long-standing tradition: in times of war, fishermen and planters, the maka'āinana, were called to battle. The men were ordered away from their work cultivating taro ponds and their ocean-going fishing canoes. The minutemen-like soldiers accompanied professional warriors who trained from childhood, becoming expert in the martial art known as *lua*, spear throwing and other battle skills.

The maka'āinana men sometimes went to battle accompanied by their 'ohana; their wives and children and other relatives serving as camp followers, providing food and water and encouragement from a good viewpoint just out of range of battle.

In the chaos following the Battle of Kaipalaoa, 'Ōpūkaha'ia's father Ke'au fled with his wife and children, making a desperate escape, heading into the highlands, up on a flank of Mauna Loa Volcano, likely somewhere outside of Hilo. He found an isolated lava tube cave, which provided a safe hiding place. Such stone outcroppings rose out of the forest floor like entrances to the underworld. Such caves were commonly used by the rulers of Hawai'i Island to protect their families during times of war. The family kept to the cave until their suffering from thirst became unbearable. Risking their lives, Ke'au led them out to a stream to drink. A party of warriors approached and Ke'au ran, leaving his family behind. He stopped, bucked himself up, and rushed back, drawn by the desperate cries of Kamoho'ula and his children. But as the warriors closed in Ke'au fled once again. In his wake, the warriors seized 'Ōpūkaha'ia, his mother and baby brother. They began to prod and torture them to draw Ke'au from his hiding place. Ke'au

Fragments of Real Missionary Life by the Rev. John D. Paris
Courtesy Hawai'i Conference - United Church of Christ

Within the Helehelekalani Heiau 'Ōpūkaha'ia erected his own heiau. Helehelekalani is located adjacent to the Hikiau Heiau and where Obookiah served his apprenticeship as a priest under his uncle Pahua. 'Ōpūkaha'ia planted three coconut trees near the platform of his heiau overlooking Kealakekua Bay. In the 1840s a report sent to New England told of a local tradition of giving drinking coconuts from Obookiah's trees only to missionaries.

---

charged, but was no match for the professional warriors. Carnage followed.

Captive in Kohala

Leaving the bodies of 'Ōpūkaha'ia's parents and baby brother to the wild pigs of the forest, Kamehameha's warriors goaded the boy north. Together they hiked along a coastal path, or perhaps sailed aboard an outrigger canoe. Past the deep, royal valleys of Waipio and Waimanu, appeared Kohala, the north tip of Hawai'i Island.

For the captured youth, Kohala was a foreign land the home of people he knew not. He had spent his young life dwelling in the arid, lava-flow strewn coast with the people of Ka'ū. Ka'ū was a district traditionally in opposition to Kohala, Kamehameha's birthplace. At Nīnole, he lived in the shadow of fiery volcanic craters erupting from the flank of Mauna Loa, the dwelling place of the goddess Pele. In Kohala he felt chilly and damp, a prisoner in a lush, rainy windward environment. In place of a boundless horizon, the island of Maui's towering Haleakalā Mountain loomed across the wind-whipped 'Alenuihāhā Channel

Here the boy lived as a captive. He was fed and sheltered, but lacked the peace a child finds in the loving home of his own parents. An existential danger permeated his thoughts; he was on edge about his own safety living in the home of the warrior who murdered his parents. In his thoughts, he rejected the fate of being raised by unloving parents, perhaps to be forced to train as a warrior, rather than cultivating his curious mind. Every day 'Ōpūkaha'ia longed to escape. The boy remained in captivity for about a year, through the fall of 1797.

Rescued by Pahua

Pahua, the brother of 'Ōpūkaha'ia's mother, served as a *kahuna pule*, a praying priest, at the Hikiau Heiau. The heiau tower and hale perched overlooking Kealakekua Bay atop a basalt stone foundation about fifteen-feet-high and one-hundred-feet square. As a kahuna, Pahua ranked just below the powerful ali'i. *Kāhuna* served as the intercessors to the pantheon of Hawaiian gods, as the judges of the strict system of laws embodied in the word kapu. Hikiau was a significant coastal, basalt rock-walled temple dedicated to the worship of Kamehameha's powerful, red-feathered personal war god Kūkā'ilimoku, a god who the ali'i nui worshipped with human sacrifices to ensure victory in war.

Kealakekua is a lei-shaped bay with an anchorage deep and wide enough to harbor a half-dozen western trading ships. Colorful coral reefs set in clear turquoise waters shimmer along its outer shore.

Pahua paraded clockwise around Hawai'i each fall during the *Makahiki*, a harvest season that lasted four lunar months.

In late fall the rainy season begins in Hawai'i, as noted in the star constellation-based Hawaiian calendar. The Makahiki is launched when the Makali'i star cluster (known in the West as Pleiades) begins to rise on the western horizon at sunset. Lono, the god of rain and harvest, ruled during the Makahiki months and received sacrifices of pigs, while the war god Kū again ascended in the season of Kau in early spring, worshipped with human sacrifices.

The Makahiki procession stopped at each *ahupua'a* (valley complex) that comprised the island. Once taxes were collected, feasting and days of Hawaiian game playing and athletics followed. It is likely that as the procession encamped in Kohala Pahua was approached by his nephew, who had grown considerably since the last time the two met. It is unlikely that 'Ōpūkaha'ia traveled sixty miles on his own down long stretches of hot, pebble-covered trails to Kealakekua.

Coming in contact with his uncle brought into the open the trauma 'Ōpūkaha'ia suffered. Later in his life he told of Pahua acknowledging his pain: "When he heard the names of my parents, he shed his tears, and he lay down trembling. He did not want me to return to the man who had killed my father and mother, but to stay with him for the rest of my life."

From his captor at Kohala 'Ōpūkaha'ia sought permission to join Pahua at Hikiau. There, his uncle told him, dwelt Hina, his maternal grandmother. The Kohala warrior threatened to kill 'Ōpūkaha'ia if the youth left for Kealakekua Bay, just as he had murdered 'Ōpūkaha'ia's parents. Pahua intervened, claiming 'Ōpūkaha'ia as his own kin. He told the warrior he would stay, too, if he forced 'Ōpūkaha'ia to stay. This was not an idle threat for kāhuna ranked above warriors; a kahuna could bring political trouble from the powerful paramount rulers, the *ali'i nui*. The warrior would know, too, of the spiritual powers possessed by *kāhuna 'anā'anā*, priests who could heal a person, or choose to pray someone to death.

The warrior relented, freeing 'Ōpūkaha'ia to make his way to Hikiau. In departing 'Ōpūkaha'ia harbored bitterness towards the man and his wife. Though they were kind to him, he could never forgive the husband for the heinous murder of his family.

Life at Kealakekua Bay

After over a year in bondage in Kohala a new world opened up for 'Ōpūkaha'ia at Hikiau along the shore of Kealakekua Bay. The love of his 'ohana reawakened, sailors and drifters off western trading ships provided him inviting glimpses of the world outside Hawai'i, and his love of learning found its true course.

'Ōpūkaha'ia, now an adolescent, set up his own thatched hale near his uncle and grandmother, his 'ohana providing safety and security within the walls of the Hikiau compound. Pahua became his adoptive father, and began training 'Ōpūkaha'ia as a priest of Lono. Under his uncle (trained by Hewahewa, the *kahuna nui*, high priest of Kamehameha) 'Ōpūkaha'ia served an apprenticeship at Hikiau.

He now lived at an international crossroads where trading ships brought ashore an array of sailors who arrived aboard ships out of ports in America, Great Britain, France and Russia. The ships provisioned, loaded firewood and filled barrels with fresh water at the bay. This was a mid-way rest stop on trans-Pacific sails to the trading factories located at the gates of Canton. Making the "Golden Round" is what sailors called these voyages. In the Golden Round savvy traders built up fortunes through collecting the raw natural resources of the Pacific Northwest, sea otter furs and fur seal skins. At the trading factories in Canton, their cargoes were sold to Chinese merchants and the proceeds were rolled over to buy a cargo of China goods. China goods were luxury goods for consumers in post-Revolutionary War America: they drank tea at home, displayed blue and white Chinaware table settings as status symbols, sewed silk fabrics into fashionable dresses; made handsome trousers and waistcoats from sturdy, khaki-colored nankeen cotton fabrics. This growing demand for China goods drove auction prices at the Tontine Coffee House (then the center of maritime trade dealmaking in Manhattan), in Boston, in London, filling the coffers of ship masters, investors and customs houses.

The coming of the western traders provided a dilemma for Kamehameha and his people. The sailors brought incredible objects and amazing insights from the western world to a people isolated from outside influence for over five-hundred years; but they also brought disease and distractions from the orderly life of Hawai'i under the kapu system. It was apparent the traders who ashore and aboard ship blatantly broke the rules of the kapu system suffered no consequences from the gods of Hawai'i.

'Ōpūkaha'ia succeeded in his priestly apprenticeship. He possessed the discipline needed to memorize chants orated sometimes throughout a night without repetition; he easily performed the intricate movements of secretive rituals performed within the heiau; and he was kind and obedient to his uncle and fellow kāhuna.

"His greatest desire was to be taught the secrets of the priesthood, and he was placed in charge of the religious rites," is how the Rev. S. W. Papaula of Napo'opo'o, writing in the 1860s, described the enthusiasm of 'Ōpūkaha'ia during his apprenticeship.

> "In pursuance of this purpose, he (Pahua) taught him long prayers and trained him to the task of repeating them daily in the temple of the idol. This ceremony he sometimes commenced before sunrise in the morning, and at other times was employed in it during the whole or greater part of the night...the prayers regarded the weather, the general prosperity of the Island, its defense from enemies, and especially the life and happiness of the King."

At Hikiau 'Ōpūkaha'ia erected a twenty-five by thirty-five-foot heiau he named Helehelekalani. His apprentice-temple stood alongside the massive basalt rock-walled Hikiau, set on the southern edge of a sacred pool. On a flat rock platform 'Ōpūkaha'ia

erected three small hale: one for the god Lono; one for Kūkā'ilimoku, the war god of Kamehameha; and one for Laka, the god of the hula. Three coconut trees served as markers.

Pahua praised his nephew's accomplishments as a student earning his place in the
priesthood brought to Hawai'i by the Tahitian Pā'ao over five hundred years earlier.

> Ancient Hawaiians believed that all things possessed a soul–animals, trees, stones,
> stars and clouds, as well as humans. Religion and mythology were interwoven in the
> culture. The gods of Ancient Hawai'i were like great chiefs from far lands who visited
> among the people, at times appearing as humans or animal and sometimes residing in
> stone or wooden images. There were powerful nature gods who controlled nature, and
> lesser gods like the 'aumukua (a family's ancient guardian spirit), 'unihipili (spirits of
> recently deceased ancestors); and those over crafts and professions. There were male
> gods and female goddesses. Chiefs of the highest rank were seen as descending from the
> gods and were shown varying degrees of veneration as prescribed by rigid kapu (taboos).
> Entwined with the religion and culture was the kapu system, a system of prohibitions
> that actually ruled the life of the land, all aspects of everyday living. It ruled ali'i, ka-
> huna, maka'ainana, and kaua alike. What was sacred to the gods had to be observed
> by all classes in the society; what was sacred to the ali'i had to be observed by ali'i of
> lesser rank, the maka'ainana and the kaua. Kahuna conducted rituals in order to keep
> the strength of the kapu intact. Rituals were performed within the heiau, attended only
> by ali'i. Maka'ainana worshipped within their families.
> (Aletha Kaohi and Stanley Lum, from *Celebrating Advocacy*)

'Ōpūkaha'ia grew taller, leaner, solidly built and toned by exercise in the ocean. Unlike Nīnole or Kohala, Kealakekua Bay was a choice location for ocean recreation, for
canoe paddling, swimming, surfing steep waves. Today the shore along the site of Hikiau
is rock-strewn and narrow due to being raked by tsunami- and hurricane-driven waves;
two hundred years ago, prior to this natural damage, the beach was a wide, sandy plain.

The beach scene at Kealakekua was a world apart from the monastic-like atmosphere cultivated at Hikiau. Just yards away from the temple, under the shade of coconut trees, and around evening beach fires, sailors and malingerers gathered night and
day. They told tales of shipwrecks and lashings with a cat of nine tails, of brave men
battling the sea behind a trading ship's wheel, of clinging to the yards when furling sails
in stormy winds, of the wild women and grog shops found in tough waterfronts around
the globe. Stewart, the brother of a young Scottish sailor who sailed aboard the HMS
Bounty and wed a Tahitian woman, told tales of the South Pacific.

Some western men settled at Kealakekua, serving Kamehameha in various func-
tions. These men married women from Hawai'i and nurtured a Hawaiian version of
their own home life as lived in New England or Great Britain.

The Hawaiians' South Pacific cousins, the Tahitians, brought connections to the
ancestral Polynesian homeland known as Kahiki. Adventure, curiosity and opportunities for work lured the Tahitians north aboard trading vessels; some settled in Hawai'i
as did their ancestors a millennium earlier.

At Kealakekua, the practice of the ancient Hawaiian religion served to quiet the
darkness in 'Ōpūkaha'ia's spirit. But deep inside his traumas haunted him; he held a
youthful hope for a new life, one he might need to leave Hawai'i to discover.

CHAPTER TWO
KAMEHAMEHA &
CONNECTICUT CAPTAIN BRINTNALL

Hawaiʻi State Archives

A portrait of Kamehameha (left) drawn from life in 1816 by artist Louis Choris. Choris traveled to Hawaiʻi aboard the Russian ship *Ruric*. The statue of Kamehameha as a young, feather-caped warrior stands in front of the Aliʻiolani Hale building in Honolulu.

THE LIFE OF ʻŌPŪKAHAʻIA, AND THE FUTURE OF HAWAIʻI were changed forever by the arrival of New Haven sea captain Caleb Brintnall, master of the seal-hunting brig *Triumph*. In late 1807 Brintnall sailed his ship along the south shore of the island of Oʻahu. His arrival set in motion a series of providential events.

Brintnall paced his quarterdeck. He stood medium-height. His warm grey eyes, set in the face of a prosperous urban merchant or Yale scholar, belied his mastery of the sea. The Connecticut sea captain ran a ship as "neat as an apple pie."

Brintnall made his home with his wife Louisa, whom the family called Lois, and their four children. The Brintnalls lived in a white, Federal Era clapboard house with black shutters close to the maritime center of New Haven. A short walk away towards the harbor was the half-mile-long Long Wharf, the backbone of the shallow-draft port.

The New Haven sea captain lived a complex life, one that embodied the turmoil and change New England was undergoing following the American Revolution. His family ties, dating back to British colonial America, showed in his refined manners and personage. Risking his life and venturing out on global sails in the China Trade personi-fied the gumption and struggle that kept the United States economically viable in its early years. Through his marriage to Lois, a member of the Mix-Beecher family, Brint-nall married into the circle of founding families of New Haven. An able sea captain, Brintnall sailed the Golden Round to acquire riches, for himself and his family, and for local investors. His success helped New Haven survive during its transition from a smaller colonial New England port to a center of the Industrial Age, the home of Eli Whitney, Samuel Colt and other innovators of mass factory production.

Brintnall kept his evangelical faith intact once around Cape Horn. His family sat in their own pew in the Brick Church on the New Haven Green. There revivals were

Western ships are anchored in the inner Honolulu Harbor in this 1816 drawing.

building up the congregation under Pastor Moses Stuart. The seed of the revivals traced back two generations to British evangelist George Whitefield. Sailing with Brintnall aboard the *Triumph* was a post-graduate Yale divinity student, upbeat Russell Hubbard.

The first decade of the nineteenth-century saw the peak of what was known in the United States as the China Trade, an industry that filled the coffers of "Old Money" families of New England and beyond. Ships from New York, Salem, Boston, and Philadelphia sailed to the chilly waters off the west coast of Canada and Alaska to barter for the luxurious pelts of sea otters hunted by Aleuts and other skilled Indian crews. A good-sized cargo of sea otter pelts, exchanged for China wares in Canton, could net a fortune for a captain and his investors at a Tontine Coffee House auction in lower Manhattan.

Being a smaller port, with a smaller pool of wealthy investors to underwrite voyages, it was logical for New Haven sea captains (citizens of a state known for its "steady ways") to turn to fur seal hunting. Going to the Pacific Ocean as a sealer allowed for scaling down the size of their ships, their crews and the capital needed to mount a lengthy voyage to China. New Haven crews did their own clubbing of four-to-six-foot-long male "wig" and female "clap-match" fur seals. They sailed to remote islands where fur seals gathered in rookeries, like "Robinson Crusoe" in the Juan Fernandez Islands (an archipelago rising out of the Pacific four-hundred miles off the coast of Chile). A beach on the Chilean coast where fur seal skins dried became known as the "New Haven Green."

Brintnall departed for Hawai'i aboard the *Triumph* a month earlier, sailing west from islands off the Pacific coast of Baja California. The lonely passage crossed about 2,500 miles of open ocean.

The New Haven captain left behind crews of sealers at barely-inhabitable volcanic black-sand beaches. The crews erected rough-hewn camps thrown together on a triangle of islands rich in fur seals: Isla Guadalupe, San Benito and Cedros. Each day the men bore the stench of hundreds of rotting, fly-infested seal corpses as they sought a new "pod" of eared, Guadalupe fur seals.

Chinese merchants bought the soft, chestnut-brown underfur of the seals to line winter garments sold to the middle class in northern China where most homes went unheated in the winter; upper class buyers favored sea otter linings. Sealers slid a filleting knife up and down the sleek seal carcass, carefully peeling off the valuable skin. Cleaned and stretched out above beach sand, attached to wooden pegs, the skins were left to dry in the Baja sun. Once cured, the tight-nap, furry skins were numbered and stacked, ready to stow aboard the *Triumph* when Captain Brintnall returned from Hawai'i.

Life for a sealer on Isla Guadalupe, even just for one hunting season, was so desolate that men were known to go mad, dashing up into the misty, mountainous interior never to be seen again. At night—in respite from the bloody, stinking work of butchering seals—the *Triumph* crew gathered around campfires to tell tales. They socialized, joked and sang, reminisced over girls left behind, speculated on how to spend their share of the voyage fortune.

In spite of the hardships, morale ran high on the sealing beaches. The men were inspired by pure capitalism. No wages were paid, the hope behind all the labor and dangers they faced boiled down to a lump-sum pay-off at the end of the voyage. This promise of a handsome profit drove the sealers. Many made only one voyage. Once back in home port they left the sea for good, the voyage pay-off big enough to buy a farm outright, setting them up for life; or they used their share to start-up a Connecticut business. Some sailed to bank the funds needed to earn a degree at Yale.

The lands-men sailors were young men, off on a grand adventure under the watch and care of veteran bluewater sailors. They trusted their lives to the judgment of stern, but caring, Captain Brintnall. He was a respected elder to them though only in his mid-thirties. Brintnall was their savior in the wild world of the sea and foreign ports; a powerful man who would steer their 85-foot-long by 24-foot-wide wood, rope, iron and sailcloth piece of Connecticut safely back to home port through any calamity or danger.

Exhaustion brought on by endless days of hard, hot work tampered down fears of being stranded on Isla Guadalupe; of suffering a lonely, miserable death should Brintnall fail to return from Hawai'i with kegs of fresh water, barrels of food, and cords of firewood.

Brintnall made the long sail to Hawai'i to dodge Spanish Navy frigates. If found in Mexican waters the New Haven captain faced boarding by a San Blas-based patrol. The Spanish government enforced a blockade of foreign vessels trading or poaching in Baja waters. Seizure by the Spanish meant imprisonment for captain and crew until a ransom arrived, and worse, the nullification of the entire voyage: the loss of the ship and their hard-earned cargo, and ending a long journey possibly in debt to their saviors.

Brintnall's uncanny navigational skills and weather-sense kept him from departing for Hawai'i until late October. He dodged the hurricane-force squalls that sweep the Pacific between Baja and Hawai'i from June into October.

Arrival in Hawai'i

On his approach to Honolulu Harbor, Brintnall sailed pass Lē'ahi, the distinctive headland east of Kamehameha's compound at Waikīkī. A skeleton crew worked the sails, lines and helm in the breezy trade winds. The opening for Honolulu Harbor lay ahead to the west. Brintnall maintained his balance as the *Triumph* rolled up and down in a deep blue sea speckled with brilliant white cat paws. The captain scanned the offshore waters for a pilot boat to lead the ship through the curving, narrow channeoncel that led to a calm, safe anchorage hidden behind a low reef and sand bar. Ashore lay several hundred thatched hale, a significant heiau, and Kamehameha's adobe-walled treasure houses: a place known as Kou Landing.

Alongside Brintnall on the quarter deck stood first officer and supercargo Elihu Mix, his brother-in-law. Mix was a family man from New Haven, the rare deep-water sailor who could navigate the sea on-deck, and keep accounts in the cabin below. Elihu left behind for his wife Nancy a detailed notebook of instructions, written in his neat handwriting. Upon the tissue-thin pages of the journal in cursive longhand he lectured his wife on when and what to plant in their vegetable garden, who to contact at a bank on the New Haven Green in time of need, and detailed other home affairs.

Elihu ranked just below Brintnall and juggled several roles aboard ship. He served as a ship's officer, a clerk who kept ledgers, and when in port as the supercargo, the buyer and seller of goods, the financial manager. Elihu–five-foot-eight and light blue eyed with chestnut hair–provided a confidential, competent ear for Brintnall's problems and thoughts. He served watches on the quarterdeck in relief of his brother-in-law.

Provisioning the *Triumph* in Honolulu was a simple chore compared to dealing with Chinese merchants up the Pearl River in Canton; a complex trading process instituted by the Emperor of China, a system required to be followed without question. In Hawai'i trading was as casual as its people. At the factory warehouses built at the gates of Canton, Chinese traders with stoic faces spoke an indiscernible foreign language, wrote out promissory notes in letters that looked like drawings. The merchants ciphered at high speed, running fingers over a wooden-bead counting machine, the abacus.

The months of sealing off Baja provided the cargo for the Canton trading. The full extent of Brintnall and Mix's Yankee trading skills would be needed in selling at a good per skin price the cargo of tens of thousands of Guadalupe fur seal skins. With the sale completed, Brintnall and Mix would switch hats and become buyers of a cargo of tea, silks, Chinaware and other China goods. Filling the hull at Canton they carefully boxed the cargo to make it secure and dry as possible during the long voyage home. Once safely unloaded at an East River dock the China goods would bring a fortune when sold to the highest bidder at a Tontine Coffee House auction.

Caleb Brintnall and the Triumph

Born in 1774, on the eve of the Revolutionary War, Captain Caleb Brintnall grew up in a seagoing New Haven family. He worked his way up in that city's South Sea sealing fleet. Through hard work and skill he rose to the rank of captain. His profits were reinvested in building a brig sturdy enough to circumnavigate the globe and as the capital to fund a new trading voyage to China. Brintnall took command of the brig *Triumph* in late 1806, departing from a mooring off the Long Wharf in New Haven Harbor.

Guilford, Connecticut shipbuilders in 1805 laid the keel and constructed the hull of the *Triumph* from Connecticut oak and other select hardwoods. Brintnall, like Captain Cook, chose a strong and steady, but relatively slow, stub-bowed merchant ship in which to sail around the earth. He held great confidence in the workmanship and ship design of the Guilford shipwrights. They proportioned her at 84 feet, 6 inches in length, 24 feet, 6 inches in beam, with a displacement of 225 tons, and a draft of 12 feet, 5 inches. A carved figurehead of a woman graced the bow.

A typical New Haven sealing crew numbered about thirty-five hands: adolescent cabin boys, able-bodied and lands-men sailors, a sea-going surgeon, the supercargo, a carpenter and his tool chest for repairing the ship and its boats, a blacksmith to forge ship parts and maintain armaments, and a cooper to hoop barrels and form crates for stowing fur pelts and skins. The *Triumph* carried twenty guns: six-pounder and four-pounder cannons, waist guns and swivel guns. The ship armory held side arms, muskets, cutlasses, and boarding pikes.

Brintnall knew the protocol of entering the fair haven of Kou, then the name of the landing that became the port of Honolulu Harbor. Offshore Brintnall waited. A casual palaver with a harbor pilot, likely the resident Englishman John Harbottle, accompanied by an ali'i sent by Kamehameha, served as a customs inspection. The inviting, spacious leeward harbor at Honolulu provided the most protected mid-Pacific anchorage for over 2,000 miles in every direction.

Brintnall ordered anchors dropped offshore of a muddy, red-earth plain dotted with hundreds of thatched hale. This bustling, haphazardly-built beachfront community was the center of action in its day, and the seed of the future metropolis of Honolulu. A canoe and boat landing set atop a coral outcropping served as its landing. The much-trodden sandy spit bore the boot prints of sea captains and sailors, adventurers, Botany Bay escapees who drifted to O'ahu, and the riffraff of the China trade. The lure of an endless stream of arriving western ships, and the curiosities and characters aboard those ships, drew Hawaiian men from outlying villages. The local men enjoyed the exciting, dynamic partying life found only at Kou. Kegs of beer, rum, wine and brandy fueled social life at the huge hangout.

The landmark structure at Kou was the sacred Pākākā Heiau, a human sacrifice (*hai kanaka*) temple built by Kamehameha. A row of human skulls taken from sacrificial victims (*po'okanaka*) lined its rafters. A forboding twenty-eight-foot high carved wooden *ki'i* image of a Hawaiian god guarded the heiau.

To the west, Nu'uanu Stream emptied into the brackish harbor. At the harbor entrance lay a rock-walled fish pond. Wooden weir openings allowed fish to enter, but not swim out. On the east bank of the stream a row of *pili* grass thatched hale served as compounds for western men prominent in the camp. These *haole* (foreigners) were held in high regard by Kamehameha for the military, trading and foreign affairs services they provided.

Kamehameha in 1808 ruled from his royal compound at Waikīkī. He favored the sweet beach life there led amongst coconut-tree-lined white sand beaches. Outrigger canoes launched easily for fishing and transport. For recreation, a row of perfect surfing waves rolled in year-round, forming over a white-sand bottom with little reef.

Kamehameha's desire for wealth and the companionship of western traders drew him to Kou, away from the comforts and pleasures of Waikīkī where his ali'i dwelt in peace away from the trading world. Kou became "the gathering place" for Kamehameha. There sea captains anchored in a safe, deep-water harbor where they sought rest from the sea and supplies for their ships.

Along the shore at Kou, Captain Brintnall chose to make his port-side base at the thatched roof compound of Isaac Davis, a Welshman known as 'Aikaka (Isaac in the Hawaiian language). In the spirit of his Welsh sense of humor, Davis designated his compound at Kou as *Aienui*–the House of Big Debt–a word play on the financial gambles made there on trading ventures, and on card-game gambling losses.

Davis alone survived the massacre of the crew of the ship *Fair American* in 1790 on the leeward side of Hawai'i Island. Kamehameha kept him alive to use Davis as an artillery advisor during sea battles. On the plains of Honolulu in 1795, Davis' accurate firing decimated the defending army at the Battle of Nu'uanu. This key turning point in the invasion led to Kamehameha conquering O'ahu.

For his loyal service, Kamehameha named Davis as governor of O'ahu when the royal court moved there from Hawai'i Island. The Welshman secured his ali'i status by marrying a high-ranking chiefess. Davis spoke fluent Hawaiian and served visiting ship captains as their translator and emissary to Kamehameha.

The Pākākā Heiau cast a shadow over Kou on *kapu* days when all activity halted and an eerie silence enveloped the entire beach complex. No one dared to move about the village nor trade, or eat openly. Such a *kapu*, a restriction practiced as part of the Hawaiian religion, was made in reverence to the presence of a Hawaiian god as determined by kāhuna. The priesthood kept track of kapu days using a moon-phase calendar.

At Kou, acquiring the riches of the West, and the East, became a sign of Hawaiian spiritual, material and political power, a new form of *mana*. Kamehameha's warehouses at Kou brimmed over, filled with silks, barrels of silver Spanish coins, western clothing, and whatever else caught his eyes in ship cargoes.

Ka'ahumanu

The one thorn in Kamehameha's life as Hawai'i's king was his tumultuous relationship with Ka'ahumanu, his favorite queen.

Ka'ahumanu descended from ali'i nui who ruled Hawai'i Island and Maui. She was a distant cousin to Kamehameha. In her youth she captivated him; she was beautiful, young, six-foot-tall, an expert at sliding down waves atop her wooden surfboard. Polynesian-patterned tattoos highlighted Ka'ahumanu's striking features.

By 1808, Ka'ahumanu had matured into a plump,cunning queen about forty years old, younger than Kamehameha, who was in his fifties. She reigned as his most powerful wife. The portly queen went to the battlefield alongside her husband, and Kamehameha listened closely to her political counsel. Ka'ahumanu's weaknesses were her infertility (she bore no heirs for her king and husband) and her promiscuity when she took lovers, angering Kamehameha.

In 1804, an epidemic, possibly of cholera or bubonic plague, devastated the army Kamehameha had gathered in windward O'ahu to attempt again to conquer Kaua'i and Ni'ihau. The deadly plague infected Kamehameha. He recovered, but Ke'eaumoku, the father of Ka'ahumanu, fell deathly ill. On his death bed Ke'eaumoku warned Kamehameha that Ka'ahumanu possessed the power to overthrow him. Kamehameha heeded the warning, and as a hedge around his throne ruled that anyone sleeping with Ka'ahumanu would be put to death.

Looking to the future of his kingdom, Kamehameha named Ka'ahumanu as *kahu*, the guardian, of Liholiho, Kamehameha's young son and heir. Liholiho's mother was Keōpūolani, Kamehameha's queen who possessed royal mana of a rank higher than that of her husband. The *kapu* system of Hawai'i relegated Ka'ahumanu, and most women of Hawai'i, to a subservient role. No women were allowed to eat with men. Ka'ahumanu saw change coming through Liholiho. She knew the young prince was the key to her own future control of Kamehameha's kingdom.

A subject of great contention between Ka'ahumanu and Kamehameha in early 1808 was a plan to send a royal prince (perhaps princes) away to New Haven to study in a western school. Brintnall offered to provide passage aboard the *Triumph* and support in New Haven for schooling. Kamehameha foresaw the future as a time when foreign powers would seek to snatch his kingdom. Knowledge of western ways might be essential to his progeny in retaining their family dynasty's control of the Hawaiian Islands.

Humehume, a son of Kaumuali'i, the king of Kaua'i, sailed away aboard the American ship *Hazard,* under a Captain Rowan, in 1804. His father loaded sandalwood aboard Rowan's ship, the equivalent of thousands of dollars in cash (tens of thousands of dollars today), to pay for the education and care of his young boy in Boston. However, by 1808 contact with Humehume had been lost.

Brintnall's plan to bring home a prince unwittingly thrust him deeply into the realm of royal Hawaiian politics. Liholiho may have been the young prince chosen to sail to New England aboard the *Triumph.*

Mix's Murder

On January, 16, 1808, a baked fish dinner arrived aboard the *Triumph,* perhaps cooked as *lau lau* (a packet of steaming morsels of fish mixed with taro leaves and wrapped in ti leaves, baked underground in an *imu* underground oven pit). One of Kamehameha's queens sent the meal specifically for the dining pleasure of Elihu Mix and Captain Brintnall.

Elihu Mix accepted the proffered meal and ate it. Unaware the fish was poisoned, Mix ingested a deadly toxicant likely laced into the baked dinner: perhaps the guts of a puffer fish, a *kēkē* (*Tetrodon hispidus*). The kēkē swam with mullet in the royal basalt-rock-walled fishpond nearby the inner harbor of the Kou settlement. Hawaiian fishermen easily spotted the fish for its head is similar in shape to a *pueo,* a Hawaiian owl.

The poison circulated through Elihu's bloodstream, causing him to struggle to breathe. A victim ingesting this poison gasps for air as their respiratory system shuts down. Foamy spittle line their lips. After an excruciating struggle to keep breathing, Elihu died.

Brintnall's cavorting ashore saved his life, for when the dinner arrived he was likely residing on land, at the Aienui compound of his friend Isaac Davis.

Combining poison with food or drink to cause death was a weapon used by kāhuna (often following the wishes of ali'i nui) and known as *'apu kōheoheo,* the poisonous cup. Kāhuna were known to mask the taste of the poison by placing it in a portion of cooked pig pulled out of an *imu* underground oven, or by spiking it in a drink of the bitter intoxicating drink awa (*Piper methysticum,* pepper plant), here baked fish was employed.

Sleepwalking Sea Captain

Brintnall skirted death a decade earlier, in mid-June 1797, aboard the ship *Betsey,* captained by Edmund Fanning out of Stonington, Connecticut. This fateful event involving Brintnall occurred in the days following Fanning's discovery of his namesake island, in waters of the Line Islands located about 900 miles south of the Hawaiian Islands. On June 11 Fanning "did...stun and mystify the evening watch by sleepwalking up onto the quarter deck, not once but three times, the last appearing in uniform at about eleven."

This is a facsimile of a map drawn by Captain Caleb Brintnall to illustrate the scene of the murder of his brother-in-law Elihu Mix on January 16, 1808 in Honolulu Harbor. The Aienui compound of Isaac Davis, and the Inner Harbor, where the *Triumph* was likely anchored, is to the far left. The foreigner burial ground where Mix was laid to rest is to left

Courtesy Mystic Seaport Collections Research Center

center, a location near the intersection of today's Piʻikoi Street and King Street. Witetee, Brintnall's spelling of Waikiki, is marked on the far right. The map was found tipped into a journal Mix left with his wife when departing on an earlier China voyage.

Fanning, sensing his sleepwalking as an omen of danger, immediately ordered sails backed, halting the movement of the ship for the night. (This corner of the Line Islands still has a reputation among sailors as a place of supernatural encounters.)

At daylight, Fanning awoke and came upon deck "just as the topmost rays of the sun came peering above a clear eastern horizon."

Dead-ahead a mass of breaking waves washed over a shark-tooth-shaped exposed coral reef. This deadly open-ocean hazard, about the size of a small city, is known today as Kingman Reef. Colliding with Kingman would have stove-in the hull of the *Betsey* leaving the crew at the mercy of the sea. Fanning wrote in his journal:

> In a moment the whole truth flashed before my eyes, as I caught sight of breakers, mast high, directly ahead, and towards which our ship was fast sailing....perceiving the manoeuvre, without being aware of the cause, casting a look at the foaming breakers, his face, from a flush of red, had assumed a death-like paleness...Still no man spake: all was silence, except the needed orders...The officer (Brintnall) to whom the events of the past night were familiar, came aft to me, and with the voice and look of a man deeply impressed with some solemn convictions, said, "Surely, sir, Providence has a care over us, and has kindly directed us again in the road of safety. I cannot speak my feelings, for it seems to me, after what has passed during the night and now also appears before my eyes, as if I had just awaked in another world. Why, sir," continued he, "half an hour's farther run from where we lay by in the night, would have cast us on that fatal spot, where we must all certainly have been lost. If we have, because of the morning haze around the horizon, got so near this appalling danger in broad daylight, what, sir, but the hand of Providence, has kept us clear of it through the night."
>
> We were so fortunate as to weather the breakers on our stretch to the north, and had a fair view and overlook of them from aloft. It was a coral reef or shoal, in the form of a crescent, about six leagues in extent from north to south; under its lee, and within the compass of the crescent, there appeared to be white and shoal water. We did not discover a foot of ground, rock, or sand, above water, where a boat might have been hauled up; of course had our ship run on it in the night, there can be no question but we should all have perished.

Poisoning Motive

Brintnall quickly determined the motive behind Mix's murder: the ongoing battle between Kamehameha and Ka'ahumanu over the future of the prince heading for New England aboard his ship.

Assuming it was Liholiho departing aboard the *Triumph*, the prince's departure, perhaps forever, would leave behind a vacuum in the power of Ka'ahumanu; she would lose one of the two pillars of her political hold on power in the court of Kamehameha. One pillar was her royal bloodlines to powerful ali'i nui on Maui; this provided an upper hand in controlling Kamehameha's access to the military and political support that kept him in power. The second pillar was her control over Liholiho; upon the death of Kamehameha she and Liholiho would corule Hawai'i. Kamehameha named her Liholiho's *kahu*, his guardian, when the prince was an infant. She had waited years to assume rule with Liholiho as an equal in the eyes of their nation, and knew she would be the prince's superior behind the scenes of power due to her seniority.

Brintnall wrote out a brief summary of Mix's murder. The report took months to wind its way back to New Haven. The news carried in the mail bag of a homeward-bound ship informed Elihu's wife Nancy that she was now a widow, that her husband lay in a grave in far away Owhyee.

Isaac Davis died the same death as Mix, poisoned on April 10, 1810. Camp followers of Kamehameha killed him. Davis, then age fifty-two, his hair gone white, invited Kaumuali'i, the king of Kaua'i and Ni'ihau, to his Aienui compound. Kaumuali'i risked the dangers of sailing to an island controlled by Kamehameha to peacefully cede his islands. The Welshman warned Kaumuali'i that a plot was afoot to assassinate him at Waikahalulu Falls along Nu'uanu Stream, a scenic spot located mauka and not far from Kou. Davis saved the life of the Kaua'i king, but in doing so lost his own.

Murder Details Revealed

Details of the murder of Elihu Mix were revealed in a biographical account of his son, written in 1886 by his grandson, Edward Townsend Mix. Edward's father was then a venerable, elderly Connecticut sailing captain long gone from the sea. Edward contributed this recollection of his father's colorful life at sea for a centennial history of his hometown of Hamden. Of the murder of his grandfather he wrote:

> "My grandfather...sailed from New Haven in the little ships of those days, circum-navigating the globe....in 1808, his ship touched for stores at the Sandwich Islands, and while there he was poisoned by the Queen of the Islands...The king wished his young sons to come (to New England) and it was understood the queen, to defeat their object, caused the baked fish she had sent to the officers to be poisoned."

The slim notebook Elihu Mix left behind for his wife provides another view of his poisoning. On the tissue-paper-thin pages Nancy added a postscript, lamenting her husband's tragic death:

> Elihu Mix Died Jan 16th 1808 aged 32 was poisoned by a female native of the Sandwich Islands and his remains are deposited on the Island of Wahoo._The Lord gave, The Lord hath taken away_Blessed be his name_That the Lord will grant me entire submission...

Also in Nancy's hand is the notation, "And was buried under a row of coconut trees on the road to Wyatiti." Mix's grave lay at the Cemetery for Foreigners, a burial ground along a coastal road located on the sandy plain that connected Honolulu and Waikīkī.

It can be assumed that Caleb Brintnall was gravely shocked by the murder of Elihu. His family and personal ties to Elihu were close-knit. Back in New Haven Brintnall's wife Lois, Elihu's sister, bore their fourth child on August 9, 1807, a child to be named Elihu Mix Brintnall.

The dark side of the exotic, and dangerous, -beach world at Kou, the tap root of the city of Honolulu, had crept aboard the *Triumph*. This surely put the captain on guard against new threats to the lives of him and his crew by the ali'i nui and their entourage dwelling on O'ahu. Brintnall saw clearly the deep darkness lying beneath the surface of the casual, festive gatherings when Kamehameha and his queen enjoyed a glass of wine and idle conversation lounging aboard the *Triumph*.

CHAPTER THREE
KEALAKEKUA BAY

Kealakekua Bay is where 'Opukaha'i departed Hawai'i in 1808, and where Captain James Cook died in 1779. 'Ōpūkaha'ia sailed away from his home at the Hikiau Heiau at the invitation of Captain Caleb Brintnall, joining the crew of the *Triumph*. In this aerial photo taken in the 1920s, the Hikiau site is located at right center. The Captain Cook Memorial is at top left. Note waves breaking around a point on south side of bay.

Kealakekua Bay, 1808

THE SAILS OF THE *TRIUMPH* luffed upon passing from the Pacific around Kā'awaloa Point into the still air of Kealakekua Bay. A single cannon shot announced the arrival of the ship to flprovisioners, shipyard workers, curious villagers, and the kāhuna at Hikiau Heiau. The shot produced a muzzle flash, then several moments later a boom which echoed across the vertical ochre-colored cliff face of fan-shaped Pali Kapu O Keōua. The face of that pali is pocked with burial caves of ali'i and overshadows and shields the bay from most winds.

'Ōpūkaha'ia, still faithfully, though halfheartedly, serving his apprenticeship at the Hikiau Heiau sensed the New Haven sealing ship was his door to another world, a world away from Hawai'i. He recalled:

> While I was with my uncle, for some time I began to think about leaving that country (Hawai'i), to go to some other part of the globe. I did not care where I shall go to. I thought to myself that if I should get away, and go to some other country, probably I may find some comfort, more than to live there, without father and mother.
>
> About this time there was a ship come from New York:—Captain Brintnall the master of the ship. As soon as it got into the harbour, in the very place where I lived, I thought of no more but to take the best chance I had, and if the Captain have no objection, to take me as one of his own servants, and to obey his word.

William Ellis - Cook's Journals
"A View of a Morai at Owhyee" by William Ellis, an artist who sailed with Captain James Cook on his third voyage of exploration. This illustration pictures images of the war god Kū mounted on a platform within the Hikiau Heiau at Kealakekua Bay.

While his quick decision to sail with Brintnall is cited as made on a lark, a "boy's notion," 'Ōpūkaha'ia also sought to move beyond the lingering anguish in his spirit brought on by the tragedies inflicted upon his family. He lamented over his years spent as an orphan. Outside of Kealakekua, after he left North Kohala, 'Ōpūkaha'ia faced death when captured during a tribal conflict. He escaped unscathed, but not before seeing warriors throw his aunt off a *pali*, a cliff, to her death. He wanted a chance at a new life, a chance at seeing what fate held for him outside of Hawai'i.

Brintnall and 'Ōpūkaha'ia Meet at Kealakekua Bay
Brintnall knew the landings on the leeward coast of Hawai'i Island, and the customs and trading practices of Kamehameha. About five years earlier the sea captain resupplied in Hawai'i while master of the sealing ship *Oneida*, out of New Haven.

'Ōpūkaha'ia intently watched the *Triumph* come around on a final tack to an anchorage in the middle of Kealakekua Bay, a few hundred yards offshore. Sails were furled, anchors dropped and the crew of the New Haven ship settled in.

Waves washed over the end of a rocky shelf at the foot of Hikiau as 'Ōpūkaha'ia, implacably drawn to the *Triumph*, stepped from rock to rock then dove into the calm bay. He quickly swam out to the *Triumph* unafraid of sharks or the large rays that ply the bay, a feat no sailor aboard the New Haven ship could match. A sentinel named Mika Alani (likely a *Triumph* sailor, perhaps a Mike Allen, known to be a friend of Hewahewa the high priest) welcomed him aboard.

> As soon as the ship anchored I went on board. The Captain soon enquired whose boy I was. Yet I knew not what he says to me for I could not speak the English language. But there was a young man who could speak the English language, and he told the Captain that I was the Minister's nephew (the Minister of that place).

Brintnall welcomed aboard 'Ōpūkaha'ia, and noted the innocent countenance of the well-mannered young Hawaiian man. Brintnall knew young sailors who had joined crews of ship involved in the China Trade. Brintnall knew such men were favored by New

England sea captains for their excellent abilities as sailors, fearless aloft in heavy seas, loyal. In the Age of Sail many Hawaiian sailors, known colloquially as *kanaka* in New England, saileded to ports around the world. Some of these kanaka settled, forming Hawaiian communities in faraway places. Having sailed several times to Polynesia (to Hawai'i and the Marquesas) Brintnall was comfortable with, and knowledgeable of, the ways of its peoples. 'Ōpūkaha'ia responded to Brintnall's invitation:

> The Captain wished me to stay on board the ship that night, and the next day go home. This very much satisfied me, and I consented to stay. At evening the Captain invited me to eat supper with him.
>
> And there sat another boy with us who was to be my fellow-traveler; by name Thomas Hopoo (Hopu).

Hopu was about twelve years old, eight years younger than 'Ōpūkaha'ia, who was now about twenty years old. Hopu may have been recruited at Kawaihae Bay, about forty miles north of Kealakekua. His birthplace was in North Kohala.

In his memoirs, Hopu wrote of living with a bleak memory of his own family trauma. He told of his mother rejecting him as a new-born. She ordered her sister to kill him, to spare her the trouble of raising another child, perhaps also in fear of a tribal attack. In a Moses-like scene, his aunt came upon him and picked up infant Hopu from the ground. She wrapped him in a blanket and moved him away twenty miles to the home of her brother. The man named the baby Nauhopoouah Hopoo, for he was his sister's *hopu*, her "catch." When he was four years old, his parents took Hopu back to their home. At age nine his mother died and his father lost their property and possessions. His father journeyed to a new place, probably in a different *ahupua'a*, a place Hopu named as Kalaikauhawah Bay, perhaps Kawaihae Bay.

'Ōpūkaha'ia agreed without hesitation to sign-on with the *Triumph* crew and sail away from the Hawaiian Islands, intertwining his fate with that of Brintnall's.

> After supper the Captain made some enquiry to see if we were willing to come to America; soon I made a motion with my head that I was willing to go. This man was very agreeable, and his kindness was much delighted in my heart, as if I was his own son, and he was my own father.

Forbidden to Leave

Leaving Hawai'i also meant ending the apprenticeship as a kahuna serving Lono he began as a child under his uncle Pahua. Being diplomatic, the Yankee sea captain avoided muddying his ties to Kamehameha, and Pahua and the Hawaiian ali'i and kāhuna at Kealakekua Bay; he knew not to sail away with 'Ōpūkaha'ia without his uncle's permission. He returned 'Ōpūkaha'ia to shore; there Pahua questioned him.

> He asked me where was I been through all that night before. I told him that I was on board the ship and staid there all the night. And I told him what my object was, and all what the Captain invite me to.

Pahua rejected the request of 'Ōpūkaha'ia and isolated him at his compound located adjacent to the tall and wide basalt rock Hikiau Heiau.

> As soon as my uncle heard that I was going to leave him, he shut me up in a room, for he was not willing to let me go. While I was in the room my old grand-mother (Hina) coming in, asked me what was my notion of leaving them, and go with people whom I know not. I told her it is better for me to go than to stay there. She said if I should leave them I shall not see them any more. I told her that I shall come back in a few months if I live. Her eyes filled with tears. She said that I was very foolish boy...I saw a little hole in the side of the house, I got through it and went on board the ship.

Finding his nephew gone, Pahua paddled an outrigger canoe out to the *Triumph* to inquire if 'Ōpūkaha'ia was aboard. A sailor on watch found 'Ōpūkaha'ia and Brintnall obliged, returning the youth to Pahua.

Before Brintnall sailed, Pahua reconsidered his nephew's request and agreed to let him sail away. But the kahuna demanded that Brintnall purchase a hog to be sacrificed at Hikiau. This act may have propitiated a god, or gods, the price paid for the young kahuna ending his worship in their temple. In his log book Brintnall signed on 'Ōpūkaha'ia as a sailor, and Hopu as a cabin boy. 'Ōpūkaha'ia later wrote:

> ...I took my leave of them and bid them farewell...My parting with them was disagreeable to them and to me, but I was willing to leave all my relations, friends and acquaintance; expected to see them no more in this world.

The *Triumph* sailed from the bay, passing the site of the death of Captain Cook at the entrance at the village of Ka'awaloa, past the lava rock point into light winds.

Honolulu to Kealakekua?

There is no mention of the murder of Elihu Mix in the memoirs of 'Ōpūkaha'ia or Hopu. Possibly the murder took place prior to their joining the crew of the *Triumph*; possibly they chose not to disclose the murder to protect the reputation of the ali'i nui tainted decades earlier in the western world by the killing of Captain Cook at Kealakekua Bay.

Considering how the murder of Elihu Mix affected the fate of 'Ōpūkaha'ia opens up an intriguing line of inquiry. It is certain that Captain Brintnall being ashore when the fish dinner arrived saved his life and preserved the voyage, leading to 'Ōpūkaha'ia's departure from Hawai'i. If Brintnall had eaten the poison fish dinner and died along with brother-in-law Elihu, the *Triumph* crew would have been in disarray. Perhaps the ship would have been confiscated by Kamehameha, dashing 'Ōpūkaha'ia's hope of experiencing life in foreign lands.

Circumstantial evidence points to a more providential scenario: the murder of Mix caused Brintnall to weigh anchor in Honolulu then sail south, fleeing the wrath of Ka'ahumanu by sailing to Kealakekua Bay. In 1808, only the ports at Kou and at Kealakekua Bay provided sufficient provisioning, watering and firewood services for western ships visiting Hawai'i. Contemporary accounts of Mix's murder offer no definitive proof that a Honolulu stop preceded the sail to Kealakekua, or if a landing in Kealakekua preceded the stop in Honolulu. Locating Brintnall's *Triumph* journal, or ship's log, would provide the answer.

Once in Hawaiian waters, Brintnall needed to sail back to Isla Guadalupe as quickly as possible to provide essential supplies to his sealing crew. It is doubtful two port stops were planned. The timing of the murder of Mix in January off Kou Landing points to a first stop in Honolulu. A New England shipping news report has the *Triumph* arriving from Baja in November 1807, likely in Honolulu according to a China trade researcher. The sail to Kealakekua Bay appears to have been unplanned, a sail of survival.

If Mix's murder did force Brintnall to flee Honolulu for Kealakekua to the southeast (a difficult, bumpy sail of about 180 miles into the northeast trade winds), then the murder of Elihu Mix becomes a catalytic, key turning point in the history of Hawai'i. No sail to Kealakekua, no departure by 'Ōpūkaha'ia for New Haven aboard the *Triumph*–thus a cutting off at the root the chain of events that culminated in American missionaries departing from Boston in October 1819, arriving in Hawai'i in late March 1820.

The account given by Edward Mix in the 1880s points to Brintnall fleeing to Kealakekua Bay. In this pre-whaling ship era (Nantucket whalers made their first stopovers in Honolulu and Lāhainā in 1819), Edward Mix cited the death of his father Elihu as a martyrdom. He wrote that his family saw the poisoning as an event that set in motion the formation and sending of the first Sandwich Islands Mission company. Edward recalled:

> This was the time of considerable missionary zeal on the part of the New England churches, and several young islanders were brought over for education under Christian societies...In a sense it may be said he (Elihu) was one of the early martyrs to the missionary zeal of New England churches. My grandmother (Elihu's widow Nancy Atwater Mix) was then, and later, one of the most active and influential women in the mission and other church work of the times.

The New England connection to Hawai'i made first by China trade captains became permanent with the arrival of the Sandwich Islands Mission. The American missionaries became residents of Hawai'i, while almost all American traders sailed away from Hawai'i for home. This church-trader connection to the United States kept other foreign powers from colonizing Hawai'i. The first commercial sugar plantation in Hawai'i developed in Kōloa, Kaua'i and was funded and run by Americans. If there was no permanent American presence in Hawai'i, Great Britain, France, Japan, or Russia would have likely become the dominant foreign power. If so, sugar plantations might not have opened, or if they did might have resembled the notorious British West Indies plantations manned by slaves. The New England Protestant missionary tie added a morality to the running of sugar plantations in Hawai'i, a benevolence lacking in other sugar-growing regions of the world. Blackbirding sea captains enslaved islanders they took from remote Pacific islands and could have become a slave labor suppliers for sugar companies in Hawai'i if a nation other than America was in control. An island society might have formed along lines similar to the policy of Great Britain in Fiji; there a sole immigrant population (Indians from India) was imported for field work.

It is certain that Captain Brintnall did sail to Kealakekua Bay prior to returning to Isla Guadalupe. At Kealakekua he recruited two adventurous Hawaiian youths ready to sail away from their home island, youths perhaps unaware they were on the way to some of the most desolate islands found on the west coast of North America.

CHAPTER FOUR
NORTHWEST SEAL ISLANDS

Isla Guadalupe, Baja, Mexico, Spring 1808

AFTER THREE WEEKS AT SEA SPENT SAILING A PASSAGE of over two-thousand miles from an island paradise, the *Triumph* approached a desolate, towering, black-cliffed volcanic island off the coast of Baja.

Soon after departing Kealakekua Bay, ʻŌpūkahaʻia took to the ship's daily watch routine of scrubbing decks and climbing black, tarred ratlines to trim sails.

Generally, in picturing the fur trade era of the early nineteenth-century, the term sailing to the "Seal Islands" on the "Northwest Coast" conjures up an image of landing on a chilly coastline lined with massive trees. However, in 1808 sea captains considered the Northwest Coast as a region encompassing a wide swath of territory running from the sea otter fur hunting regions of chilly British Columbia and Alaska, down to temperate Alta California and Baja California.

Back in Baja

By May, 1808, the *Triumph* was cruising between the sealing islands off central Baja. In the fall of 1807 Captain Caleb Brintnall left behind at least two sealing crews, one on Isla Guadalupe and one on nearby Isla San Benito, and possibly another crew at Isla Cedros. The crews went all out in gathering the soft under-fur skins that sold in Canton for about a tenth of the price of the plush pelts of sea otters hunted on the Northwest Coast. In addition to the obvious superiority of a sea otter pelt, the higher price reflected the need to rely on an Indian hunter trained from childhood to spear a wily sea otter in the currents, winds and waves of cold offshore waters; any green Connecticut sailor bold enough to face a pod of four-hundred-pound seals could club a fur seal to death.

Prior to his Sandwich Island sojourn of 1807-1808, Brintnall sailed thousands of miles north after reconnoitering the sealing rookeries of the Juan Fernandez Islands off Chile. There he found the beaches and coves of the mountainous islands stripped of fur seals. Over a span of about ten years, New England crews clubbed, skinned and sailed away from the Juan Fernandez Islands to China with an estimated one to three million fur seal skins.

With his plans to seal on the Chilean islands scuttled, the pressure was on the relentless New Haven sealing captain to find an unexploited sealing ground. Being desperate for a cargo to trade with in China, he gambled, plotting a course north to the islands offshore of the Baja peninsula, perhaps counting on a tip passed along to him on an earlier voyage to the Pacific Ocean. This change in plans added an unexpected sail of over 4,900 nautical miles up the coast of South America. The sail north cost Brintnall an unbudgeted extra month of supplies, and placed him in waters patrolled by Spanish frigates on the lookout for Yankee ships. The *Triumph* crew knew heading north was a gamble, their voyage north the equivalent in sea miles of a sail from New Haven to London and back–all without any assurance the *Triumph* would come upon an island teeming with fur seals.

Desolate Isla Guadalupe

The first landfall away from Hawai'i for 'Ōpūkaha'ia and Hopu brought them to a chilly sea and a foggy island unlike balmy Hawai'i, to the coast off Isla Guadalupe. This unpeopled island presented a harsh first look for them at the world outside Hawai'i. Just a 180-mile sail away to the northeast lay civilization at the busy port town and Spanish mission of San Diego in Alta California. One other youth from Hawai'i joined them on the voyage; his identity (unlikely a royal prince) is unknown.

Isla Guadalupe casts a foreboding presence from the sea. Veteran globe-trotting sea explorer Jacques Costeau described the island and its spirit of place as "High, hostile, and huge...." Isla Guadalupe runs twenty miles north to south and six miles across at its widest point. Great White sharks flock to its coast, which is rich in marine life. The black, basalt vertical walls of the volcanic island reach up 4,500 feet from its rocky shore to its highest peak.

'Ōpūkaha'ia recalled arriving at Isla Guadalupe: "On these Islands the Captain left twenty or thirty men for sealing business on his way to Owyhee. We found them safe."

The crew of hardy men dwelt together in beachfront lean-tos roofed with seal skins. Their world was the island's beaches. They kept a close tally of their work for one skin in a hundred went to each of them.

Fur seals were shepherded upland, off the downward-tilted, black sand and pebbled beaches onto smooth sand tablelands for clubbing, then skinning. The furs were spread out to dry near the crew's camps and held down with wooden pegs.

'Ōpūkaha'ia and Hopu might have stayed aboard the *Triumph* during their months off Baja. Brintnall sailed his ship from island to island as an offshore supply base for his beached sealing crews.

'Ōpūkaha'ia noted the attention shown him by crewman Russell Hubbard, an adventurous Yale theology student from Hamden, Connecticut off on a post-graduate adventure. The friendly Yalie was a classmate of author James Fenimore Cooper, both members of the Yale Class of 1806. Yale students were known to be pranksters. Cooper was expelled for sending a flash of gunpowder through a student-room keyhole, blowing away the door. Hubbard introduced 'Ōpūkaha'ia to Christianity and western education.

Black paper, hand-cut silhouette profile of Russell Hubbard, from Yale College Class of 1806 class album. Author James Fenimore Cooper graduated along with Hubbard. Cooper afterwards went to sea and wrote fictional accounts of New England sealers. This class album is notable, credited as being the first-ever college, or high school, yearbook.

Among these men I found a very desirable young man, by name Russell Hubbard, a son of Gen. H. of New Haven (his father was a War of 1812 general). This Mr. Hubbard was a member of Yale College. He was a friend of Christ. Christ was with him when I saw him, but I knew it not. "Happy is the man that put his trust in God!" Mr. Hubbard was very kind to me on our passage, and taught me the letters in English spelling-book.

Fourth of July Far From Home

Overcoming the dark spirit of the island, the upbeat morale of the young Connecticut men turned their stay into a lark. The crew of the Boston ship *Amethyst* joined them at a beachside Fourth of July party and feast in 1808. Two pigs, likely traded for in Hawai'i, were roasted; baskets of mussels substituted for a Connecticut clam bake; Johnny cakes and draughts of rum added a New England flavor. For entertainment, the African-American cook of the *Triumph* played Yankee doodle on his violin, and

Life on the Ocean

A crew from a sealing ship clubs fur seals on a remote island in the Juan Fernandez chain located west of Chile. Sailors from the *Triumph* crew clubbed seals in the same manner on Isla Guadalupe. The *Triumph* took away 50,000 skins.

Hubbard sang "Hail Columbia," one of the unofficial national anthems of the United States throughout the nineteenth-century.

An account found in the journal of the *Amethyst* notes that an Indian (a generic term often used in the China trade era to describe a Hawaiian or Tahitian sailor) served food and drink during the celebration, known as a "gam," a social gathering of two ships' companies; this server may have been 'Ōpūkaha'ia or Hopu.

Adding a Yale prank to the festivities, Hubbard (possibly his brother) dressed up in a makeshift toga. Climbing atop a beach rock, he delivered a humorous oration in Latin to the assembled crews.

As the seal mating season off Baja drew to a close, the isolated crews of sealers were picked up by Brintnall. Their final chore was transporting Guadalupe Fur Seal skins aboard boats out to the *Triumph*, to be stowed in its cargo hold.

In all, about 50,000 fur seal skins left the Spanish-owned Baja islands aboard the *Triumph*. Such skins were one of the few western trade goods Canton merchants accepted from Yankee sea captains. The capital needed to underwrite a crew of sealers was affordable compared to using barrels of silver coins bought on credit from a bank in New Haven to buy China goods in Canton.

With the sealing in Isla Guadalupe complete, Brintnall set his ship on a return course to Honolulu to make a brief provisioning stop on the way to China.

Brintnall told 'Ōpūkaha'ia and Hopu that once back in the Islands they were free to leave the crew of the New Haven ship, to stay at home in Hawai'i, or to stay aboard the *Triumph* for the long voyage across the Central Pacific to China and beyond.

CHAPTER FIVE
China Trade

ʻŌPŪKAHAʻIA AND HOPU FACED A MOMENTOUS DECISION as the *Triumph* approached Oʻahu on its return from Isla Guadalupe. A short provisioning stop was scheduled prior to the long sail west to Canton. Should they stay in their homeland and return to the good and the bad of the lives they knew? Or should they take up the invitation of Captain Brintnall to join him on a sail half-way around the globe, final destination the East River in New York?

Honolulu to China

The *Triumph* made port in Honolulu Harbor in the balmy late summer, early autumn Island season of 1808. Brintnall knew to sail west before the variable kona winds of the Makahiki season of late autumn blew, winds that drove ships upon a lee shore.

The New Haven captain wanted ʻŌpūkahaʻia and Hopu to sail on, but by their own choice, not due to his prodding. Brintnall ordered his crew to not wander from the anchorage at Honolulu. The *Triumph* would sail in just a day or two. The captain needed to resolve any lingering political intrigue over Kamehameha's wish to have his son, the young prince, depart for New England. Hopu wrote in his memoirs:

> In our absence to the northwest coast of America, the King had changed his mind (about sending his son to New England with Brintnall for a western education), because he feared that some evil would befall the prince, and he would never return to his father again: So that he stayed in Oahhoo, one of the Sandwich Islands. Both of us, however, who were to have been the attendants of the young prince, having our expectations excited, and having a strong curiosity to see America, we both of us continued in the ship, expecting to return to our native island, by the first favorable opportunity, after gratifying our curiosity of seeing America.

ʻŌpūkahaʻia noted that Brintnall, "...delayed no longer than a few days, and we set out for China, on our direct course to America."

Brintnall timed the five-week passage from Hawaiʻi to Canton to avoid sailing in seas roiled by late-winter to early-summer typhoons that turn the South China Sea into a maelstrom. The calm-weather months of fall follow the typhoon season and mark the opening of Chinese fur trading establishments known as *hongs*.

The journey went smoothly covering thousands of miles of empty, warm Pacific waters, along a line of north latitude that lays just a few degrees south of Hawaiʻi's. Sailing in the right season meant little change of sail beyond trimming along the straight-shot, westward course plotted by Brintnall from Hawaiʻi to Canton.

The winds and sea currents of the empty ocean gradually changed as Brintnall and his crew approached the Ladrones. ("Thieves Islands," islands known today as the Northern Marianas, north of Guam.) They sailed south of the coral reef-lined lower tip of Formosa, and entered the murky waters of the South China Sea.

During this passage, a wave swept Hopu overboard as he washed dishes with salt water while standing out onto the chains, the exposed side of the ship's gunwales.

'Ōpūkahaʻia wrote of almost losing his closest friend to the deep:

> The Captain calls all hands upon the deck, and ordered to have all the sails pull down in order to let about....my friend Thomas was out of sight. While he was in the water, he pulls all off his clothes in order to be lighter. We turned our ship and went back after him. We found him almost dead. He was in the water during the space of two and a half hours. O how glad was I then to see him for he was already gone.

Hopu recalled in his memoirs his faith-building, near-death ordeal:

> ...I fell overboard. It was early in the morning, while my Captain was fast asleep in the cabin. But while I was in the water, longside of the ship...At this time, the wind blew very high, so that the waves roared, and the ship was going at about nine knots an hour....I lost sight of the ship...though I was an expert swimmer, I gave myself up for lost. Then I cried to my god, Akooah, for help, and made my vow to him, in the hour of trouble, that if he would save me out of the great and mighty waters, and I might reach the ship, I would devote to my god, Akooah, a fine jacket, which I had received from my Captain, as a present. And I also made several short prayers to the great Spirit...I considered myself in the greatest danger of being swallowed up in the mighty ocean. I expected to die before the ship would reach me. While the waves of the sea were breaking over my head, every moment, I then thought that it must be a very hard thing for me to die, in the full strength of this mortal body....I saw a bird come from God, as I thought, out of the clouds, down to me, on the water....I was greatly rejoiced to see such a messenger sent down to me from the great Spirit....Then the ship again reached me, and I was taken on board: but I could not speak a word to any one of my shipmates, because I was almost dead when I got on board the ship. Immediately after I got on board, a great shark came alongside the ship. I suppose the shark followed my track. O! What a wonderful mercy of God is this, that God who is infinite in kindness to so unworthy a creature as I am; and whose hand is not shortened, that it cannot save, neither his ear heavy, that it cannot hear....When the poor cry for help, in their troubles, He is always near to save them.

Trouble off Macao

The *Triumph* entered the waters offshore of Cathay, the Celestial Kingdom of China, anchoring off the island of Macao. The Portuguese leased this colony in 1557 and were allowed to stay to promote trade and ward off pirates for the Chinese. Here 'Ōpūkahaʻia and Hopu were reprieved from a cold first winter away from Hawaiʻi, instead they landed in the warm sub-tropical climate of South China.

"Very early in the morning, we met the Chinese fleet, on the coast of China, about three thousand boats," Hopu wrote of the muddy sea brimming with lateen-sail fishing boats and merchant junks sailing in a hundred different directions.

Captain Brintnall gathered his ship's papers and pulled from a cabinet his heavy cashbox, loaded with Spanish silver coins. From experience he knew to forego his Yankee thriftiness in navigating the complex Chinese trading protocol known as

Captain Caleb Brintnall set a course west from Honolulu in 1808 across the west Pacific Ocean to Canton, passing through the Ladrone Islands (present day Northern Mariana Islands), south of the southern tip of Formosa, and into the South China Sea.

---

cumshaw. At Canton, bribing officials, and sliding under the table extortionate payments to bureaucrats, were anticipated transactions.

The upriver sail to Canton began with the hiring of a Macao pilot to guide the *Triumph* up to the gates of the Pearl River. But before a pilot could respond to the ship's cannon shot, the *Triumph* was accosted by a British frigate. Unknowingly, Brintnall had sailed into an international incident involving Great Britain and China. His crew had spotted the British East Indies warship anchored off Macao, a signal of trouble ahead. ʻŌpūkahaʻia described spending tense days at anchor off Macao when the safety of their captain and the future of the voyage hung in doubt:

> ...we fired one of our cannon for a pilot. When we had fired once or twice, there was another ship of war belonging to the British, which stood about four or five miles apart from us. As soon as they heard our cannon they sent one of their brigs. We were taken by it for a while. They took our captain...he was there for a number of days.

Brintnall's captor may have been British Royal Navy admiral William O'Bryen Drury, naval commander of Britain's East Indies Station, aboard HMS *Russell*. About three months earlier, Drury sailed from his India station to Macao with a squadron of three ships of war to occupy the Portuguese Island. It was the height of the Napoleonic Wars and Great Britain feared France would remove their Portuguese allies from Macao. Some three-hundred British troops landed at Macao. The Chinese government in Canton threatened an armed battle with the British due to drunken British soldiers vandalizing Chinese tombs and generally raising hell throughout the cosmopolitan island.

Satisfied the *Triumph* was no threat, the Royal Navy released Brintnall: the Canton trading was on. The destiny of ʻŌpūkahaʻia and Hopu would have changed if Brintnall had been imprisoned, if the *Triumph* had been seized by the Royal Navy. If the voyage stalled in Canton they would have secured a berth on another merchant ship, as Hawaiian sailors often did. American ships departing Canton rarely headed for Hawaiʻi, most headed for the Indian Ocean, the Cape of Good Hope, final destination a port in America or Europe.

Thomas Allom *China, In a Series of Views*
A view of Whampoa Island where the *Triumph* lay at anchor. A climb to the top of the
pagoda on the island provided visiting sailors expansive views of the Pearl River.

Up the Pearl River to Whampoa Anchorage

Brintnall foresaw being in the Chinese port for about three months. The *Triumph* anchored off Macao on December 20, according to British customs records archived in Canton. The first step was paying a substantial fee to a *hoppo* (customs superintendent) to begin the trading process.

Guided by a pilot the *Triumph* sailed about forty miles north to the citadel guarding the entrance to the Pearl River, to a narrow opening known as Boca Tigris (mouth of the tiger). The wide, shallow, muddy, fast-flowing river beyond led to the fabled walled city of Canton. The shallowness of the river served as a guard against attack upon wealthy Canton by foreign frigates. Western captains relied on their Chinese pilot to keep from going aground as their ships weaved around river bars. The pilots knew which channels were deep enough, knew the time of the tides.

The Pearl River pilot departed after finding an anchorage for the *Triumph* at Whampoa Island. This Chinese island served as an official gathering place for foreign trading ships and their crews. Here the crews stayed behind while ship's officers were rowed upriver to warehouse buildings known as factories built along a neat row of narrow streets at the gates of Canton. Cargoes of furs, silver specie, sandalwood, and other imported trading goods followed, loaded on lighters and junks, transported under guard to the trading factories upriver.

A handful of wealthy financiers gathered in a collective known as the *Co. Hong* were appointed by the Emperor of China as emissaries to the western traders. The Co. Hong representative stepped in to finance and facilitate trading with Chinese merchants. He was responsible for all aspects of the dealing, for any debts incurred, and to resolve any disturbances a crew might become embroiled in while in port.

The trustworthy *hongs* patiently dealt with the western traders, always looking towards long-term profits. Promissory notes underwrote the deals, the contracts written in classical Chinese characters. Funds from banks in New Haven, New York, Salem and elsewhere might be years in arriving in Canton to conclude the exchanges.

The sterling reputation and honest dealing of the hongs generated huge fortunes for American maritime merchants. The hongs became revered figures in American ports, long remembered by returning sea captains. Brintnall signed a promissory note to repay funds fronted him by the hong Consequa, with a due date of 1810 in Canton.

At the factories, captains and supercargoes from New England, New York and Philadelphia, from London, Amsterdam, Stockholm enjoyed each other's company and were wined and dined by the Chinese hongs.

Brintnall turned a good profit from the sale of the thousands of Guadalupe fur seal skins brought upriver from the *Triumph.* The proceeds paid for a return cargo of export China goods: a variety of teas carefully boxed for shipping, bolts of silk and durable nankeen cotton fabric, sets of Chinaware, cinnamon and spices, and more.

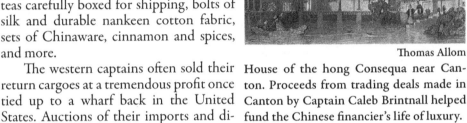

Thomas Allom

The western captains often sold their return cargoes at a tremendous profit once tied up to a wharf back in the United States. Auctions of their imports and direct selling of the cargo in transactions House of the hong Consequa near Canton. Proceeds from trading deals made in Canton by Captain Caleb Brintnall helped fund the Chinese financier's life of luxury.

made over week or so in home port determined the profit of a voyage that might take three years to complete.

Brintnall's personal purchases of Chinese goods included a set of prized paintings. The oil paintings are set pieces, ones repeated again and again for the traders to take back to their home port to show their families and friends what they had seen and experienced. The set selected and brought home to New Haven could have been used by Captain Brintnall to show his passage to Canton. The set starts with the island of Macao, then Boca Tigris, then Whampoa, and finally, the grand view of the trading hongs at the gates to Canton. Sometimes the Chinese painters, aptly employing non-Asian, European painting techniques and styles, would toss in a fifth painting of a significant place along the Golden Round China Trade route, one heading out or en route from Canton. In the Brintnall set, the fifth painting was a landscape of Table Bay at Cape Town, near the southern tip of Africa.

The Chinese artists took meticulous care in keeping current the historical changes of the views they were presenting. In the Brintnall paintings, they added specific buildings at Macao and placed new sheds in the distance at Whampoa; Dutch flags on the ships at Table Bay date the scene to one prior to 1806 when the British took over the African port town.

Along with his paintings, Brintnall brought home rattan furniture, personalized Chinaware and other gifts for his family, friends and himself.

A Sailor's Life at Whampoa

Back at Whampoa, a *compradore,* a local caterer-buyer, served 'Ōpūkaha'ia and

Life on the Ocean

Western trading ships and Chinese junks mingle on the Pearl River near Whampoa Island downriver from the city gates of Canton.

Hopu and the working crew aboard the *Triumph*. Henry and Thomas perhaps sampled rice and Chinese dishes, and fruits like lychee, and tried to eat using chopsticks. Taro, the pasty mainstay of the Hawaiian diet, sold in abundance in Whampoa markets and could have been mixed with water and smashed into *poi*. On Whampoa Island "joss" house altars held statues of Chinese deities venerated with burning sticks of aromatic incense. Across the river, villages and rice fields checkered the landscape. At evening wood fires heated up crew dinners. Inviting whiffs of sizzling meat alleviated for a time the stench of the Pearl River in the soft light atmosphere cast by Chinese lanterns. Ornate flower boats passed by, decorated with carved birds and flowers and colored windows, transporting attractive young women. The arrival of a Mandarin boat carrying armed Chinese officials and marine police usually meant trouble, especially if wandering crewmen caused trouble in a Chinese village.

Crews often idled at Whampoa for months. To keep up morale, and minimize mischief, daily maintenance chores were ordered to fill idle days and ensure the ship was ready to sail on time: painting, rerigging lines, sail mending, cleaning the cargo hold, and major jobs such as replacing tall masts.

As was the custom when weighing anchor at Whampoa, merchants and sea captains satisfied with both ends of their dealing, feeling in harmony with each other, funded the lighting of a good luck *chin chin*. This huge pack of red firecrackers, suspended on the end of a pole, lit up like an exploding exclamation point, clearing the air after weeks of intense trading.

Departure from Canton

In March 1809, the *Triumph* departed from Whampoa, sailed downriver past Macao and headed for the Sunda Straits and the Indian Ocean. For the young sailor 'Ōpūkaha'ia and cabin boy Hopu, content and well fed during their weeks in China, their adventure into the world outside Hawai'i continued.

CHAPTER SIX
CHINA TO NEW YORK

CAPTAIN BRINTNALL KEPT HIS CREW on watch for attack by Malay pirates during the four-week passage south from Macao through the South China Sea to the Java Sea. With the right timing, a ship might catch the trade winds of a northeast monsoon. The final, most dangerous leg of the passage passed the coast of Borneo, weaved through the narrow Sunda Strait that separates Sumatra and Java, ending at Java Head, the entrance to the Indian Ocean.

Brintnall warned the crew to be on alert for boarding by Sumatran pirates; of ramming into unmarked jagged hull-piercing reefs; of being pulled off course by unfamiliar currents or being struck by an equatorial lightning bolt that might ignite the gunpowder magazine; to be ready to dodge pumice stones sent skyward by eruptions on smoldering, sulphurous-smelling volcanic islets they might pass.

On this passage sailors doubled up during watches. Weapons in the armory lay ready for action: cutlasses, pikes and pistols. Bags of gunpowder were stacked nearby cannons and swivel guns. Nets hung from the lower yard arms, circling the main deck, ready to snare nefarious boarders.

The humid, hot. light-wind tropical equatorial climate of this passage–so unlike the temperate, four-seasons climate of New England and Great Britain–tried the patience of China trade crews. The blazing sun melted tar coating ratlines and ropes, making a mess of their hands and clothes, and dripping on deck, adding misery to the daily scrubbing of decks. In light winds sailors climbed in the heat of the day to wet down sails to increase the force of what little wind blew.

Java Head served as a landmark, marking the entrance to the wide reaches of the Indian Ocean. There a ship was free to sail far offshore of coastline dangers.

A Visit by King Neptune

Captain Brintnall ran a tight ship, but wasn't above enjoying a spell of fun. Well into the Indian Ocean passage he ordered 'Ōpūkahaʻia and Hopu to the main deck. In a sonorous voice, King Neptune, wearing ragged nautical regalia, announced his arrival from the deep and climbed aboard over the gunwales, his court following behind. This nautical tradition marks a crossing of the equator (the "line" to sailors). Sea captains hold the comic ceremony to break up the monotony of a long voyage.

"Pollywogs" (sailors who had yet to cross the line) were doused with salt water and dung before a court of the mop-headed ruler. This day only 'Ōpūkahaʻia and Hopu stood before Neptune. The remainder of the crew were "shellbacks" (veterans of a crossing of the line and an anointment by King Neptune). 'Ōpūkahaʻia recalled his initiation:

At the Cape of Good Hope, or before it, our sailors on board the ship began to terrify at us. They said that there was a man named Neptune who lived in that place and his abiding place was in the sea. In the evening, the sailors begun the act. One of them took an old great coat and put on him, and with a speaking trumpet in his hand, and his head was covered with a sheep-skin; and he went forward of the ship and making a great noise. About this time friend Thomas and myself were on the quarter deck, hearing some of them telling about Neptune's coming...we heard the sound of trumpet as follows. "Ship hail! from whence came you?" The Captain immediately giving an answer in this manner: "From Canton." "Have you got my boys," said the old Neptune. "Yes," answered the Captain. "How many boys have you," added the old Neptune. "Two," said the Captain...As soon as we both heard the Captain says "two," we both scared almost to death; and wished that we were at home. The old Neptune wished to see us; but we dare not come near at it. ...After our conversation with him he wished for drink....I went and filled two pails full of salt-water...he took his speaking trumpet and put it in my mouth for funnel, in order to make me drink that salt water which I brought.

...I took hold of the speaking trumpet and hold it on one side of my cheek, so that I may not drink a drop of salt water: did not any body knew it for it was dark. But friend Thomas he was so full of scare, he took down a great deal of salt water. On the next morning he was taken sick, and puked from the morning until the evening.

Sailors new to the crossing of the Indian Ocean anticipated a break from the dangers and hard work they faced when crossing the Atlantic, the Pacific and rounding Cape Horn; they assumed the Indian Ocean would present just a short hop from the East Indies to Africa...until they actually sailed this passage. It was a long sail across the Indian Ocean (about 4,500 nautical miles); the roughest part of the voyage came off the British-controlled south tip of the African continent. Portuguese explorer Bartholomew Diaz named the massive headland Cape Tempestuoso (the "Cape of Storms"), but his king quickly renamed it the Cape of Good Hope to calm the fears of Portuguese sailors.

Once the Cape was doubled, Captain Brintnall plotted a course up the South Atlantic Ocean, avoiding the coasts of West Africa and South America. It is unknown if the *Triumph* made a rest stop at lonely Ascension Island or at St. Helena (islands below the equator that lay midway between the horn of Brazil and Africa), a common practice in those days by American sea captains.

During the long Canton-New York voyage, Christians among the crew taught the Lord's Prayer to ʻŌpūkahaʻia and Hopu, and Russell Hubbard continued his tutoring.

Lower Manhattan Sojourn

A marine report published in the *Connecticut Herald* newspaper announced the arrival of the *Triumph* in New York. The voyage from Canton ended on Saturday, August 5, 1809. The passage took 157 days from the Pearl River to a berth at Schermerhorn's Wharf on the East River in Lower Manhattan.

In port, culture shock hit ʻŌpūkahaʻia and Hopu. In and around the wharf roamed drunken sailors from up and down the eastern seaboard and both sides of the Atlantic. Free African-American sailors comprised a good percentage of American

Harper's Weekly

A wharf scene on the East River near Schermerhorn Wharf where dockworkers unloaded the *Triumph*'s cargo of China goods. This mid-nineteenth-century view looks west towards the Tontine Coffee House and the tall steeple of Trinity Church.

---

crews. These sailors crossed paths with black slaves toiling at loading and unloading cargoes, including bales of cotton grown on southern plantations being transshipped from New York to London. The profane sailors rollicking about were a breed unlike the *Triumph* crew out of Connecticut: the Yalies, the sober and friendly veteran sailors, and New Haven-born lads on their one and only circumnavigation.

The bustle of the city outmatched Whampoa. Peddlers of goods and flesh hawked their wares. Music rang out from bawdy port-side taverns; a forest of bowsprits shaded the waterfront up and down the East River, "belted around by wharves as Indian isles by coral reefs."

"On our arrival to this country, I perceived many new things, that I never had seen before in all my life," Hopu wrote in his memoirs. "It seemed sometimes that it would make one almost sick, to see so many kinds of curiosities, in the city of New York."

The timing by Brintnall of the departure and arrival of the *Triumph* was perfect. In early 1807, he sailed out of New Haven Harbor just three months before President Thomas Jefferson enacted the Embargo and Non-Intercourse Act; this act shut down foreign shipping from American ports. Now in summer 1809 foreign trade from American ports had just reopened, merchant ships were just departing for China when Brintnall sailed up the busy East River with a full cargo of China goods. The pent-up consumer demand for the luxury China goods with little or no supply in stock was driving bids high at the auction blocks in lower Manhattan.

Brintnall paid off his crew. The men pocketed the payoff from their substantial shares and departed for home. This left their captain, 'Ōpūkaha'ia, and Hopu to man the unusually quiet ship.

Auctions for the variety of China goods brought aboard the *Triumph* were advertised. Merchants and traders placed bids at the Tontine Coffee House auction room located a short walk from Schermerhorn's Wharf. From this bustling Tontine public room grew the Wall Street Stock Exchange. Brintnall forwarded a portion of the proceeds to his underwriter Consequa back at the factories in China.

In a separate transaction, Brintnall advertised the *Triumph* for sale in the financial newspapers of Manhattan. This was a common practice, like ending a commercial truck lease.

Two friendly New Yorkers invited 'Ōpūkaha'ia and Hopu to a night out at a Lower Manhattan theater. Theatergoers in 1809 enjoyed a variety of performers who appeared on a candlelight-illuminated stage backed by the lively music of string and horn bands. Shakespeare's plays were popular, and actors orating selections from the Bard became celebrities. A beer garden concession served refreshments in warm weather.

> One evening two gentlemen called on board the ship to see us. After our conversation was made with them, they wished us to go with them into a playhouse to show the curiosity. We then went with them into the playhouse and saw a great number of people, as I ever saw before. We staid during the fore part of the evening, then went on board the ship.

The next day 'Ōpūkaha'ia and Hopu reflected on their own daily life under the *kapu* system back in Hawai'i.

> ...the same two gentlemen called again and invited us to come to their house that forenoon. So that we both went. I thought while in the house of these two gentlemen how strange to see females eat with men.

Home to New Haven

With the auction of his cargo and sale of the *Triumph* in the works it was time for Brintnall to head home. He paid for passage for himself, 'Ōpūkaha'ia and Hopu aboard one of the single-mast, fore-and-aft rigged packet sloops that sailed overnight to New Haven. Departures were timed to the incoming Atlantic tidal surge; the tide powered the packet up the East River, through treacherous Hell Gate, towards Long Island Sound. 'Ōpūkaha'ia and Hopu sat back, passing the spacious estates of the then rural East River shoreline north of Wall Street. In a role reversal, they were paying passengers, able to sit back and relax and enjoy life in a new world as a *haole* crew worked the sails and served food. The Hawaiians were an uncommon sight to the passengers making the eighty-mile passage from lower Manhattan to the Long Wharf at New Haven. Despite the stares, the two close friends felt secure in this foreign Yankee world, safe under Captain Brintnall's wing. After a stay in New Haven, Brintnall promised he would find them a berth on a ship headed back to Hawai'i.

While Brintnall, 'Ōpūkaha'ia and Hopu enjoyed their sail to New Haven, trouble was brewing back in Macao. On the morning of August 23, 1809 Captain William Sturgis of Boston anchored the China trade ship *Atahualpa* in Macao Roads. Twenty-one pirate junks carrying two thousand men led by their admiral Apootsae attempted to board. Sturgis fought them off with small six-pounder cannons; he cut the cables to his anchors and set sail to escape and come within protection of a Macao fort. Apootsae faced torture and death by Mandarins after being captured. Sturgis was ready to blow up the *Atahualpa* to keep his crew from being tortured.

A world away, 'Ōpūkaha'ia and Hopu were peacefully headed to the city of New Haven, the home of their captain, their starting point for whatever lay ahead.

CHAPTER SEVEN
NEW HAVEN

Story of the Morning Star

Edwin Dwight approaches Obookiah in 1809, Obookiah weeping on the steps of Yale over
his lack of learning, in this American Tract Society illustration published in 1860.

New Haven Harbor, Late Summer 1809

THE FIRST SIGNS OF NEW HAVEN came into view for 'Ōpūkaha'ia and Hopu as
they sailed along the Connecticut shoreline of Long Island Sound. Ancient East Rock
and West Rock ridges loomed up on the horizon, framing New Haven like two giant
bookends set two miles apart.

Captain Caleb Brintnall served as the youths' guide and host into this realm, a land
until now only envisioned in their imaginations. Brintnall anticipated his arrival home
as a glorious one, a successful return to the wharf from where almost three years earlier
he ventured out on a circumnavigation of the globe.

'Ōpūkaha'ia and Hopu looked forward to exploring New Haven. Russell Hubbard
and the crew of the *Triumph* told tales that presented an idealized view of the city for
months aboard ship. 'Ōpūkaha'ia, now about twenty-two years old, and Hopu in his
mid-teens, anticipated the joy of embarking on yet another youthful adventure in the
world outside Hawai'i.

Brintnall, with 'Ōpūkaha'ia and Hopu alongside him, would have stepped down
the packet gangplank at the Long Wharf. This wharf, the longest in New England, jut-
ted out for over a half mile across the shallow inner-harbor to the harbor channel, like
an outstretched arm greeting ships arriving at the port of New Haven.

Anticipating the return home of Captain Brintnall was his family: his wife Lois
and the couple's children, Nancy, nine, Charles, seven, Henry, four, and the two-year-
old infant born while Caleb was in Hawai'i, a child to be named Elihu Mix Brintnall.
The children knew father's return meant gifts from the far-off exotic land of China.

They weren't disappointed. Stevedores piled upon the deck of the wharf a multitude of their father's wooden boxes, all marked with mysterious Chinese writing.

The captain's biggest surprise stood alongside him: his two young brown-skinned "heathenish" crewmen. Brintnall invited 'Ōpūkaha'ia to earn his keep by being the family's household servant. Hopu was to board with the captain's neighbor, physician and apothecary Obadiah Hotchkiss, who lived just around the corner.

'Ōpūkaha'ia accepted that Henry Obookiah was the name he would be known by in New Haven, and Hopu that he would be called Thomas Hopoo.

The New Haven cityscape appeared to be a miniature version of Manhattan. Tall church steeples pierced the late summer blue sky behind a long row of commercial buildings built right to the harbor's edge.

Obookiah recalled, "...(We) went home with Captain B. to New-Haven; the place where he lived. There I lived with him for some time...." Henry roomed in the comfortable two-story, white wood frame home owned by Captain Brintnall and his wife Lois on Chapel Street. The coming of the day, noon, and evening were marked by church bells rung in the center square of New Haven, located just a few streets away.

Henry, the name the family used in all dealings with him, felt somewhat at home with the Brintnalls, but sensed a reserve in their hospitality.

Captain Brintnall considered Obookiah as a short-term guest, a visitor who earned his keep until he moved on. He would soon find a berth for the friendly Hawaiian sailor on a sealing or trading ship bound for Hawai'i. As at sea, in his home Brintnall was firm, but fair and kind too.

"There I lived with him for some time...I could understand or speak, but very little of the English language," Obookiah remembered.

Swaggering, tawny strangers from the South Seas, Obookiah and Hopoo became known by name as they roamed about New Haven, a city of steady ways and Yankee ingenuity, of thrift and order.

"Town-born" (a superlative term for native-born residents of New Haven) Brintnall and Hotchkiss descended from prominent New England families. Both worshipped as voting members at the First Congregational Church, commonly known as the Brick Church. The church was set in a grassy field separating Yale College and the New Haven Green.

Henry sat through Sunday services with the Brintnall family, who took up almost a full hardwood pew. The congregation looked upon Henry as a visiting South Seas sailor kindly taken in by the Brintnalls. He was a curiosity, a Polynesian recast in the role of a young New England man, a "heathen" nattily dressed up in a collared shirt, waistcoat and trousers (A heathen then meaning someone from the non-Christian world who worships multiple gods, not Jehovah the Christian's supreme being; this simplistic view of native peoples included their opinion of Native Hawaiians and Tahitians.).

Among the Congregation only Captain Brintnall fully appreciated the transformation of Obookiah. At Kealakekua Bay he was 'Ōpūkaha'ia, his kahuna uncle Pahua's apprentice; at the Hikiau Heiau he chanted through the night to the Hawaiian god Lono, costumed in *kapa* cloth patterned regalia, wearing atop his head a fragrant green-leaf lei, standing before the wooden *ki'i* figures into which the spirit of the Hawaiian gods manifested. Now, Henry pondered the Christian world he stepped into when he decided to leave Hawai'i. He glanced around the spacious, white-walled, unadorned

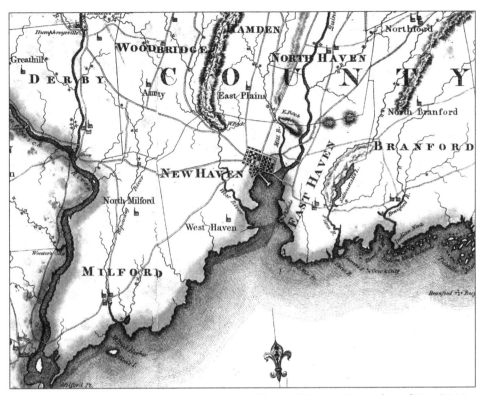

Library of Congress, Geography and Map Division
New Haven and surrounding towns as surveyed in 1811. New Haven Harbor and its Long Wharf are pictured in center of map. East Rock and West Rock lay north of the city.

Congregational sanctuary. He looked up and down the rows of pews filled with well-dressed men, women and children gathered, he presumed, to seek the favor of a god still unknown to him. He was baffled by the English words of the long sermon delivered by a black-robed New England minister who stood above him, perched behind a wooden pulpit. Relief came through the universal sound of music; the congregation clutching Watts hymnals sang in harmony; the melodious tune soothed his spirit.

Old Lights and New Lights

Obookiah stepped into the New Haven church in the culminating year of a decade of great change and division within the Protestant churches of New England. He had no perception of the significant role he would play in the upcoming decade in advancing these changes, which would manifest in new and surprising ways.

The Rev. Moses Stuart likely met Obookiah at the First Church in New Haven while greeting his congregation at the church door following the service. The entrance of a youth from faraway Polynesian islands into New Haven's Protestant-centric community came in an auspicious season. An explosion of interest in foreign missions was brewing. Interest in the islands of Polynesia was sparked by lengthy reports of the trials and triumphs of missionaries sent to Otahitie by the London Missionary Society.

A proponent of the revolutionary New Light theology, Stuart supported the wave of revivals then lighting up churches across New England. Staid ministers still clung to the old church ways in churches pastored by Old Light ministers. The Old Light ministers criticized the revivals as emotional sensationalism, threats to church authority and the traditional practices of the church. They overlooked the deadness enveloping their congregations. Church attendance was declining and the youth were being drawn into following atheistic tenants of the Enlightenment over following Christ.

The Old Lights condoned the Half Way Covenant, a ministerial compromise that allowed communion and infant baptism without a commitment to avidly following Christian beliefs.

The New Light evangelical wave flowed across Connecticut and western Massachusetts. But the opposite happened in Congregational churches in Boston and eastern Massachusetts. Some of those churches took to liberalizing, even eliminating, long-held Trinitarian beliefs of their Puritan New England heritage; that is the belief in God as Father, God as Son, and God as Holy Spirit, and of the Bible as the literal word of God.

In the post-Revolutionary War era, New England suffered a crisis of the soul amongst its people. The vast majority were Protestants. However, their long-held orthodox Christian beliefs were being challenged by Enlightenment ideals and disbelief in the Puritan way. The free-thinkers championed science, idealized nature and called Polynesians "noble savages" though they knew little or nothing about the Pacific peoples. They looked to progress and human reason over biblical-based Christian beliefs. Such thinking was espoused by widely-read agnostic commentators Thomas Paine and Benjamin Franklin. Rational thinking guided life, they said, over and above the irrational religious faith of the evangelical, Bible-believing churches. Men and women could reach a level of perfection through their intellect; the fear of God, belief in the Puritan God a hindrance to progress in this idealized crusade.

New, modern, liberal Protestant denominations sprang up. Most denied the Trinity and espoused a neutered gospel. They affirmed that people are basically good, rather than having a nature tainted by the Puritan belief that humans are cursed with a sinful nature. Most radically, they rejected the need to seek redemption from sin through the Protestant savior Jesus Christ. Liberal theology permeated churches in Boston, a traditionally Puritan city nearby Cambridge, the home of Harvard College. Unitarian churches in Boston drew Deists who saw God as a disinterested creator, a "force" who left man alone. Their God left behind a "natural law" visible in nature as a moral guide for man. They saw Jesus as a great moral teacher, but not a divine one. Deist-follower President Thomas Jefferson abridged his *New Testament*, expunging with a pair of scissors the miracles of Christ and passages he felt too spiritual. There was no worry, the Deist commentators wrote, about the path of sin leading you into the flames of hell, as so espoused by Jonathan Edwards in his famous brimstone sermon "Sinners in the Hand of an Angry God," preached at Enfield, Connecticut in July, 1741.

The evangelical wing saw as heresy the renunciation of God's absolute sovereignty over man and denying the divinity of Christ, of the Trinity and active work of the Holy Spirit, disbelieving the Bible as being the inspired word of God. Deism, they claimed, led to atheism, and then to infidelity, which resulted in a looseness of morals and the decay of society. The evangelicals saw the main goal of life as knowing God and his son Jesus Christ; strident Puritan belief saw life as foremost a preparation for death and eternal judgement.

The rationalist distanced themselves from the evangelical's hope that God was active on the earth, loved all but through free will allowed humans to choose eternal life or damnation, the God carried on a personal relationship with his followers.

Committed New Lights saw themselves, and the young United States, as having a role to play in ushering in the return of Christ to redeem the earth, to launch a New Millennium in which the "saved" ruled with Christ.

Timothy Dwight, the grandson of theologian Jonathan Edwards, was named president of Yale in 1795. Dwight found his student body enamored of the Enlightenment and the French Revolution. Few, sometimes no one, from the student body professed to being a Christian. Evangelical minister Lyman Beecher of Litchfield, Connecticut, who entered Yale in 1793, recalled classmates hailing one another as "Rousseau" and "Voltaire" in allegiance with the French. Evangelical students then cowered in fear of bullying, embarrassment and persecution if they expressed their faith on campus.

At Yale in 1800–through Dwight's sermons and his Bible chapel teachings–a revival broke out. This was a surprising development in New Haven, though dozens of revivals were breaking out in towns large and small across New England.

The New England revival manifest a calm and reserve when the Holy Spirit fell. The revivals led to the launching of significant Christian movements: Foreign missions, temperance societies to battle the highest levels of drunkenness ever faced by the United States, formation of national and state Bible societies, inner city missions, outreaches to Indian tribes. Better known today are the emotion-fueled revival camp meetings gathered in Kentucky, Tennessee, Ohio and other new western territories.

Timothy Dwight birthed the revival at Yale through a simple classroom study that questioned students about the truth of the Bible. He preached chapel sermons such as "The Nature and Danger of Infidel Philosophy." Dwight's meetings drew a few students at first, then snowballed into a surge, resulting in Christian commitments by a third of the students at Yale by 1802. A noticeable Christian presence in the college continued for years afterwards. A network of like-minded evangelical ministers holding Yale degrees spread out throughout New England.

Renowned pioneer American chemist and Yale natural science professor Benjamin Silliman observed that by 1802, "Prayer and praise seem to be the delight of the greater part of the students."

A monthly, weeknight service known as the Concert of Prayer united across the Atlantic American and British Christians experiencing what is now known as the Second Great Awakening. The inspiration behind the Concert of Prayer was theologian and minister Jonathan Edwards, a man many say possessed the most brilliant mind in America during the eighteenth-century. From his church in Northhampton, Massachusetts Edwards distributed a tract with a title almost as long as its text: "An Humble Attempt to Promote Explicit Agreement and Visible Union of God's People in Extraordinary Prayer for the Revival of Religion and the Advancement of Christ's Kingdom on Earth." Edwards called for extraordinary prayer sessions to be held corporately in New England churches on the first Monday of each month.

Ushering in the New Millennium

The New Light vision of helping to bring about a peaceful thousand-year New

Millennium and the return of Christ to the earth fueled the Second Great Awakening.

Dwight and other significant preachers spread a vision for transforming America and the entire world to bring in the New Millennium and the return of Christ to the earth by about the year 2000.

Dwight delivered a New Millennium-focused sermon to ministers and foreign mission supporters gathered at the American Board of Commissioners' annual meeting, held in Boston in September, 1813:

History of the Colony of New Haven

A brick-walled Yale College building circa 1800. In the student rooms of such a building Obookiah and Hopu socialized with Yale students, and were taught the basics of reading, writing, and speaking English.

The present is the proper time for this glorious undertaking. It is the proper time, as it is marked out by the Spirit of prophecy. Almost all judicious commentators have agreed, that the Millennium, in the full and perfect sense, will begin at a period, not far from the year 2000. Christ, referring immediately at least, to this great event, says, "Behold I come as a thief;" i.e. suddenly; and sooner than the world will expect...the dawn of the succeeding day will be earlier than mankind have been accustomed to believe.... The voice of his Providence, powerful and full of Majesty, calls to us, "Go forward."

The American youth of the Second Great Awakening were hailed as a generation providentially called to play a role in bringing forth this new Zion. Within the churches it became exciting, even romantic, to consider a life as a missionary, going out to the frontier at home, or in foreign fields, to spread the Gospel. Preparing faraway peoples for the coming of Christ required elevating their societies as well as their souls: bringing literacy needed to read the Bible, medicine to heal their bodies and moral rules based on biblical principles to guide them on their paths towards salvation. Social ministries rose up too: ministering in prisons, bringing an end to the slave trade and the institution of slavery in the United States, inner city reform, outreaches to sailors in port.

A collegiate and theological controversy arose in 1805 following the appointment of a Deist as head of Harvard's theology school. This divergence from Trinitarian Christianity drew a deep divide between the two emerging wings of the almost two-hundred-year-old Puritan church in America. Bombastic letters published by both sides as widely-read tracts drove the debate and polarized the churches further. In response, the Theological Seminary at Andover, the first evangelical seminary in America, was founded in 1808. The seminary opened alongside the Phillips Academy at Andover, on a hilltop site about twenty miles north of Boston. Its buildings were designed to reflect the look of the Old Brick Row at evangelical-leaning Yale College.

A band of college men meeting under a haystack in a lightning storm in the fall of 1806 (1808 is also cited, the exact date is uncertain) began the American foreign missions movement. The students, led by pastor's son Samuel J. Mills Jr. of Torringford,

Connecticut, formed a secret foreign missions-advocating society at Williams College. Williams is set in a rural valley ringed by the Berkshire Mountains in northwest Massachusetts. The Brethren recruited foreign missions-minded students and met in college rooms, boarding houses and outdoors in nearby woods and fields.

Holoholo in New Haven

While the Second Great Awakening revivals brought a fresh, encouraging spirit to the students of Yale and in the Connecticut churches, Obookiah and Hopoo found their own joy in exploring the city's streets. They went *holoholo*, wandering for fun.

The fashions of the turn of the nineteenth-century made a bold, modern statement, and were adopted by Obookiah and Hopoo. Men favored ankle-length pantaloons, or trousers, only worn in the past by working men, long stylized top coats, and beaver fur top hats. Men's hair cuts were short with curly, Romanesque flourishes around their hairline in the French style. Older men, such as dictionary author Noah Webster, still wore Colonial Era knee-length breeches, white stockings and silver-buckled shoes, and pulled their long hair back into a pigtail. Women turned to soft cotton, muslin dresses, moving away from fancier, colonial-era silken garments; they wore no makeup.

As Native Hawaiian sailors, frequently roaming New Haven in their everyday clothing of sailor togs, the two youths became readily identified as men from the South Seas.

However, racial prejudice against people of color did exist in New Haven in 1809, prejudice that Obookiah and Hopoo faced. In his statistical account of New Haven, Timothy Dwight presents a scathing description of what he saw as the low life of African Americans in general in the port city of his day.

Dwight's stance exposed a conundrum for the evangelical Christians of his day. They strove to save the world for Christ by spreading the Gospel to foreign nations, yet at home accepted the lowly status and social barriers faced by blacks, free and slave.

Obookiah and Hopoo, intrigued by the multitude of things to see in New Haven, were surely attracted to the curios at the Mix Museum located along Olive Street near the entrance to the Long Wharf. The museum's collection of oddities and wonders featured side-show-style wax figures of popular, and historical, celebrities. Among its artificial curiosities was a display of parts off a Hawaiian canoe brought home by a sea captain or sailor. On the museum roof a visual wonder, an oversized camera obscura, projected a photograph-like, wide-angle oval landscape view of New Haven.

Obookiah worked out his stiff swimming muscles by taking late-summer, warm-water harbor swims. The shallow, muddy water of New Haven Harbor in that season almost matched the warmth of the surf at Kealakekua Bay. Nearby the Mix Museum was a shore-side bathing house where waders sought to cool off and to find companionship at an adjoining ice cream parlor and public garden. However, rather than wading in the harbor shore amidst genteel society, Obookiah swam where the rough and tumble sailors and dockworkers hung out, far out on the Long Wharf, away from the city. He amused the wharfies and drunken idlers when he duplicated his swim out to the *Triumph* in Kealakekua Bay by swimming towards the mouth of the harbor on Long Island Sound. Obookiah's long swims were notable feats. His display of Hawaiian waterman skills came a century before Olympic swimmer and champion surfer Duke Kahanamoku of Waikīkī Beach introduced surfing to the East Coast.

For a shellfish snack there was an abundance of fresh New Haven oysters to stand-in for the *'opihi* limpets found on the rocky coasts of Hawai'i.

Through his contact with sailors, perhaps *Triumph* crewmen, Obookiah got word of a merchant ship soon to depart from New York for the Pacific Ocean and the Sandwich Islands. He discussed with Captain Brintnall whether he should join the ship's crew; in the end Henry chose to stay in New Haven.

"The Captain was willing that I might take leave of this country and go home if I wish," he later wrote. "But I was not agreeable to this."

Weeping on the Steps of Yale

Just a few blocks from the New Haven homes of Obookiah and Hopoo were the brick buildings and commons of Yale College. Students of Henry's age spent idle hours on the college lawn, playing ball, idly leaning on a white wooden fence along the New Haven Green. Hopoo began mingling with the Yale students who lived just a short walk from Doctor Hotchkiss's home. He was befriended, invited in to be tutored by students drawn to him both by his uniqueness, and by a sincere hope they could help Hopoo .

Yale student Edwin Welles Dwight one day found Obookiah weeping on the steps of the college. Obookiah wept openly over being unable to comprehend western learning. Henry saw clearly that language, cultural and literacy barriers kept him from joining the Yale students in their studies. Dwight's response became a noted chapter in Yale's heritage. A biographer of American foreign missions pioneer Samuel Mills described the scene: "...he could understand little or nothing, and that the treasures of knowledge which were open to others, were locked up from him; he sat down and wept on the threshold of the College buildings." Obookiah wrote of Dwight's helping hand:

> In this place I become acquainted with many students belonging to the College. By these pious students I was told more about God than what I had heard before; but I was so ignorant that I could not see into it whether it was so. Many times I wished to hear more about God, but find no body to interpret it to me.
>
> Friend Thomas went to school to one of the students in the College before I thought of going to. I wished to continue in this country a little longer. I staid another week-saw Mr. E. W. D. (Edward Welles Dwight) who first taught me to read and write. The first time I saw him, he enquired whether I was one who came over with Thomas, (for Thomas was known among many scholars in College.) I told him I was one who come over with Thomas. He then asked me if I wished to learn to read and write. I told him that I was. He wished me to come to his room that night and begin to learn. So that I went in the evening and began to read in the spelling-book. Mr. D. wished me to come to his room at any time when it is agreeable to the Captain with whom I then lived. I went home that night and the next morning I mentioned all this matter to the Captain. He was pleased, and he wished me to go to school to Mr. D. Thus I continued in school with him for several months.

Edwin Welles Dwight and Samuel Mills Jr.

As a collegian Edwin Dwight was known to have a pleasant voice and is described as dark-haired, side-burned, with bright eyes and a Roman nose, of above medium height with a well-proportioned body.

Edwin grew up in Stockbridge, Massachusetts in the Berkshire Mountains, down the pike from Williams College in Williamstown. In his childhood, Stockbridge was considered a missionary outpost on the young nation's frontier where Stockbridge Indians were evangelized and schooled. Edwin was born in Stockbridge on November 17, 1789, and was a distant cousin to Yale President Timothy Dwight.

Edwin's Indian-mission upbringing gave him a familiarity with, and acceptance of, Native Americans becoming Christians, and thus equals to him. For the descendants of the Pilgrims and Puritans in New England this was an uncommon trait in the first decade of the 1800s. This gave Edwin a familiarity with the plight of Obookiah as a young, non-white, Polynesian seeking his place in a white, Puritan-based society.

Edwin Dwight enrolled at Williams College in 1806. There he joined the secret foreign missions society known as the Brethren. He attended many of their prayer meetings, but was absent when Mills led the legendary Haystack Meeting. That day, a handful of Brethren members met for prayer just a short walk from the Williams campus, in a grove of leafy maple trees located near the Hoosac River. A lightning storm drifted down from the Berkshire Mountains that ring Williamstown. This forced the students to seek shelter under a haystack lifted off the ground by a wooden support.

Mills advocated the evangelization of the unsaved world to be undertaken by the American students of his generation. Sensing a fulfillment of the *Mayflower* Pilgrims vision for spreading the Gospel out from the New World, Mills exclaimed:

> We can do it if we will. O God, strike down the arm, with red artillery of heaven, that shall be raised against a herald of the cross.

Samuel's father, the Rev. Samuel J. Mills, Sr., better known as Father Mills, led perhaps a more colorful life and ministry than any other pastor or preacher in New England. Father Mills laced his sermons with words he coined off-the-cuff, words spoken in an unwittingly humorous manner, like a Christian W. C. Fields. Mills Senior was the long-time pastor of the Torringford Congregational Church in east Litchfield County. This rural region spread out upon the forested Litchfield plateau above Hartford.

Following the graduation of Samuel Mills from Williams in 1809, the Brethren moved their base of operations to the newly-opened Theological Seminary located atop Academy Hill in Andover, Massachusetts. To enroll in the all-male Brethren a student swore in writing that he would dedicate himself to going out for life to a foreign mission field. The vows were made almost unto the pain of death. Minutes were kept in a cryptic cipher, their plans and membership roll hidden to keep any presumptions about their missions society out of public purview should their efforts fail.

Tutored at Yale

Edwin, who graduated from Yale in September, 1809, described how learning transformed Obookiah from a downcast tarred-suited sailor fresh off a China trading voyage to a hopeful student. In a self-depreciating manner, Edwin wrote his own comments in the third person.

When Obookiah was discovered at New-Haven by the person of whom he speaks, his appearance was unpromising. He was clothed in a rough sailor's suit, was of a clumsy form, and his countenance dull and heavy. His friend had almost determined to pass him by, as one whom it would be in vain to notice and attempt to instruct. But when the question was put him "Do you wish to learn?" his countenance began to brighten. And when the proposal was made that he should come the next day to the college for that purpose, he seized it with great eagerness.

It was not long after he began to study, and had obtained some further knowledge of the English language, that he gave evidence, that the dullness, which was thought to be indicated by his countenance, formed no part of his character. It soon appeared that his eyes were open to every thing that was passing around him, and that he had an unusual degree of discernment with regard to persons and things of every description that came within his notice.

Obookiah displayed his sparkling wit and distinct intellect while being tutored in a Yale dorm room by Edwin. Henry soon grasped enough English to begin reading an elementary primer spelling book. He attempted to express into English words his thoughts, which ran through his mind in the Hawaiian language:

...there were certain sounds which he found it very difficult to articulate. This was true especially of syllables that contained the letter R...In pronouncing it, he uniformly gave it the sound of L...."Try, Obookiah, it is very easy.,"–the attempts to correct the error were at last successful, the circumstance was soon forgotten. A short time after this, long enough however for Obookiah to have made some improvement in speaking the English, his instructor was spending an evening pleasantly with him, in making inquiries concerning some of the habits and practices of his own country....Obookiah mentioned the manner in which his countrymen drank from a spring when out upon their hunting excursions. The cup that they used was their hands. It was made by clasping them together, and so adjusting the thumbs, and bending the hands, as to form a vessel that would contain a considerable quantity....after preparing his hands, (he) was able, from the pliableness of his arms, to raise them entirely to his mouth, without turning them at all from their horizontal position. The experiment was attempted by his instructor: but he found that before his hands were raised half the distance to his mouth they were so much inverted, that their contents would have been principally lost. He repeated the trial until he began to be discouraged; when Obookiah, who had been much amused with his efforts, with a very expressive countenance said to him, "Try, Mr. D., it is very easy." The former mystery was now unraveled, and an important lesson taught with respect to the ease or difficulty, with which things are done by us that are or are not natural to us; or to which we have or have not been, from early life, accustomed.

Obookiah was a natural mimic who spoke in broken English as he learned to read and write.

About this time it was discovered that Obookiah noticed with un-common acuteness and interest every singularity in the speech and manners of those around him.

And in the midst of his own awkwardness, to the surprise of all who were conversant with him, he suddenly began to shew himself dexterous as a mimick. He one day placed himself upon the floor, drew up his sleeves half way to the elbow, walked across the room with a peculiar air, and said, 'Who dis?' The person intended was instantly known by all that were present. He then put himself in a different position, changed his gait, and said again, 'Well, who dis?' This imitation also was so accurate, of another of the members of College, that no one doubted with regard to the original. The extent of his own awkwardness at this time may be learned from the effect which an exhibition of it produced upon himself. After he had completed his own efforts at mimickry, his friend said to him, "Well, Obookiah, should you like to know how you walk?" He seemed much pleased with the suggestion, and the imitation was attempted. He was greatly diverted, though almost incredulous, and said with earnestness-several times repeating the question, "Me walk so?" After being assured that it was a reality, he burst into a loud roar of laughter and fell upon the floor, where he indulged his mirth until he had exhausted his strength.

Hopoo, Hotchkiss and Hawai'i

Like Obookiah, Hopoo continued his tutoring by Yale students in handwriting and speaking. Meanwhile Dr. Hotchkiss, who had stepped up his own commitment as an evangelical Christian, overwhelmed Thomas with Calvinist theology. Hotchkiss likely read to Thomas from a student version of the Westminister Catechism. Hopoo recalled:

A few weeks after our coming to this place, I was taught to know about the true God, and Jesus Christ whom he has sent into the world to die for sinners.... He told me I must immediately believe, and love that God, who made the heavens and the earth and all the people in the world: then when I came to die, he would take me up into heaven, where he is: but if I did not believe and love him, he would send me to Hell, when I came to die.

Hotchkiss probed him about the Hawaiian religion and the gods of Hawai'i:

What does your father worship in Owhyhee, generally? My father generally worships wood, and he believes that the Spirit sometimes comes into the wood. So he takes an axe, and cuts the wood into shape; then sets it up by the altar, and when the time comes for the evening sacrifice, or morning, to be offered, then the spirit comes into the wood. And when this is done, they offer up the sacrifices unto God; then the priest goes away from the images....

What are the gods which you, Hopoo, worshipped, in Owhyhee, before you came to this country? The gods which we worship, in Owhyhee are wood and stone, sun, and moon, and stars of heaven.

Any heaven and hell in Owhyhee, Thomas? No, no heaven, no hell, in my country, where I came from.

What place do you go to when you die, Thomas? Go into the earth.

Do you believe that you have a soul to live in another world? No, I have no idea that I have any soul to live in heaven; for my father never did tell me that I had a soul....

What do you give these things to them (idols) for, if they eat not? Because they must eat, and they must have all these things, or else they would be poor, or be angry with us, all the days of our lives; for it is generally the case with us, if we do not eat, we shall die; and if no man give us anything for our living, we shall feel bad and be angry.

At Home with Yale President Dwight

An offer of employment from Yale President Timothy Dwight allowed Obookiah to continue his New Haven sojourn. He moved out of the Brintnall's home. This, freed Captain Brintnall from the responsibility of providing day-to-day support and oversight for Henry. In supporting Obookiah Brintnall politely deferred the full attention he needed to settle back in with his wife and children after being away on voyage of almost three years.

Henry became a servant for the Dwight family. They lived in a stately two-story frame home built in Georgian architectural style to serve as the home of Yale's President. Obookiah boarded in the servants' quarters, an annex located to the rear of the President's mansion, just a short walk away from Edwin's room in Yale's Connecticut Hall. Henry later recalled his reaction to the daily prayers said by the Dwights.

I lived with this pious and good family for some time...Here was the first time I meet with praying family morning and evening. It was difficult for me to understand what was said in prayer, but I doubt not this good people were praying for me while I was with them; seeing that I was ignorant of God and my Saviour. I heard of God, as often as I lived with this family, and I believed but little.

On an evening in the fall of 1809 a visit by Obookiah to Edwin's room led to a fateful encounter. That night a door opened for Henry that led inland, to Litchfield County, and away from a quick return to Hawai'i and into the center of the world of American foreign missions.

CHAPTER EIGHT
SAMUEL MILLS & OBOOKIAH

In 1809 Henry Obookiah lived in the servants' quarters located at the rear of the Georgian-style, fifteen-room home of Yale College President Timothy Dwight. The white clapboard home was located adjacent to the campus of Yale College.

DRESSED FOR THE COLD FALL NEW HAVEN WEATHER, Obookiah entered the room where Edwin Dwight boarded in Yale College's brick-walled, three-story Colonial-style "college house" dormitory. Pine logs ablaze on the fireplace took the chill off the autumn night. With Edwin was someone a bit older, perhaps a minister. He was introduced to Obookiah as Samuel, Samuel Mills.

Mills, the Haystack Meeting leader, enrolled at Yale following his graduation from Williams College, in September, 1809. Officially, Mills was at Yale for a term of graduate theological study. In fact, he was seeking missions-minded recruits for the Brethren.

Standing next to handsome, well-coiffed Edwin Dwight, Mills seemed plain in appearance and demeanor. "He has an awkward figure and ungainly manners, and an unelastic and croaking sort of voice," is how Mills was described by Timothy Woodbridge, his roommate at the Theological Seminary at Andover. Woodbridge continued, "...but he has a great heart and great designs. His great thoughts in advance of the age are not like the dreams of a man who is in a fool's paradise; but they are judicious and wise."

Mills was taken aback by discovering a young Hawaiian man being tutored in a Yale student's room. Inspired by meeting Obookiah, and quick to act, Samuel added the Sandwich Islands (as Hawai'i was known in New England until after the Civil War), to his plans for launching an American student foreign mission movement.

Obookiah recalled, "Mr. D. wished me to make acquaintance with Mr. M. So did I (and shook hands with him.) Mr. M. continued in New-Haven for several months..."

Mills' first biographer, the Rev. Gardiner Spring, pastor of the landmark Brick

Presbyterian Church in New York City, remarked, "...Mr. Mills, on his arrival at New-Haven, became the companion of Mr. (Edwin) Dwight, and was deeply interested in this heathen boy. He soon conceived the plan of educating him as a Missionary to his native islands..."

Mills–an enthusiastic young Christian man–boarded with like-minded Rev. Moses Stuart, pastor of the Congregational church attended by the Brintnalls. Samuel wrote in detail about his hopes for Obookiah and the Sandwich Islands in a letter written December 20, 1809, sent to Andover, to fellow Brethren student Gordon Hall, a future American Board missionary to Ceylon.

> Mr. Dwight...was instructing a native Owhyean boy....As I was in the room with Mr. Dwight, I heard the youth recite occasionally, and soon became considerably attached to him. His manners are simple; he does not appear to be vicious in any respect, and he has a great thirst for knowledge. In his simple manner of expressing himself, he says, "The people in Owhyee very bad, they pray to gods made of wood. Poor Indians don't know nothing." He says, "Me want to learn to read this Bible, and go back then, and tell them to pray to God up in heaven."
>
> I called into Dwight's room last evening, and had not been long there, before Henry, for this is his English name, came into the room with a very gloomy countenance. Says he, "Me feel very bad." I asked him why he felt bad? "Me got no place to live." I then asked him if he was not going to live with (Timothy) Dwight. He said, "No; he say, me may go away, he no more want me." I told him he need not be concerned; I would find a place for him. He said, "Miss (apparently a head servant in Timothy Dwight's home) say she take away my new clothes." I told him he need not be afraid of that, for I had clothes enough for both of us. He did not appear to know what course to take.

Mills noticed that Obookiah expressed in his countenance and chats the difficulties he faced living and working as a servant in the household of Yale President Dwight. This trouble might have been due to Henry's lack of understanding the Yankee, or perhaps African-American, dialects spoken by the other servants, thus hindering their work. Obookiah, uncertain of his standing in the Dwight staff, feared facing the rejection and destitution of his childhood should he fail at his job, this time during a freezing New England winter.

Samuel freed Obookiah from his indeterminate commitment to Dwight, plus removed his fear of abandonment. Mills opened the door to Obookiah advancing in his studies. Samuel promised Henry his family who would show him unqualified love, and always care for him. Henry felt the Mills family had made him an hānai (lovingly adopted) family member. Mills wrote to Hall, "I told him he might go home with me, and live at my father's, and have whatever he wanted."

With practicalities taken care of, Mills began to disciple Henry in the Christian faith. "I heard him read his lesson, and attempted to instruct him in some of the first principles of Christianity, of which he was almost entirely ignorant. He then retired for the night."

Mills pressed his suggestion that Obookiah move with him to his family home in Torringford. Henry wrote, "During this time he wished me to go home with him; he says he has a good father, mother, brother and sister." Mills told Hall:

> This morning I repaired to Mr. Dwight's room. He (Edwin) felt interested in be-half of Obookiah, and thought he had best endeavour to find a place for him, where he could work a part of the time, and pay for his board, and recite as he had done. I told him I did not think he had best stay in town, as he would be ex-posed to bad company,...

Harper's Weekly

Students linger along the white rail fence bordering Yale College near the New Haven Green. Obookiah and Hopoo walked in this area on their way to study in the Yale student rooms.

Mills then echoed the slogan of the British anti-slavery movement–"Am I Not A Man and a Brother?"–when he wrote, "... and most likely be treated as a slave, rather than as a friend and brother." Mills stated the obvious. People on the street in New Haven were misidentifying Obookiah as an African slave still in bondage, with all the prejudice that might entail. Mills explained Obookiah's dilemma to Hall:

> I told him he would be glad to go; he was without a home,—without a place to eat, or sleep. The poor and almost friendless Owhyean would sit down disconsolate, and the honest tears would flow freely down his sun-burnt face; but since this plan has been fixed upon, he has appeared cheerful, and feels quite at ease.

To Obookiah, Mills also held out a promise of financial support for his educa-tion. Funds were available, Mills said, from the Litchfield Missionary Society, and his father was a trustee. Mills' long-term goal was, "...to attempt so far as that he may be able to instruct his countrymen, and by God's blessing, convert them to Christian-ity." He wrote to Gordon Hall:

> What does this mean? Brother Hall, do you understand it? Shall he be sent back unsupported, to attempt to reclaim his countrymen? Shall we both rather consider these southern islands a proper place for the establishment of a mission?

Obookiah recalled choosing a path in this crossroads in his life:

> This requesting was very pleasing to me-so that I consented. I then left New-Haven and went home with Mr. M. I lived with this family in the year 1810.

Samuel and Henry boarded a mail-coach at a terminal located on Church Street, south of Chapel Street. The ride through the Connecticut countryside went along turnpikes and stopped at inns during the half-day ride to Torringford.

The busy port cities of New York and New Haven had framed Henry's life in America. Now he was heading inland to a tranquil rural village, taking a ride in a Litchfield Turnpike coach. The bustle and noise, streets stinking of horse manure, the big city social pressures were giving way to rural quiet, pine-scented forests and close-knit communities.

Torringford is a village founded by farmers in the mid-1700s, located in the southeast corner of Litchfield County, a county located in the northwest corner of Connecticut. The town of Litchfield is the county seat and business center. Goshen, Cornwall, and other crossroads villages dot the county to the northwest. Torringford is set upon the eastern edge of the Litchfield plateau. Vistas of lowlands open up below that tableland in a striking manner, the view looking out in the direction of Hartford and New Haven. The village's name takes the "Torring" from Torrington and blends it with the "ford" from New Hartford, the town nearest to the east.

Samuel Mills introduced Obookiah to his family, who welcomed Henry. His belongings were placed in a bedroom made up just for him. The Mills lived in the church parsonage located across Torringford Road from the white-steepled Congregational church where his father served as pastor.

The Torringford church was the center of Christian activity in a rural village peopled by farmers and the craftsmen who supplied them with tools and other goods. Nearby was Battell's general store, the hub of Torringford's commercial life; at Battell's local residents lingered in winter around a wood stove when picking up mail and newspapers brought by coach from the cities below.

The Mills family reassured Obookiah that he was welcomed to live with them as long as he wanted. Obookiah rejoiced. Samuel's petite mother, Esther Robbins Mills, continued Henry's exposure to the basics of Christianity, employing a child's version of the Westminister Catechism. While politely spending his allotted time being read to from the small leather-bound book, Obookiah's interest focused on experiencing life in his new community, practicing penmanship and improving his reading skills. Obookiah recalled:

> These, people were the most judicious and kindest people. I was treated by them in the most affectionate manner (yet not knowing who brought me there, for I was very ignorant of him who gave me so many good friends, in this country). It seemed to me as my own home....

Father Mills
Samuel's father, the renowned Father Mills, held no qualms about bringing Obookiah into his family. Unlike some of his congregation, Father Mills held no racial prejudices; he saw all people as equals under Christ. Using the power of his status as a pastor, he had since the early 1790s publicly advocated for the end of slavery in Connecticut. He traveled to Hartford for regular meetings of an anti-slavery committee, joined by his friend, dictionary compiler Noah Webster.

Jeremiah Mills, Samuel's older brother, carried on with the work of Edwin Dwight in tutoring Obookiah. Henry studied basic spelling, reading and writing. For his keep, Obookiah worked on the Mills' nearby farmland, perhaps on the farm Samuel had inherited from his grandmother, or in the fields adjacent to the Torringford Congregational Church.

While Jeremiah and Samuel stepped in as older brothers to Obookiah, Father Mills became his adoptive father. Father Mills possessed an outgoing, unforgettable personality. A biographer of Samuel described his father as *sui generis*, one of a kind. In person, the Torringford pastor presented a striking figure: white-wigged, hefty but well-proportioned, recognized immediately when riding atop the horse that carried him around Litchfield County.

As Obookiah had, Samuel faced an existential dilemma in his youth. Samuel knew that at birth his parents had dedicated him to missions. Even so, he felt passed over by the redeeming, revival wave of the Holy Spirit his brother and sister and other youths at Torringford reveled in. He felt no joy of the presence of God in his spirit, while they did. This troubled his soul. Was this a sign he was damned by the te ne   t of pre-destination, the foundation of the Calvinist theology as taught by his father? He obsessively worried that his soul stood irretrievably outside of God's kingdom, haunted by a pre-determined curse.

When blessing Samuel as an infant, his parents dedicated him with domestic missions in mind, like the mission to Vermont Father Mills undertook in the 1790s. Now they feared Samuel's leadership of the Brethren, and his unrelenting hope to be sent overseas as a missionary, would prove to be a death sentence for their beloved son. Father Mills recalled his son's rebuttal to his father's fears:

> I thought he was growing wild, and I felt it my duty to admonish him, so the next time he came home I said to him, "Samuel! who taught you to be a missionary?" "It was you, father," said he, "when in my childhood you talked of the Millennium, and prayed for the heathen." With tears in his eyes the good man added, "I had not a word to say."

Father Mills frequently traded pulpits with the Rev. Lyman Beecher, pastor of the Congregational church in Litchfield town, the churches being only about ten miles apart. Beecher's daughter Harriet, the minister's daughter who grew up to write *Uncle Tom's Cabin*, was born in Litchfield in 1811. Harriet often spent childhood Sunday mornings in the presence of Father Mills. In *The May Flower and Miscellaneous Writings*, Stowe's first book to be published, she based her Father Morris character upon Father Mills:

> He was a...man, in a powdered white wig, black tights, and silk stockings, with bright knee-buckles and shoe-buckles; with round, dark snapping eyes; and a curious high, cracked, squeaking voice, the very first tones of which made all the children stare and giggle....
>
> Although the old man never seemed to be sensible of anything tending to the ludicrous in his own mode of expressing himself, yet he had considerable relish for humor, and some shrewdness of repartee. One time, as he was walking through a neighboring parish famous for its profanity, he was stopped by a whole flock of the youthful reprobates of the place....
>
> "Father Morris, Father Morris! The devil's dead!" "Is he?" said the old man, benignly laying his hand on the head of the nearest urchin; 'you poor fatherless children!'

Back to Andover

Once Obookiah settled in with the Mills, Samuel departed for the Theological Seminary at Andover to prepare for the ministry. Being ordained as a Congregational minister was a necessary step in qualifying to promote, and perhaps lead, foreign missions. At Andover, Mills continued his unceasing advocacy for support for foreign missions, recruiting carefully selected students to join the Brethren.

To fulfill his hopes for sending foreign missionaries from America, Mills began looking beyond seminary and college campuses. He saw the Brethren needed to acquire financial, administrative and organized spiritual support if they were to send missions to faraway nations. The means of transporting the Brethren missionaries to foreign ports was in place through connections to New England's maritime trade. The missing link was a board of senior missions-minded ministers who would provide credibility, leadership and raise financial support through a network of churches and local missions societies.

Harvesting, Learning

In the spring of 1810 warm weather returned to Torringford. Obookiah joined the Mills family in the fields hoeing and plowing like a veteran Yankee farmhand. Samuel was absent, studying at Andover. In the farm fields Obookiah excelled, perhaps showing he had spent time cultivating taro in a rock-walled taro *lo'i* pond. Henry's great dexterity in swinging farm tools surprised the Mills family. Father Mills recalled:

> His attention to what passed before him and his talent at imitation, were singular. He had never mown a clip until he came to live with me. My son furnished him with a scythe. He stood and looked on to see the use he made of it, and at once followed, to the surprise of those who saw him. We had a spell at reaping. We furnished him with a sickle. He stood and looked and followed on. It was afterwards observed by a person who was in the field that there were not two reapers there who excelled him. In these respects and others, he was truly a remarkable youth.

His time spent in 1810 at Torringford provided a foundation for the remainder of Obookiah's life, and lasting security for him. He now had a sure place to come home to. But it was soon time to move on, to grow, and gain a greater education, and if Samuel Mills' hopes prevailed, to prepare Henry for the day he would depart on a mission to Hawai'i.

Obookiah's scholarly side benefitted from Samuel Mills' intervention. Within a year of his arrival in New Haven Obookiah had mastered the primary spelling-book, a task begun aboard the *Triumph* with Russell Hubbard. He began to grasp the basics of Christianity and read selections from the *King James Bible*. He wrote cursive script in a clear hand. The practical need to speak in English everywhere he went improved his speech, though his pronunciation and grammar sounded more like pidgin English than Yankee English. Content and secure, he began to look beyond his own needs, showing concern for the fate of other Hawaiians youths roaming in New England.

It became apparent Henry felt pleasure in learning, a love that went above and beyond any attraction to Christianity. Despite the emphasis of his tutors in providing him Christian books and Bible studies, Obookiah felt no need to become a Christian, nor talked of returning to Hawai'i as a Christian missionary. Edwin Dwight wrote of this opposition:

> ...he rankled against their entreaties regarding God, saying he lacked a knowledge of the one true God, and that he felt he was just as happy as the ministers who knew much about God. In that light, Obookiah wrote that he ignored them when they spoke to him.

In late 1810, Obookiah departed Torringford for the Theological Seminary at Andover. Henry traveled by coach 140 miles east across Connecticut and into Massachusetts, to Academy Hill, a rise just south of the town center of Andover. Prosperous Andover lay about ten miles south of the Merrimack River, twenty miles north of Boston, and about twenty miles west of the seaports of Salem and Newburyport. Upon arriving in Andover Henry found his way to the campus and to brick-walled Phillips Hall, a building strikingly similar to Connecticut Hall at Yale where Edwin Dwight boarded. He opened the door, got in out of the cold and climbed the stairs to Samuel's comfortable student room, room No. 21 in Phillips Hall.

One morning Henry was said to have come "bounding" into the Andover dining hall "at breakfast and announced his discovery of water so hard you walk on it."

A tragedy befell the Mills family soon after the departure of Obookiah. Samuel's mother Esther fell gravely ill in chilly, wintertime Torringford. Upon receiving word of his mother's condition, Samuel rushed home, embarking on an anguished homeward journey. The slow pace of winter travel aboard coaches hindered his woeful journey. Walking down the path from the Torrington stage he discovered the freshly-covered grave of his mother in the graveyard located adjacent to his father's church. He was too late, his mother had died on December 30, 1810 at age 61.

Henry felt compassion for Samuel. From Andover Obookiah wrote a letter of condolence, recalling the death of his father Ke'au and mother Kamoho'ula:

> Dear Sir. Mr. Samuel J. Mills. Now I no Father and no mother, and your mother very good to me. now I hope she go to God. So I mind what she say so I must be a good man if I come to good man I hope I see her again. she very kind to me now I lost my mother and my friend your mother. Behold I am not feel very well.
>
> I am, Henry Obookiah

Father Mills mourned the wife he loved in his own distinct manner. For a year after Esther's death the Torringford minister replaced the full-length white wig he wore in public with a black handkerchief wrapped around his head.

Upon Samuel's advice, Obookiah traded the comfort of the Mills' homestead in rural Torringford for town life at Andover with the Brethren at the New England evangelical church's chief seat for educating ministers. At the Theological Seminary, Samuel hoped, Henry would embark on the schooling needed for his return to the Sandwich Islands as a leader of the first, pioneering missions party.

CHAPTER NINE
ANDOVER & BRADFORD

American Missionary Memorial
The roster of the Brethren in 1808, written in a
secret cipher at Williams College.

SAMUEL MILLS EASED HENRY OUT into the world beyond rural Torringford by making space for him in the Phillips Hall room he shared at the Theological Seminary at Andover.

"There was no small degree of interest excited among the people of God, who were acquainted with his history," Mills wrote of Henry's arrival at Andover in late 1810.

Like his days being tutored by Yale students in New Haven, Obookiah roamed around Andover town and the Seminary campus, asking questions, seeking new friends,.

The close-knit circle of the Brethren at Andover welcomed Obookiah. Samuel requested they join in teaching him, to encourage his conversion to Christianity with hopes Henry would join the Brethren in launching a mission to the Sandwich Islands.

Obookiah soon endeared himself to the seminary students and staff.

"Whenever he had learned a lesson prescribed to him by his guardian, he was at liberty to go to any student he could find, and recite it," an account from Andover recalled.

Henry met Timothy Woodbridge, the blind seminary student who roomed with Samuel. Andover students put their faith to work by helping blind Timothy overcome his seemingly impossible task of earning a graduate degree in theology. Timothy listened as they read their assignments out loud; he dictated his class papers to his helpers. Using his sharp mind, Timothy interpreted difficult passages of text for the sighted students.

The Theological Seminary at Andover was founded in 1808 for, "the preservation of Calvinist puritanism in the face of liberalism...." A theological civil war erupted in 1805 when Harvard appointed a Unitarian theologian as head of its divinity school.

From *Old Andover Days* by Sarah Stuart Robbins, daughter of Moses Stuart, photo c. 1870
Obookiah found lodging at Andover by staying with Samuel Mills and Timothy Woodbridge in room No. 21 in Phillips Hall (far left) on "Seminary Row" at the Andover Theological Seminary located on Academy Hill. The brick-walled buildings closely resemble the
"Brick Row" buildings of Yale College, an architectural statement symbolic of the closes
ties between the two institutions, reflecting their Second Great Awakening evangelical
missionary spirt of the early nineteenth-century.

Harvard was dedicated to the training of Calvinist ministers upon its founding in 1636,
but had now become a center of those espousing non-trinitarian, liberal theology.

At Andover, the Seminary's founders sought to emphasize the connection between Yale, then a bastion of orthodox Christianity, and the Seminary, the first evangelical seminary gathered in the United States. In building Phillips Hall, architects
copied Yale buildings right down to the red brick patterns of walls.

Missions-minded students enrolling at Andover swelled the ranks of the Brethren.
Haystack Meeting-like prayer sessions began forming along the banks of Rabbit Pond, a
scenic spot located just a short walk away from Phillips Hall.

A New Wave of Brethren Interest

Students from colleges besides Yale and Williams joined the Brethren at Andover
including Providence College graduate Adoniram Judson. Judson's minister father led
the Pilgrim's church at Plymouth, Massachusetts.

Adoniram became a leading proponent of foreign missions at Andover in 1809
when Samuel Mills was absent, dwelling in New Haven, studying at Yale.

After graduating from Providence College with honors, Adoniram departed New
England, venturing into the bohemian world of actors residing in lower Manhattan.
He was lured there by an idealistic vision of arty city society, through the "infidel senti-
ments" espoused by his college roommate. This student named in Judson biographies
only as "E.," led him, a pastor's son, away from the Bible to the Enlightenment writings
of Rousseau and Thomas Paine.

Once in New York and living the life of an actor, Judson's idealism soured when his
companions habitually ran out on their rent. He became disillusioned by experiencing
within his own soul the consequences of their dissolute ways.

Escaping the city, Adoniram borrowed a horse from an uncle and headed for the Hudson Valley to further seek his way outside his family circle. En route, seeking a room after dark at a country inn, he found only one open for the night. The room shared a wall with that of a very ill young man whom Judson had been warned was dying. Edward Judson, his father's biographer, described the scene:

Sounds came from the sick chamber, sometimes the movements of the watchers, sometimes the groans of the sufferer; but it was not these which disturbed him. He thought of what the landlord had said, the stranger was probably in a dying state; and was he prepared? Alone, and in the dead of night, he felt a blush of shame steal over him at the question, for it proved the shallowness of his philosophy. What would his late companions say to his weakness? The clear-minded, intellectual, witty E, what would he say to such consummate boyishness? But still his thoughts would revert to the sick man. Was he a Christian, calm and strong in the hope of a glorious immortality? Or was he shuddering upon the brink of a dark, unknown future? Perhaps he was a "freethinker," educated by Christian parents, and prayed over by a Christian mother. The landlord had described him as a young man; and in imagination he was forced to place himself upon the dying bed, though he strove with all his might against it. At last morning came, and the bright flood of light which it poured into his chamber dispelled all his "superstitious illusions." As soon as he had risen, he went in search of the landlord, and inquired for his fellow-lodger. "He is dead," was the reply. "Dead!" "Yes, he is gone, poor fellow! The doctor said he would probably not survive the night." "Do you know who he was?" "O, yes; it was a young man from Providence College, a very fine fellow; his name was E." Judson was completely stunned.

After hours had passed, he knew not how, he attempted to pursue his journey. But one single thought occupied his mind, and the words, Dead! Lost! Lost! were continually ringing in his ears. He knew the religion of the Bible to be true; he felt its truth; and he was in despair. In this state of mind he resolved to abandon his scheme of traveling, and at once turned his horse's head towards Plymouth.

Once united at Andover, Judson and Mills joined forces to promote foreign missions. They recognized it was time for the Brethren to connect with Congregational Church leaders from Massachusetts and Connecticut in launching foreign missions out of New England. Mills and Judson contacted the Rev. Samuel Worcester of Salem, a missions-advocate and leader of the Congregational Church in Massachusetts. Worcester traveled to Andover on June 25, 1810 to confer with the Rev. Moses Stuart (Stuart was now the professor of Biblical Studies at Andover, released from the First Church in New Haven) and the Rev. Gardiner Spring. The three ministers knew of the plans of the Brethren, and trusted in the sincerity, leadership and capabilities of Mills and Judson. Worcester, Stuart and Spring agreed that a formal missions board was needed to underwrite and oversee the Brethren's plans.

The next morning a statewide meeting of Congregational church leaders was scheduled to gather at Bradford, a village located eight miles north of Andover. The Brethren chose a contingent of four to travel to Bradford to present a plea for support. Mills and Judson, along with Seminary students Samuel Nott and Samuel Newell, ambled down a country road rich in leafy summer foliage. Bradford village lay ahead, nestled along a double oxbow in the Merrimack River. From Bradford, workers walked over a bridge to the industrial town of Haver-hill, finding jobs in tanneries, shoe manu-facturing and boat yards.

The Brethren students presented a letter seeking the organization of a formal Ameri-can foreign missionary society to support, and guide, the sending out of missionary candidates recruited by the Brethren. Do-mestic missionary societies who supported short-term missions to the wilds of New York, Vermont, and Ohio were by then well established in New England. The work of the London Missionary Society in Tahiti, and British Baptist missionary William Car-ey in India, were both well known to New

The home of Deacon Hasseltine in Brad-ford, Massachusetts where Obookiah board-ed while attending Bradford Academy. The home has been moved from its original lo-cation along the green where the American Board of Commissioners' formation me-morial now stands.

England Christians. Even so, it would be revolutionary for churches to support sending young men and women on one-way, likely life-long, voyages to faraway lands.

"They were confident the voice of God had spoken," a Judson biographer wrote of the bold Brethren statement. "The assembly waited, hushed and uncertain, listening in-tently, as each of the young men told why he believed it was his duty to give up home and friends and go on the long perilous journey to the heathen world."

The committee conferred overnight and the following morning announced their support of the Brethren plan. This meant that the United States' first-ever foreign mis-sions organization had been created. The board would organize and promote support for missionaries going out to foreign shores, including the Sandwich Islands. A name was suggested, a cumbersome one that would become known throughout the United States and around the world: the American Board of Commissioners for Foreign Mis-sions.

The Brethren and the American Board of Commissioners were made for each oth-er. The Brethren, along with professors at Andover, would identify, recruit and train missionary candidates within the student body. The American Board would send out the students to a foreign mission field chosen by their Prudential Committee, provid-ing spiritual, financial and other logistical support. Once out on a mission, the Breth-ren members would correspond back to Andover, sending back confidential, real-life accounts of life on the mission field to help train and educate mission candidates.

Obookiah and Bradford Academy

By early 1811, while residing in Phillips Hall, Obookiah made his first attempt at praying in public in a style that reads like a Hawaiian *kahea*, a prayer cry:

His friend, having knelt down and prayed, turning to him before they rose, said, "you may pray." When he delivered himself, in substance, in the following terms.

"Great and eternal God-make heaven-make earth-make every thing- have mercy on me-make me understand the Bible-make me good-great God have mercy on Thomas-make him good-make Thomas and me go back Owhyhee-tell folks in Owhyhee, no more pray to stone god-make some good man go with me to Owhyhee, tell folks in Owhyhee about Heaven-about Hell-God make all people good....."

As the year 1811 unfolded, a year when foreign missions came to the forefront in New England, Samuel saw it was time for Obookiah to be properly educated. Henry had been learning haphazardly, acquiring bits and pieces of grammar, reading and math, taught by helpful, but busy, Seminary students.

Samuel chose nearby Bradford Academy, a school opened in 1804 to educate the boys and girls of that riverside town. Samuel raised the funds in Andover to pay Henry's tuition and boarding fees for the three-month winter term. Samuel boarded Obookiah in the home of Deacon John Hasseltine, a leader in the Bradford Congregational church.

Henry studied in a classroom in a one-story school topped by a belfry. He was now in his early twenties. In 1811 older students often studied alongside younger students. A lack of family funds to pay for an education might require years of farm labor to be saved in advance to pay for tuition.

The Bradford Academy board divided their academy building into two rooms, one for boys, one for girls. The rooms shared a fireplace set down the middle of the building. Henry sat on a hardwood plank seat, and recited lessons "in every branch of useful knowledge": English, Latin, Greek, reading, writing, geography, arithmetic.

A revival had crested at the Bradford Academy prior to Obookiah's enrollment. With the revival fervor waning, the Hasseltines had no qualms over making their home a "favorite resort of the boys and girls" by opening a "hall at the rear of the second story to be used for their parties and entertainments."

BRADFORD ACADEMY, 1803.

The winter months at Bradford set Obookiah off on a tangent, attracting him to worldly interests. Away from the godly influence of Samuel and the Brethren, Henry became sidetracked. Samuel hoped he would become a model Christian and prepare to bring the Gospel to Hawai'i. Instead, Obookiah observed:

I become prayer-less and thoughtless-no hope for mercy-never attempted to be alone, as I had done before. I sit and walked about all day-took no opportunity to be at the throne of grace, but rather to be stupid-from the morning until evening never thought of him who kept me alive; neither when I lay down upon my bed, nor when I rose up. I was in this situation for a long time, while I was at school.

Captain Cook's Death

Ensconced in an upstairs bedroom in the Hasseltine home, Obookiah began telling Hawaiian stories to his roommates. This helped Obookiah improve his grasp of speaking English, and provided entertainment for the boarding house friends.

A glimpse of his Bradford days appears in a letter published in the 1860s in *The Friend*, the Congregational newspaper edited in Honolulu by the Rev. Samuel Damon. Joshua Coffin wrote the letter. Coffin was an orphan from Newburyport on the Massachusetts coast who boarded at Bradford as a teenager.

Coffin, in his recollections of studying and living with Obookiah, wrote, "He was a great favorite with all the family. He had so much frankness, honesty and simplicity that no one could be offended with him."

Obookiah would tell tales of his life at Kealakekua Bay to Coffin, then about seventeen years old, in "many interesting conversations which I had at various times with this very interesting young man. He gave me at different times a particular account of his life, adventures, &c. He gave me a particular account of the death of Captain Cook, and the causes which led to it." Obookiah told Joshua his tale of Cook's demise was told by his grandfather to his father, and related by his father, Ke'au, to him.

Andover Sojourn

In spring 1811, Obookiah returned to Andover. As someone beholding to another for support might do, he hedged in telling Samuel Mills about the frivolous life he led at Bradford.

> Mr. M. was not there. It was vacation. I staid until he returned. When he returned he enquired how I have been and how I was pleased with the school. I answered well. But I did not let him know what was my situation, and what trouble I had met with while I was there, but kept all these things in my own mind.

That spring Obookiah worked about two months felling trees and doing chores for a Mr. F., who lived about five miles away from the Theological Seminary. At this homestead Obookiah experienced an epiphany of faith. He felt God spoke a sure word directly to him, a revelation. He received it in his soul, not through his intellect. The experience was personal, not the indifferent feeling that came over him when hearing the words of Samuel and the other New England Christians who preached to him.

> I took an axe and went and worked there till towards noon....Many thoughts come into my mind that I was in a dangerous situation. I thought that if I should then die, I must certainly be cast off forever. While I was working it appeared as it was a voice saying "Cut it down, why cumbereth it the ground." I worked no longer-but dropped my axe, and walked a few steps from the place...I fell upon my knees and looked up to the Almighty Jehovah for help. I was but an undone and hell-deserving sinner. I felt that it would be just that God should cast me off whithersoever he would-that he should do with my poor soul as it seemed to him fit. I spent some time here until I heard a boy calling for me-and I went. The people in the house asked of my sadness-to which I gave but little answer. In the night my sleep was taken away from me. I kept awake almost the whole night. Many of my feelings

and thoughts in past time came into remembrance–and how I treated the mercy of God while I was at Bradford Academy. The next morning I rose up before the rest, and went to a place where I was alone by myself. Here I went both morning, night and noon. At this little place I find some comfort. And when I go there I enjoy myself better all the day.

Obookiah left the forest for another season in close contact with Samuel and Timothy Woodbridge. Henry again hid his uncertainty over whether he was meant to live out his life as a Christian. Despite his encounter in the forest outside Andover, he dodged questions when pressed about his salvation. He wrote, "Many times Mr. M. asked me about my feelings, and I was neither willing to answer much, nor could I on account of my unfruitfulness and wickedness."

Obookiah hired himself out during the mid-summer haying season, this time on the Abbot Farm in Andover, a farm owned by Nehemiah Abbot, the steward of the Theological Seminary. He wrote:

"Mr. A. was a good man and it was a religious family. I had here the same seriousness in my mind as before, but never did meet with real change of heart yet."

During Obookiah's two years living and studying in and around Andover he became a favorite of the steward and his wife, Sarah Abbot. Sarah is the namesake of the renowned girls-only Abbot Academy opened in 1829 just down Academy Hill from the Seminary.

"This family bear very favourable testimony to the excellence of his character," Edwin Dwight wrote. "They speak of him with tears. Said Mrs. A(bbot) to a friend, 'He was always pleasant. I never saw him angry. He used to come into my chamber and kneel down by me and pray. Mr. M. did not think he was a Christian at that time, but he appeared to be thinking of nothing else but religion. He afterwards told me that there was a time when he wanted to get religion into his head more than into his heart.'"

Nehemiah Abbot noted the inquisitiveness of Obookiah, who educated himself on whatever caught his eye, especially phenomena that brought to mind his youth in Hawai'i, "...(he) could never be satisfied until he saw the whole of a subject. This was peculiarly observable during an eclipse of the sun, concerning which he asked many troublesome questions..."

Obookiah took an interest in the Andover town council's tax system, "...particularly the mode of levying, collecting and appropriating taxes." This unlikely interest perhaps recalled to Obookiah's mind the autumn Makahiki Festival tax collecting procession.

Obookiah foresaw western, New England-style buildings being one day erected in Hawai'i; his insight came true. "He was seen one morning very early with a rule measuring the College buildings and fences," Nehemiah Abbot observed. "He was asked why he did it. He smiled, and said, 'So that I shall know how to build when I go back to Owhyhee.'"

"When he heard a word," Nehemiah recalled, "which he did not understand or could not speak, it was his constant habit to ask me 'How you spell? How you spell?' When I told him he never forgot."

Obookiah left his comfortable home with the Abbots in 1812 to travel northwest from Andover on a fateful journey to the rural village of Hollis, New Hampshire.

CHAPTER TEN
HOLLIS HEALING

Henry Obookiah convalesced in Hollis, New Hampshire in the home of Deacon Daniel Emerson. The Emerson home, constructed in 1768, is the oldest standing building in Hollis. The house was preceded by the family's pioneer log cabin erected in a forest in 1744.

IN THE SUMMER OF 1812 Samuel Mills sought a temporary, secure home near Andover for Obookiah. The domestic missions societies of Connecticut and Massachusetts had recruited Mills to head out for six months on his first mission: a Bible distribution and church survey tour beyond the Allegheny Mountains, out to, and down, the Mississippi River.

Riding with Mills was John Freeman Schermerhorn from the Society for the Propagation of the Gospel of the Dutch Reformed Church. Mills and Schermerhorn planned to start out on horseback from Torringford the day before the Fourth of July. Their mission: demarcate for the first time the spiritual, moral, and temporal state of an area that is today the heart of America's Bible Belt.

Ralph Emerson, a student at the Andover seminary, likely offered to arrange for Henry's care by the pastor and deacons of the Congregational Church of Hollis, New Hampshire. Another connection to the rural town of Hollis was American Board of Commissioners' Corresponding Secretary Samuel Worcester. Worcester was born in the village in 1770, the son of a farmer.

Henry traveled thirty-five miles from Andover to the picturesque country town. The town center of Hollis is the quintessential image of what a rural New England town should look like. The Congregational Church of Hollis is set across the road from a grassy commons. Obookiah dwelt in several Yankee homes, all located just a short walk away from the church.

At Home in Hollis

Obookiah found that in Hollis the Congregational church, as in most New England villages, served as the center of spiritual and social life. In the early nineteenth-century, Sunday services began in the morning, paused for a short lunch break followed by an afternoon service. A prayer meeting in the evening concluded their Sabbath. The evangelical, Calvinistic theology the Hollis congregation worshipped under was reflected in a mysterious black thunder cloud painted on the ceiling of the church; the icon said to remind worshippers of the wrath of God upon the unrepentant sinner's head.

The people of Hollis were known to be churchgoers, honest and fair, hard working and prosperous but not ostentatious. They were patriotic: some 125 men from the area served in the Revolutionary War. The war caused a split in the town with tory Royalist families departing.

Ralph Emerson was born in Hollis on August 18, 1787, and graduated from Yale College with honors in 1811. His family tree branches out to a distant cousin of almost the same name, Ralph Waldo Emerson, the famous Transcendental philosopher.

Ralph Waldo Emerson was born in Boston in 1803, the son of a Unitarian minister. He graduated from Harvard and likely emphasized his middle name to dis-

The Rev. Ralph Emerson

tinguish himself from his older relative. During the philosopher's early life Ralph Emerson of Hollis was the pastor of the Congregational church in Norfolk, Connecticut.

The lives of the two Ralph Emersons portray the divergent paths New England churches followed in the early- to mid-nineteenth century: evangelical Bible-as-literal-word-of God vs. Enlightenment-influenced Christianity. Ralph Waldo Emerson left the ministry and turned to humanist philosophy. In his writing he denied Jesus was the son of God, and doubted accounts of miracles told of in the Bible.

Ralph Emerson studied at Yale in 1809 when the students in the college boarding rooms began tutoring Hopoo and then Obookiah. Ralph enrolled at the Theological Seminary in 1811, boarding in Phillips Hall where Obookiah slept and studied in Samuel Mills' room.

Ralph's grandfather, the Rev. Daniel Emerson, studied at Harvard in the 1740s. In Cambridge, the open-air preaching of Great Awakening English preacher George Whitefield changed his life. He went on to serve for fifty years as the founding pastor of the Congregational Church of Hollis. Daniel volunteered to be a chaplain in the French and Indian War. An anecdote from that war has the Hollis pastor presenting his Bible during a parade-ground roll call when asked by the commanding officer to "present arms."

The construction and blessing in 1804 of the Third Congregational Church of Hollis followed a revival in 1801 that added 150 persons to the congregation. Here Obookiah attended church with the Emersons and Burges while Pastor Eli Smith led services.

Hollis Congregational Church Pastor the Rev. Eli Smith lived in this home. Smith built his wood frame home about 1800, during the Federal Era. Obookiah spent time with the Smiths while convalescing. In this home and in others in Hollis, the conversion of Obookiah to Christianity took place.

The gravestone of Deacon Ephraim Burge in the graveyard of the Hollis Congregational Church. Burge and his family helped to nurse Henry Obookiah during his near-fatal illness suffered in Hollis, New Hampshire in 1812. Burge enjoyed a long life in the rural town.

Taken Ill, Taken In

"Here," Obookiah wrote of Hollis, "I lived with two good men, Dea. E(merson) and Dea. B(urge) and with the Rev. Mr. S(mith). While I was in this place, I became more thoughtful about myself. I attended many of the young people's meetings, and I was quite happy. But I was now taken sick of a fever at the house of Dea. B. I was very weak and was not able to answer to the questions of those who came to visit me."

Obookiah became gravely ill, nearly dying of a fever at the onset of cold fall weather. In his weakness, the kindness and care of the pastor, deacons, physicians, and the people of Hollis—all strangers to him—made the difference in his battle with death. He spent weeks recuperating in their homes. His faith grew through the selfless love that surrounded him, and the connection he made with God during the stillness of his long, bed-ridden recovery.

> Then thought I, where shall I go for a physician, but unto thee! Death had but a little fear. I continued sick for five weeks. The whole family of Dea. B. were very kind....Doctor C (Benoni Cutter) was a very kind and friendly man. He was a pious and good Christian. Many times he prayed with me while I was upon my sick bed.
>
> One day Mrs. B. asked me whether I was willing to die and leave this world of sin and go to the better. To which I replied that I should have no objection if God should do with me as it seemed to him fit. She added, 'Do you remember the goodness and the kindness of God toward you?' I answered yes-For I have neither a father nor a mother, nor a brother nor a sister in this stranger country but He.... the greatest part of the time I took much comfort and happiness, both in my secret prayer and in serious conversation with others. I thought now with myself that I have met with a change of heart.

The obituary of Deacon Ephraim Burge reflects the change of heart Obookiah underwent during his close call with death at Hollis:

> ...Henry Obookiah, the first convert among the Owyhean youth then in this country, was led to hope in Christ during a summer which he spent in his family and that of another deacon in the same church. The important bearing of the conversion of this youth, on the establishment of the Sandwich Islands mission, will be recollected...The great results which God may connect with the humblest instance of christian faithfulness, can be fully known only at the judgment day. "Them that honor me I will honor."

Native Hawaiian Diaspora

If Henry had died in rural Hollis, he would have been one among many Native Hawaiians to suffer untimely deaths in the early 1810s. A diaspora of young Native Hawaiian men lured to the sea spread out along the trade routes of western maritime commerce.

Estimates of the numbers of people living on all islands prior to the arrival of Captain Cook at Kaua'i in 1778 ranges from about four-hundred thousand to one-million-plus. Living in the most isolated island group in the Pacific was a blessing and a curse for them. Prior to western contact they lived free from most contagious diseases, untouched by the great plagues that swept through the masses of people inhabiting Europe and Asia. Their curse came from their lack of immunities to diseases spread from Cook's arrival onward, from the bilges and cabins of western trading and naval ships. By the time of Obookiah's departure from Kealakekua Bay in 1809, the population of Hawai'i had been cut at least in half by epidemics of smallpox, measles, tuberculosis; by the spread of venereal diseases, especially in the ports where canoe-loads of young women slept with western sailors, which brought infertility as well as sickness.

Back to Andover

In late fall 1812, Obookiah left Hollis, returning to Andover to live with the Abbot family over the winter. From Andover he wrote about his growing vision for Hawai'i, one that might bring him back home. His letter to "A Christian Friend," perhaps written to Edwin Dwight, is dated Dec. 15, 1812: "I hope the Lord will send the gospel to the heathen land the words of the Saviour never yet had been. Poor people worship the wood and stone and shark, and almost every thing their gods; the Bible is not there, and Heaven and Hell they do not know about it...."

In January 1813, Obookiah wrote to Samuel Mills about his outreach to a fellow Hawaiian living nearby. His friend, whom Obookiah failed to name, lived in the Merrimack River town of Tyngsboro (Tyngsborough), about 30 miles west of Andover. At Tyngsboro Henry took on the role of a tutor and mentor, just as Edwin Dwight had been to him. Obookiah wrote in his journal:

> He arrived last June (this is not Thomas that came with me.)As the distance from this place was small I went to visit him. I hope the Lord will have mercy upon his poor soul. He knew nothing of the Saviour before I told him.
>
> ...mentioned to him Genesis 1:1 &c. telling him that God made the world by his own power. I spoke in Owhyhee.

This mention of his having translated scripture into the Hawaiian language is significant. Obookiah with limited western education had taken an early step in the creation of a Hawaiian-language Bible. Henry received the response he sought:

> ...then he said, O how foolish we are to worship wood and stone gods; we give them hogs and cocoa nuts and banana, but they cannot eat...Then he asked me where that man was, that made every thing. I told him, he was every where with us. Does he hear when you and I talk? says he. I told him yes, and you must believe in him if you would be his friend....I told him what God did for him in keeping him alive, and bringing him to this country. He said he liked that man very much, (meaning God.) He asked me many questions again and again about God, which I answered. After we went to bed he said he never would forget what I had told him. He said when he eat he would remember who gave him food.

With his health restored, in the spring of 1813 Obookiah returned to the Mills home in Torringford. Samuel had completed his Bible-planting tour out to the Mississippi River, and Obookiah his basic schooling. Both were ready to move on in their lives to face new and greater challenges, Henry now as a Christian.

CHAPTER ELEVEN
TORRINGFORD & MORRIS ACADEMY

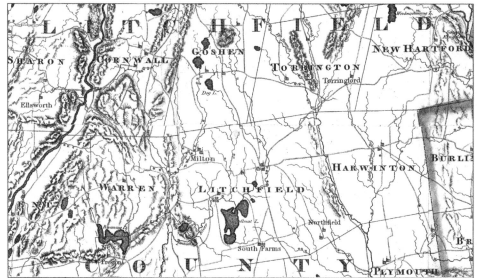

Key events in the life of Obookiah and Hopoo happened in the Litchfield County towns of Cornwall, Torrington, Torringford, Litchfield, Sharon, South Canaan, South Farms, and Goshen. Goshen is considered the birthplace of the Sandwich Islands Mission. This Litchfield, Connecticut topographic map was drawn based on a survey made in 1811 for the General Assembly of the State of Connecticut.

OBOOKIAH WALKED WEST DOWN TORRINGFORD ROAD in the fall of 1813, leaving the Mills' parsonage-home to board at a school founded and run by Revolutionary War hero James Morris. The walk took Obookiah through Torrington. He then continued east to Litchfield town, and then hiked directly south, to South Farms. The Morris Academy building stood on a central corner of this crossroads village.

A decade earlier Samuel Mills began his college-prep education at the Morris Academy.

At home in Torringford, Samuel reunited with Obookiah after returning from his Bible surveying tour of the West. Samuel was then at work composing a report compiled from the notes and statistics he and John Schermerhorn had collected. The report was to be published to champion domestic missions, to gain support from churches and enlist volunteers to distribute Bibles, and to plant churches across the new frontier.

Obookiah had followed Samuel back to Torringford, following Samuel's graduation from Andover Theological Seminary. At the Morris Academy Henry was enrolled as an upper-level academy student, a grade equivalent to that of a high school sophomore or junior. His rapid progress in his studies proved to the ministers of Litchfield that he was an able student, a worthy candidate for financial support from the churches.

Elderly James Morris and his youthful wife Elizabeth welcomed Henry, providing him room and board in their colonial home in South Farms.

Obookiah enrolled in the winter quarter at the Morris Academy, a school noted for being one of the few academies in New England where girls sat alongside boys, though the boys were being groomed for college, the girls to be wives. The previous summer Henry worked on the Mills' farm to help to pay for his wintertime schooling.

Morris, along with the Rev. Lyman Beecher in Litchfield, and Father Mills in Torringford, offered a solid circle of pastoral support in maturing Henry as a Christian. It was presumed that Henry would within a few years return to Hawai'i with Samuel Mills, to evangelize his people and to introduce the Bible and evangelical Christianity.

James Morris

Morris was raised in a Christian home and grew up desiring to be a minister. He entered Yale in 1771 and was tutored by a young Timothy Dwight. Morris took his graduation exam to earn his Yale degree in July 1775, right at the outbreak of the Revolutionary War. His ministry plans were shelved when he joined George Washington's Continental Army as an officer prior to graduation exercises.

Morris fought as a first lieutenant in the Battle of Long Island on August 27, 1776. He rode in an open boat when General George Washington and his Continental Army troops made a miraculous night-time escape across the East River, from Brooklyn to Manhattan, avoiding capture and a likely end to the war against the British.

The British Army later captured Morris and imprisoned him in Philadelphia. He wisely spent his time as a prisoner of war in studying books he managed to borrow from the library of Benjamin Franklin; many American prisoners idled their time away playing cards and socializing. Following the war Morris taught school in South Farms. He opened his namesake academy in 1800.

Obookiah's Chrysalis

Morris tied his hopes for his academy to the foreign missions movement by enrolling Obookiah in 1813. Through Morris' assistance Henry's ability accelerated in reading, speaking, and writing in English. His fervor for reading the Bible grew. Being enrolled at the Morris Acacedmy was encouraging for him both intellectually and spiritually, "...seldom would any object of circumstances prevent his reading daily some portion of the Scriptures."

A scholarship was offered to Henry in acknowledgment of his growth as a scholar, and as a Christian. He gained the support of Father Mills and Lyman Beecher along with other Congregational ministers and lay church leaders in Litchfield County.

Henry enjoyed a reunion with Edwin Dwight during a visit to the Beecher's spacious white frame home located in Litchfield town. Henry shared with his Yale-days mentor his adventures in Hollis and Andover. Edwin wrote, "Occasionally, when requested, he has prayed and spoken in social religious meetings; and always performed these services to the acceptance, and, it is believed, to the edification of those present."

The transformation of Obookiah was a wonder to Edwin. The rough-shod, sullen, sailor-suited Sandwich Islander found weeping in the summer of 1809 on the steps of Yale was now a handsome young man. Obookiah and Edwin shared the same hair cut, the neo-Roman style of that time, short except for a frame of longer hair stylishly framing the face. Henry shared with Edwin how he had found salvation in Andover and

In the Fall of 1813, Henry was invited by James Morris, Esq. of Litchfield, to spend the winter in his family,

History of Five Sandwich Islanders

This British woodcut presented an English view of Obookiah's walk from Torringford to the Morris Academy in 1813.

Hollis in his own way, and at his own pace.

Edwin pictured his brown-skinned young friend in a pulpit sharing his faithful story in Connecticut churches, living proof that native missionaries could return to their homelands to share the gospel.

Hearing a Christian native of Owhyee alternatively praying in English and in the language of the Sandwich Islands validated Samuel Mills' vision. Samuel foresaw the Brethren joining forces with Obookiah in leading an American Board of Commissioners' mission to Hawai'i.

Recalling Samuel's' hopes for Obookiah to lead a mission to his home islands, Dwight questioned Henry on how far he had advanced in his knowledge of the Bible, and of biblical concepts.

Dwight surmised, "...he gave answers which clearly evinced that on this subject he had thought and felt for himself; and furnished much reason to hope that he had been savingly instructed by the Holy Spirit." As Henry had painstakingly memorized the many chants required in his training as a kahuna at Kealakekua, so did he acquire, "...a very considerable knowledge of the Scriptures. He quoted passages appropriate to almost every subject of conversation."

And as Obookiah would have had continued to learn the deeper meanings of the chants and prayers of the kāhuna had he followed his uncle Pahua at Kealakekua, Henry took on a detailed study of the nuances of the Bible. Edwin remarked:

> It was evident that his mind dwelt upon the truth of the Bible, and that he found much of his habitual pleasure in searching out the less obvious treasures which it contained. He manifested great inquisitiveness with regard to passages of Scripture whose meaning he did not entirely comprehend. Many passages were the subjects of enquiry. One only is recollected. "What our Saviour mean," said he, "when he say 'In my father's house are many mansion-I go prepare a place for you.' What he mean, go prepare a place?..."

Back to Torringford

In the spring of 1814, Obookiah returned to the Mills' home in Torringford "and spent the summer principally in labouring on the farm." There he reunited with Samuel Mills.

> In the beginning of summer my friend Mr. M. whom I loved, returned from his missionary tour. I received him with joyful salutation. Several times he asked me how my wicked heart get along while I was hoeing corn. But I was still fearful to tell whether my heart was changed or not.

Samuel departed in 1814 from Torringford on a second horseback surveying tour, planning to follow roughly the same route as his first tour. Daniel Smith of Natchez, Mississippi rode with him on this tour. Mills and Smith arrived in Catholic New Orleans in the weeks following Andrew Jackson's victory over the British army at the Battle of New Orleans. They ministered in hospitals to wounded men from both sides, handing out Bibles to the soldiers. Mills in a bold move met with a Roman Catholic bishop who surprisingly agreed to distribute Protestant Bibles to his Catholic parishioners.

Henry completed his course at the Morris Academy, then moved about twenty miles north, to the crossroads village of Goshen. There the pace of his learning accelerated. He was now ready to take college preparatory classes, including biblical language studies, one-on-one with the Rev. Joseph Harvey, pastor of the Congregational church in Goshen.

Goshen villagers warmly welcomed the studious young man who seemed to be on his way to accomplishing great things for the American missions movement, and for his own people in Hawai'i. Obookiah, who attended Sunday services in the town church, became a familiar figure around the rural town, friendly, sincere, apt to quote the Bible and offer a word of good cheer. Soon Tennoe (Kanui), another kanaka sailor landed in New England, arrived to join Henry in boarding with the Harveys.

Hopoo Returns to the Sea, War of 1812

Thomas Hopoo for several years boarded with Dr. Obidiah Hotchkiss in New Haven, staying long after Obookiah departed. While Dr. Hotchkiss and Thomas formed a close friendship, the doctor's efforts to convert Thomas came to naught. The many distractions and worldly influences of life in urban New Haven surely lured Thomas.

Life changed for Hopoo in June, 1812 when President James Madison declared war on Great Britain. Hopoo found a berth aboard a privateer, a merchant ship given a letter of marque by the President allowing its owners to act as legal pirates, to be free to capture British merchant ships. He wrote in his memoirs:

> ...my wicked disposition seemed inclined rather to rove to sea, than to stay on land. I had rejected very many of the best invitations of my friend Hotchkiss, to stay with him, and be taught to know more and more about the Saviour of this sinful world. I had however learned to write, and to spell some easy words, in the spelling book, before I chose the life of a sailor. So I went to sea, about twelve voyages, out of New Haven, in several vessels: And during the late war, more frequently to the West India Islands.

Hopoo suffered through trials at sea. On one voyage his ship was captured by the Royal Navy and he found himself imprisoned on the island of St. Kitts. There he observed the plight of Africans enslaved by a sugar plantation owner:

> ...I had often seen the white people, on these Islands, put chains on their slaves' necks, and on their legs, as long as they lived. While I was on these Islands, I had a great desire to return to America, because I did not like to see all these things....

After four months behind bars, Hopoo was released and returned to New Haven in wintertime. The lure of the warm Caribbean climate drove him to find a berth aboard a West Indies trader. The voyage abruptly ended in disaster:

> I was shipwrecked, and very narrowly escaped from a watery grave. It was about 400 miles distant from the West India Isles, our little vessel was turned upside down, by the strong Northeast wind....We had to swim to save our lives from the morning until almost sundown that day in the water....I found that my shipmates were almost sinking down...Every time the waves broke over them, they made a dreadful noise in the water: but I told them, you must now look to God for help, while danger is near, rather than cry out. At all times, in your troubles, if you know the Bible is the word of Christ, you ought to pray to the God of Heaven, more than the heathen; but if you do not, you will never see America again.

Hopoo's waterman ocean skills learned as a child in Hawai'i saved him and his companions. Retrieving a rope from the wreck he lashed their swamped whale boat to a section of a mast found floating nearby. He struggled to bail the boat out on his own, while his helpless shipmates clung to the boat's gunwales. Once squared away, Thomas employed Polynesian navigational skills, using the sun and stars and currents, along with direction he sought from God, to sail over 400 miles to safety. Once ashore, black West Indian islanders provided water, a handful of fish and clothing.

After being paroled by the British, Hopoo landed a berth on a captured American ship heading back to New England.

Obookiah's Plan

Back in Litchfield County Obookiah's vision for returning home to Hawai'i took shape. He sought out Edwin Dwight, challenging his tutor and friend and cohort of Samuel Mills to return with him as a missionary to the Islands. Edwin recalled:

> ...it was his object to converse...upon that subject of accompanying him to Ow-hyhee. He plead with great earnestness that he would go and preach the Gospel to his poor countrymen. Not receiving so much encouragement as he desired, he suspected that his friend might be influenced, by the fear of the consequences of attempting to introduce a new religion amongst the heathen. Upon which, though he had now just began to lisp the language of the Scriptures, he said, "You afraid? You know our Saviour say, He that will have his life shall lose it; and he that will lose his life for my sake, same shall save it."

Obookiah also presented his plan to return to Hawai'i to a minister, perhaps Father Mills. The minister challenged Henry's commitment:

> His own fearlessness and zeal on this subject he exhibited about the same time to an aged Minister who asked him why he wished to return to Owyhee. He replied-"to preach the Gospel to my countrymen." He was asked, what he would say to them about their wooden gods. He answered, "Nothing." "But," said the clergy-man, "Suppose your countrymen should tell you that preaching Jesus Christ was blaspheming their gods, and should put you to death?" To this he replied with great emphasis, "If that be the will of God, I am ready, I am ready."

Obookiah's Life Publicized

The first full account of the life of Obookiah in Hawai'i, and of his adventures in New England, appeared in the fall of 1814, in the pages of *The Adviser*. The Rev. Chauncey Lee and others edited this monthly magazine published for the evangelical churches of Vermont out of the college town of Middlebury.

Lee wrote a short biography of Obookiah to accompany a letter written by Henry to the minister's son. Lee served as pastor of the Colebrook Congregational church in a town located in the northwest corner of Connecticut. He hoped to encourage his son's Christian faith through correspondence with Henry.

Lee's son first met Obookiah at Battell's, the general store and informal town gathering place located a short walk from the Mills' home in Torringford.

The minister's words provided the first-known published account of Obookiah's life in Hawai'i, and of his odyssey in New England.

Lee, who apparently met Obookiah along with his son, described Henry:

> ...being a sprightly active lad, of uncommon agility of body—tall in stature—straight built—his limbs well proportioned; and his complexion a medium between the redness of the American Indian, and the sable hue of the Mulatto—his hair straight, but his features resembling neither.—Mildness and modesty are the most prominent expressions of his countenance.

Lee reported that Obookiah was creating a grammar and vocabulary of the Hawaiian language, steps necessary in translating Bible scripture into his native language.

He has made some few essays in translating certain passages in the New Testament; but he tells me, that tho he retains a perfect knowledge of his own language, yet the task of translating is difficult and discouraging...For instance, he has no word for heaven, but that, which means clouds, not for hell, but under ground.

Obookiah later described his Bible translating work undertaken at this time:

And a part of the time was trying to translate a few verses, of the Scriptures into my own language! and in making a kind of spelling-book; taking the English alphabet and giving different names and different sounds-(for this language was not written language.) I spent some time in making a kind of spelling-book, dictionary, grammar, &c.

Obookiah was later able to translate sections of the Book of Genesis directly from the Hebrew language into the Hawaiian language. A Litchfield-New Haven-Andover connection likely aided him.

Andover seminary biblical languages professor Moses Stuart (the pastor of Caleb Brintnall's church in New Haven back in 1809 when Obookiah attended services) wrote out his own Hebrew grammar lessons for use by his students. Stuart employed the Book of Genesis as the text for his lessons.

Using one of these manuscript copies, along with tutoring by Andover student Eleazar Fitch, Obookiah likely began studying biblical Hebrew.

Obookiah's extraordinary memory skills employed in the service of his uncle Pahua at the Hikiau Heiau were revived in his study of Hebrew. He found the grammar and sound of the ancient language of the Jews close in spirit and sound to the Hawaiian language.

The Rev. Lee spent time with Obookiah at Goshen. He wrote:

SELECT PORTIONS OF THE HEBREW SCRIPTURES,
IN PROSE AND POETRY.

I. *The original creation of the heavens and the earth, and the primitive state of the latter;* Gen. I. 1, 2.

בְּרֵאשִׁית בָּרָא אלהים אֵת הַשָּׁמַיִם וְאֵת הָאָרֶץ׃ 1

וְהָאָרֶץ הָיְתָה תֹהוּ וָבֹהוּ וְחֹשֶׁךְ עַל־פְּנֵי תְהוֹם וְרוּחַ 2
אֱלֹהִים מְרַחֶפֶת עַל־פְּנֵי הַמָּיִם׃

II. *The work of the first day;* Gen. I. 3—5.

וַיֹּאמֶר אֱלֹהִים יְהִי אוֹר וַיְהִי־אוֹר׃ וַיַּרְא אֱלֹהִים 3 4
אֶת־הָאוֹר כִּי־טוֹב וַיַּבְדֵּל אֱלֹהִים בֵּין הָאוֹר וּבֵין
הַחֹשֶׁךְ׃ וַיִּקְרָא אֱלֹהִים לָאוֹר יוֹם וְלַחֹשֶׁךְ קָרָא לָיְלָה 5
וַיְהִי־עֶרֶב וַיְהִי־בֹקֶר יוֹם אֶחָד׃

This selection from Moses Stuart's *A Hebrew Chrestomathy* was designed as an introduction to a course of Hebrew study at Andover Theological Seminary where Moses served as professor of sacred languages. This printed sample is a refined version of the hand-written Hebrew lessons Stuart distributed to his class in 1812. His student Eleazer Thompson Fitch likely passed along a copy of the paper to Obookiah, and from this paper Obookiah began translating Genesis from Hebrew into his version of the written Hawaiian language.

He is now pursuing his studies with Rev. Mr. Harvey at Goshen, who informs me that his genius is both quick and retentive. Indeed his letter to my son...which may be relied on as a genuine composition, in point of penmanship, style and subject, is perhaps the best index of his literary improvement, and his moral state of mind. It is such in every view, and especially when accompanied with the reflection that five years ago, he was an unlettered, ignorant savage; that, many of our American youth who from infancy have enjoyed the liberal means of literary and Christian education, may even blush to read it.

Lee foresaw Obookiah sailing back to Hawai'i, as a member of a mission to the Sandwich Islands, and called for the churches to support him.

He promises, in due time, to be, either an excellent interpreter, to a gospel missionary—or a preaching missionary himself, or a school instructor; or all three, to his benighted countrymen....

Obookiah's letter in the *Advisor* described his embracing prayer and seeking Jesus:

While I was in this place with Rev. Mr. H. I took more happiness upon my knees than I ever did before; having a good room to study, and being alone the greatest part of the time. Many happy and serious thoughts were coming into my mind while I was upon my bed in the night. Every thing appeared to be very clear to my own view. Many times the Lord Jesus appeared in my mind to be the most great grace and glorious. O what happy hours that I had in the night season!...

Time of the New Millennium

At Goshen, grooming Obookiah as a missionary to Hawai'i was tied to the words of the Hebrew prophets in a key sermon delivered by the Rev. Joseph Harvey. Harvey strongly supported sending a foreign mission to Hawai'i. In his sermon, Harvey foresaw a soon arrival of the New Millennium and the return of Jesus Christ to the earth.

Harvey delivered this influential sermon at the annual meeting of the Foreign Mission Society of Litchfield, held on February 15, 1815. This resulted in sending from Goshen a formal request to the American Board of Commissioners for a mission to be sent to the Sandwich Islands. Obookiah, Kanui and Hopoo were likely sitting in a pew listening to Harvey deliver his sermon.

Harvey pictured the world of 1815 bookmarked in an island of time that covered 7,000 years. Creation, as described in Genesis, being year-one; 1815 being near a glorious, and catastrophic, global completion of this phase of existence. In this dispensationalist view, Harvey predicted that within about two-hundred years what New Light theologians called the New Millennium would be ushered in, in about the year AD 2000. Life as lived on the earth would end, he preached. Satan would then lose his influence over the world, and Jesus Christ would return, ending Satan's reign and establishing a New Jerusalem on the earth to be peopled by faithful Christians. Christians were to spend their lives as dwellers of two nations–their waking world and the heavenly New Jerusalem that would be soon brought down to earth. The material world of 1815 was not the ultimate reality, Harvey declared.

This timeline, as presented by Harvey, was a foundational tenet of the Second Great Awakening movement. The tipping points, the main foreign missions goals of American Christians in bringing in the New Millennium, would be the return of the Jews to their homeland in Israel, and the translation of the Bible into the languages of people groups throughout the world. Harvey preached:

...The increasing spirit of missions is another prominent sign of the present time.... Let it never be said that the children of the Pilgrims, who came to this wilderness for the sake of their religion, are the last to convey its blessings to those who are perishing for lack of vision...

In early 1815, Henry sought to join the Torringford church. Church membership was a serious commitment in New England in the early nineteenth-century, one that provided benefits and obligations, both spiritual and temporal.

Obookiah traveled to Torringford for the Sunday service where he would be baptized by Father Millis. His acceptance by the congregation would be announced that day. Henry recalled:

I thought I was traveling, that I was going home to New Jerusalem-to the welcome gate. As I walked along I repeated these words, "Whom have I in heaven but thee? and there is none upon earth that I desire besides thee." I was received into the church of Christ in Torringford, on the ninth day of April, in the year 1815.

Obookiah sought out Father Mills prior to the service and requested to speak before the congregation. He was baptized that day by the name Henry Obookiah and surrounded by the Torringford congregation. The minister, likely due to his self-absorption, closed the service without calling up Obookiah to say his piece. This upset Obookiah, who likely felt his adoptive father had purposely overlooked him for racist reasons.

In 1815, Joseph Harvey sent a formal request for the formation and sending from New England of the pioneer company of the Sandwich Islands Mission. The letter was filed and tabled at the Boston headquaters of the American Board of Commissioners for Foreign Missions. Obookiah was the obvious choice to be a leader in the mission party, the man the American Board would need to connect with the ali'i nui. American Board commissioners voted on November 15, 1815 to take Obookiah under their care.

During the fall season of 1815 a reunion in Litchfield encouraged Obookiah, both in his growth as a Christian, in his retaining his Hawaiian identity in the Protestant, white society of New England, and in his hope for returning to Hawai'i.

CHAPTER TWELVE
HOPOO'S ADVENTURES

Samuel F.B. Morse painted this portrait of Thomas Hopoo in 1819. The image was engraved in 1822, appearing in the illustrated broadside "Four Owyhean Youths."

THOMAS HOPOO MOVED INLAND IN 1814 to work in the rural village of Whitestown, New York as a servant for former U.S. Postmaster Gideon Granger. It was time for a peaceful interlude for Thomas following his perilous adventures at sea.

But even on land, the sea continued to engulf him. One memorable night he dreamt an apocalyptic dream, envisioning the earth being destroyed by a flood. This frightened Thomas. He abandoned a plan to return to Hawai'i on his own separate from any Christian missionaries in fear of retribution from the ali'i nui:

> ...I often thought, that I was as good a Christian as any other people in the world: but when I came to hear more about God's word, saying, "Except a man be born again, he cannot see the kingdom of God," the more I thought about these words, and my dream, the more did they go down deeper and deeper, until they got hold of my wicked heart....
>
> ...If the Lord had not had pity on my soul, or led my mind to fear him, from this time, I should have gone back to Owhyhee with my unbelieving heart, and with the spirit of the evil one, and become a worshipper of those wooden gods, which can never save the souls of any of the human race. Often did the spirit of Satan tell me, that I must not believe what the ministers said to me, or embrace their doctrines or religion; for if I should believe the Christian religion, when I came to go back to Owhyhee, said Satan, Kummahamaah will cut my head off.

By September, 1815 Hopoo landed back at the East River docks where he and Henry had lived aboard the *Triumph* in 1809. Scuttlebutt spread along the waterfront had Captain Brintnall recruiting a crew to sail back to the Pacific Ocean and Hawai'i. Hopoo decided to return to New Haven to seek a berth on Brintnall's newly-launched ship.

Back once back in New Haven Hopoo decided to stay in America:

> ...my Christian friends at New Haven again proposed that I should stay and obtain
> an education; and offered their assistance for that purpose....(I) immediately went
> into the country to join with Henry Obookiah, who was then studying at Goshen.

Four years earlier the lives of Obookiah and Hopoo diverged. Now they were
reunited. In Goshen. Thomas sought solace from his friend:

> There I found Henry Obookiah, in his chamber reading the Bible. I said to him,
> "Obookiah, what shall I do to be saved in the life to come; for my mind is full of
> darkness, and I feel guilty on account of God's law which I have broken, from day to
> day; and do you tell me that I may go to Jesus and lay my soul at his footstool; that
> I may go with you to Heaven where God is." Then Obookiah kneeled down at the
> side of his bed and prayed to God for me; and after he rose from his prayer he said
> to me, "Thomas, God be merciful to your soul this day; go to God, repent of your
> sins, that you may be made a happy subject of his grace and pray to him for a new
> heart. You cannot see God in peace." I said to him, "How can I pray to God? for I
> have no heart to pray to him; my prayer is nothing but sin." But said Henry, "Ask
> right and it shall be given you and knock and it shall be opened unto you." Here I
> asked of God, but I found no forgiveness; and knocked, but I found no door open
> to me; nothing but gloom and fear filled my mind—no peace of mind—no rest of
> soul, while I was under this ever pungent distress, on account of my sins; because I
> had lived so long in a land of gospel light with-ought (sic) embracing the Saviour.
> The things which I heard of God's eternity and judgment pressed me down.

In October, 1815 Obookiah and Hopoo relocated again, this time to South
Canaan, a village in north Litchfield County set just below the Massachusetts bor-
der. The Rev. Charles Prentice, pastor of the town's Congregational church, boarded
them and provided instruction. Prentice encouraged Obookiah to write down an
account of his life. Hopoo continued to be troubled over his Calvinistic theology-
influenced visions of hell. He was haunted by the sins of his boyhood in Hawai'i, and
by the dissolute way of life he lived during the War of 1812:

> On the day we left Goshen, the fears of hell were more increased in my mind than ever
> before; so that I could not sleep many nights until Christ spoke peace to my wounded
> soul. On the evening after we got into Canaan, Mr. Prentice had a prayer meeting ap-
> pointed at his house. But my awful distress, which I had before I came to this place was
> increased more and more; so that I could no longer conceal it. While Mr. Prentice was
> praying for the blessing of God upon my poor soul, I felt that I could not so much as
> lift my head before the people, on account of my shame in the sight of the eternal God.
> These sins of my infancy, and childhood, and youth, were all set in order before my eyes,
> so that I could indeed see them, as plain as noon day, while I was in this awful situation.

Soon Hopoo's focus would be off himself and onto helping a prince, a son of an
ali'i nui born on Kaua'i, but now stranded in New England.

The Zephyr Voyage

In 1815, the life of New Haven Captain Caleb Brintnall again crossed paths with Obookiah and Hopu. Brintnall offered Henry and Thomas passage back home to Hawaiʻi aboard his "new and elegant ship," the 110-foot-long *Zephyr*. But they both turned down the captain inspite of his promise to depart for Hawaiʻi within months,

New Haven harbor reopened to international trading following the signing of the Treaty of Ghent in Paris and the end of the War of 1812. For three years the city had suffered through a British blockade, and the lingering threat of being again attacked and pillaged by British soldiers and sailors, as had happened during the Revolutionary War. The war ended the glory days of New Haven sealing ships making China Trade voyages, so Brintnall instead found support in Providence, Rhode Island.

The sleek lines of the black-hulled *Zephyr* hinted at its speed under sail. The fine ship showcased the work of top-notch Connecticut shipbuilders working in Middletown, a town located northeast of New Haven along the Connecticut River. The *Zephyr* lived up to her name, fast as a fierce wind. The ship was one of a new generation of Connecticut vessels that gained an advanced design inspired by the fast-running privateers built in Baltimore during the War of 1812. The hull of the *Zephyr*, at 530 tons displacement, held a cargo twice the size of the hold of the *Triumph*.

Due to President Jefferson's "Dambargo" of 1807, and then the War of 1812 blockade by the Royal Navy, major capital investments made by New Haven merchants turned from the sea to land. Industries developed: carriage building, a precursor to America's automobile industry, and pioneering work involving mass production of rifles and pistols by cotton gin inventor Eli Whitney.

By 1815, the enlistment of a crew and raising investment funds for a China trade voyage lacked the support shown to sealing captains in the era of the *Triumph* voyage. The local merchants lacked assuredness of turning a profit, let alone making a fortune off the *Zephyr* voyage.

His new voyage began on a poignant note for Brintnall. He weighed the desire for securing a new fortune, and adventure at sea, with leaving behind his wife for up to three years. Lois would be left alone to ʻparent their four children. Nancy was now fifteen, Charles, thirteen, Henry, ten, and Elihu eight and named for his late uncle who was poisoned in Honolulu. It is unclear if Brintnall knew upon departing that a deadly illness was developing in his wife's body. Within months the illness struck and took her life away, about when Caleb was mid-way in his voyage to the Pacific Ocean.

Brintnall took a great risk in purchasing the *Zephyr*, and investing his funds and those of investors in a China voyage. He knew of reports claiming the herds of fur seals in the southeast Pacific were decimated. Even so, the risk was outweighed in the mind of investors by Brintnall's reputation for bringing home profitable cargoes from Canton. Investors from Providence, Rhode Island and a few from New Haven took on the gamble and backed the voyage and the costly construction of the speedy *Zephyr*.

As a fatherly gesture, Brintnall offered a berth to his wife's nephew, Edward Mix, the young son of his late brother-in-law Elihu Mix. Edward would grow up to be an illustrious sea captain, and in his old age told tales of his voyage aboard the *Zephyr*. His adventures with Brintnall were recalled in his lengthy obituary that detailed his life at sea. "While Mix was with Brintnall he enjoyed diving a surf of 'three rollers'–a very

Dodds family collection
New Haven artist Thomas Prichard Rossiter painted this portrait of
Captain Caleb Brintnall sometime
between 1840 and 1845, over thirty
years after Brintnall's voyage aboard
the sealing ship *Triumph*. The portrait
once hung in the New Haven Colony
Historical Society gallery.

difficult thing–and once upon being battered by the captain, attempted to ride a sea lion but was, as a matter of course, thrown off."

The *Zephyr* was well-armed to fight off the Ladrones, the pirates and thieves of the South China Sea, carrying twelve twelve-pound cannons, two large swivel guns, along with a supply of muskets, pikes, and other hand-to-hand combat weapons.

The crew comprised thirty-seven young Connecticut men, most of whom had sailed aboard American privateers during the War of 1812; in particular the *Sabine*, the crew of which captured one of the most valuable British prize ships taken during the war. As aboard the *Triumph*, the crew all sailed knowing they would be paid no wages. Their pay would be in shares of the sealing voyage profits, a pay-off put in their hands only when the dangerous voyage ended back in the United States.

"Thoroughly equipped and out-fitted, the ship sailed from our port early in the morning of the 25th of October, 1815," New Haven historian Thomas Trowbridge wrote in the 1880s. "A large concourse of citizens had assembled at the pier head to witness her departure."

Brintnall penned a note in his journal upon departure, one that may show he knew his wife was ill: "...(We) left all we hold most dear bound on a long voyage may the Almighty in some way prosper us that we may yet make a short voyage."

The *Zephyr* departed sailing northeast along Long Island Sound to round Montauk Point, then headed south for the Falkland Islands. There the crew prepared for the severe weather expected while doubling Cape Horn. En route in the Atlantic, off the northeast tip of Brazil at Cape St. Roque, the *Zephyr* logged a fast fourteen knots per hour while being chased "by a swift French man-of-war...with wind abeam, and ran the Frenchman out of sight."

CHAPTER THIRTEEN

GATHERING IN LITCHFIELD COUNTY

GEORGE TAMORREE

George Tamorree (George Prince Kaumuali'i) prior to his departure for Hawai'i aboard the brig *Thaddeus* in 1819. Engraving is taken from a portrait painted by Samuel F. B. Morse.

NEWS THAT A ROYAL PRINCE OF KAUA'I resided in the Charlestown Navy Yard in Boston reached Obookiah in 1816. George Prince Tamorree, the son of the ali'i nui Tamorree (Kaumuali'i), the king of Kaua'i and Ni'ihau islands, found himself in Boston, destitute, mustered out of the navy, a wounded combat veteran.

In 1804 Humehume (as George Prince was known in Hawai'i) departed as a young child from his father Kaumuali'i's royal compound at Waimea, Kaua'i. The boy spent two years at sea under the care of Captain James Rowan of the China trade ship *Hazard* out of Providence, Rhode Island. Rowan accepted guardianship of Humehume. Kaumuali'i paid Rowan with a cargo of sandalwood, bundles of the fragrant Kaua'i wood worth about $7,000. This payment would cover Humehume's expenses at sea, and pay for his education in New England schools.

No sure reasons have been found for the decision by Kaumuali'i to send his son so far away at so young an age. Possibly Kaumuali'i sought to preserve the royal Kaua'i bloodline by saving his son from being captured or killed by Kamehameha.

On his voyage Humehume sailed to the Pacific Northwest, south to San Diego, west to China, around the Cape of Good Hope, finally up the Atlantic to Providence.

The funds given to educate the boy ran out after several years. Some of the money may have been stolen or misspent. Humehume was then cast out on his own to wander in New England. Taking on the name George Prince, the youth labored in farm fields and as a carpenter, sometimes supported by friends he met along the way.

George found a way out of his predicament by enlisting in the Marines. He later told of being in sea battles during the War of 1812. He became disabled by being speared by a pike thrust into him by a British sailor during a fierce sea battle against a Royal Navy warship. His life was saved, he said, by a marine who hauled him off the deck of the ship during the pitched boarding fight.

Once Obookiah heard the Prince of Atooi resided in Boston he sought to find him. He wrote to Benjamin Carhooa, a Hawaiian sailor settled in Boston who attended the First African Baptist Church. Carhooa appraised Humehume's situation for Obookiah. The Prince no longer spoke Hawaiian, Carhooa observed, and he worked as a servant for the purser of the Boston Navy Yard in Charlestown.

The Kaua'i prince was then seeking a berth as a civilian aboard the USS *Congress*, a ship the navy was sending on a post-War of 1812 cruise to the Pacific Ocean.

The Rev. Jedidiah Morse of Charlestown located George in straitened circumstances. Morse had led in bringing the naval facility to Boston, and was well known at the yard. The pastor and his wife Elizabeth welcomed George into their home.

Jedidiah offered the youth, then in his late teens, a chance for an education alongside fellow Native Hawaiians. Morse impressed on him that this would raise his status when the young prince to return home to Kaua'i possessing an academy degree.

George put his trust in Morse. He agreed to join Hopoo and Obookiah in Connecticut. In September, 1816 Morse and George Prince rode in the overnight stage to New Haven where the annual Yale College commencement exercises were underway.

Yale President Timothy Dwight greeted them. Jedidiah graduated from Yale, as did his sons, Samuel F. B. Morse, who is credited with inventing the telegraph, and Sidney Morse, publisher and editor of a successful Christian newspaper in New York City. The two brothers attended Yale in 1809 when Edwin Dwight invited Obookiah to study with him in a student room Edwin shared with Sidney.

Morse was on his way to Hartford to attend the annual meeting of the American Board of Commissioners. He sent a note back to his wife in Charlestown:

> George (the Owhyean Prince who came with me) is much noticed here–is put into good clothing & looks like a new man–his countenance is brightened–& his dejection gone. He will go back with me to Hartford where the 4 other Owhyean youths are to meet him, we think it is important to see them all together. Mrs. Dwight has been very kind in clothing him, & giving him his food...

From Hartford, George Prince was to join William Tennooe (Kanui) and John Honooree (Honoli'i) at the home of the Rev. William Vaill, pastor of the North Guilford Congregational Church, a town located east of New Haven. Obookiah and Hopoo then lived in South Canaan with the Rev. Charles Prentice, near the north end of Litchfield County.

Though about sixty miles apart, the Connecticut 'ohana kept in touch. They all found new lives in New England after facing tragedies back in Hawai'i. Obookiah's parents had been murdered; Hopoo survived a close call with infanticide; Kanui's father was slain in a tribal battle, throwing his family into disarray, and more recently his brother had died while they were on the road in New England.

The "welfare of the Owhyhean youths now in this country" was the focus of a meeting called in New Haven by the Foreign Missions Society of Litchfield in June 1816. Attending were Lyman Beecher, Charles Prentice, Joseph Harvey and James Morris. All held personal ties to Obookiah and his countrymen. They formed a "board of trust...to take charge of the youths who are in this country from the Sandwich Isles, pursuing an education; to receive and appropriate any donations made for their benefit...." With their support being raised the Obookiah and his friends focused on learning and growing as Christians.

From *Henry Ward Beecher - A Sketch of His Career*

The home of the Rev. Lyman Beecher and his family during the second decade of the nine-teenth-century. Obookiah, Hopoo, and Kanui enjoyed the hospitality of the Beechers in this home when *Uncle Tom's Cabin* author Harriet Beecher Stowe was a child.

The Rev. Vaill recalled overhearing Hopoo speaking to a Yale student on summer break in North Guilford, "O how much better, go back to college with a new heart. Then you get the best education; the Holy Spirit teach you." "Press Forward" became Hopoo's signature exhortation.

George Prince moved in with the Vaill family. He wrote a letter sent to his father back on Kaua'i. William Heath Davis, captain of the American fur trade ship *Eagle,* carried the letter. George also wrote a letter to Timothy Dwight's wife Elizabeth:

I hope I shall not meet with the hardships that I have been through for a few years past. We thank Providence that I have fallen into the hands of Christians. I hope it will be provided so that I can go back to my country and do good among the people....I have seen Obookiah.—You told me to tell him to write to you and let you know how he proceeds in his learning. I am now learning the Owhyhee language. This friend that lives here with me is a great benefit to me, for he can learn me the Owhyhee language. I can learn him the English language....I think it will be better for me to stay here a few years longer than to return to my native country... I should have been on my passage now if I had not come here...I hope I shall be a benefit to my father if I should ever return. I hope it will be provided so that I may return again, but I must seek after God. He will help me through this world. I hope I may be prepared for another....I hope I shall for time to come endeavor to do something towards God....

Mr. Vaill has put an addition to my name, it is George Prince Kummoore, that is my father's name...Obookiah thought it would be better for me to have the name of my father Kummooree....

CHAPTER FOURTEEN
FOREIGN MISSION SCHOOL

Memoirs of Thomas Patoo

Obookiah and Hopoo studied in the Foreign Mission School building in Cornwall, Connecticut. Note the distinctive weather vane and school bell. Of the school it was said in the nineteenth-century: "The vale of Cornwall became known in almost all the world by this singular, interesting, and highly prosperous seminary."

EDWIN DWIGHT PREPARED Hopoo, George Prince Kaumuali'i, Kanui, and Honoli'i for a move. Over the winter their 'ohana studied basic education courses together at the Morris Academy's "Heathen School" at South Farms in south Litchfield County. Their sojourns with the Prentice and Vaill families prepared them for the academy; their paths back to Hawai'i passed another milestone towards home. The Morris Academy school year began in fall 1816. Classes were tailored for the Hawaiian students and held separately from other Morris Academy students, in the parsonage of the Rev. Pettingill of South Farms.

The makeup and traits of the Brethren, and of Obookiah's New England 'ohana, reflected their respective cultures.

The Brethren were secretive, held intense showdowns where members tore apart each other with critical words, verbal scourgings. The Brethren looked upon overcoming the Yankee trait of self-dependence as a spiritual quest, a necessary step in gaining the mind-set of disinterested benevolence. The Brethren were literate, educated through the written word; proper, keeping to punctual schedules where time rather than empathy determined when meetings and church services should begin and end; they were raised to be reserved, thinking before they spoke.

Obookiah and his close circle of friends transposed the best qualities of their Native Hawaiian lifestyle to Puritan New England. The close-knit 'ohana opened up freely to each other; without hesitation they sought help when needed. Conflicts were resolved amiably, as a group, probably in a form of mediation known as *ho'oponopono*. Though wearing western clothing, dining Yankee style and studying at New England academies, underneath the American trappings they were convivial Hawaiians; they were Polynesians who lived life as a family though unrelated by blood, experiencing come what may as a group, everyone freely and honestly expressing their opinion. They openly shared their thoughts on the joys and trials, the challenges and surprises of their New England pilgrimage. In the Hawaiian manner, the 'ohana were primarily oral learners, though they readily adapted to book learning. Words flowed easily. The natural start and denouement of an event determined its timing for them, not a clock or set schedule. Obookiah served as the elder, their *kahu* (overseer, guardian), a natural leader of his crew; he led them also as their spiritual leader, their kahuna. George Prince played the *kohole*, the rascal.

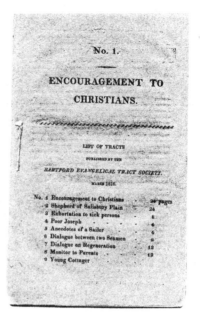

Obookiah handed out tracts following his fund-raising speaking engagements in and around Amherst, Massachusetts. Picutured is the first tract in the series provided to him by the Hartford Tract Society. Note tract #5, *Anecdotes of a Sailor*, a fitting tract for the former *Triumph* sailor.

Departure from the Morris Academy

At the gate of the parsonage in late April 1817 a driver hitched up a team of horses to a carriage. The students began placing in its boot parcels and bags holding the few possessions they owned: donated clothing, Henry's library of books and papers, and his hand-written Hawaiian language and grammar notes.

The warm mid-spring weather was a welcome change from the cold Connecticut winter. Springtime brought much hope to their hearts. They were heading to a new school, a school in many ways created for them to prepare them to return to Hawai'i: the Foreign Mission School in Cornwall, Connecticut.

Weeks earlier, Obookiah had returned to South Farms from an American Board missions fund-raising tour. The tour lasted longer than expected thanks to its success, keeping him away over the winter of 1816-1817. He made appearances at churches in and around Amherst, Massachusetts, under the care of American Board of Commissioners agent the Rev. Nathan Perkins Jr., a minister from Amherst.

Perkins tutored Obookiah during the tour, and shared the pulpit with him in packed churches, the audience drawn by the curiosity of having a Hawaiian evangelist stand in the pulpit. In churches and meeting halls many were amazed to see a student from the faraway Sandwich Islands preach, providing proof in the flesh that the peoples of pagan lands could be as much a Christian as any New Englander.

Perkins began a typical tour service with a sermon on the importance of "spreading the gospel among the Heathen," then espousing "...an affecting view of their deplorable situation...." and concluding with a request for donations, what he called an "appeal to the liberality of his audience."

Then Obookiah, the star attraction, rose to the pulpit. He spoke the concluding prayer in clear English, his pidgin twists of the tongue mostly ironed out. As a finale, he enthralled the audience by reading a selection from his work in translating scriptures from the Hebrew Bible into the Hawaiian language, repeating "a few verses from the 1st Chap. of Genesis, in his native tongue."

After the services Obookiah greeted the churchgoers. He pumped their hands, looked them in the eye, smiled with aloha. As a remembrance of meeting him, Henry handed out pamphlet-size tracts, ones with teal-blue, rag-paper covers like "Anecdotes of A Sailor," supplied to him by the Hartford Evangelical Tract Society.

Edwin Dwight noted Obookiah's fervent, heartfelt prayers made on these tours, both in public and behind closed doors:

> Rev. Mr. Perkins, who often witnessed his performance of his duty in public assemblies, and had also a favourable opportunity of becoming acquainted with his secret devotions, it is observed, "Prayer seemed to be his daily and nightly business: in this duty he not only appeared to take great delight, but he was pertinent, copious, and fervent. It was almost impossible to hear him pray and not be drawn into a devotional frame. I have repeatedly witnessed great numbers in a meeting melted into weeping, and in one instance the greater part of the assembly, and several sobbing, while he stood before the throne of God, filling his mouth with arguments and pleading for Christian and Heathen nations."

Perkins wrote of Obookiah's studious personality, and of a pocket-size New Testament the student carried with him everywhere he went.

> I have rarely, if ever...seen a person who seemed to set so high a value on time as Obookiah. What others would call leisure hours, would be busy hours with him. When alone he was delighted in his literary studies. When in company improvement was his object-and if the conversation was not immediately interesting to him, he would take his Pocket Testament and read, or repair to his study and his books....
>
> ...The Bible was his best and constant companion. He always carried in his pocket a Testament, which was presented to him by a friend who is now a Missionary to the Heathen. At a certain time he went about ten miles to visit one of his countrymen (to see George Sandwich, a Native Hawaiian then living in Enfield, Connecticut). In changing his clothes, he left his Pocket Testament, On his return, he pleasantly said to me, "Blind man don't walk very safely without his staff."

Henry also avidly reached out to people he sensed needed help.

> ...his habitual practice, to converse, as he had opportunity, with persons whom he

supposed to be destitute of grace, and urge upon them the necessity of immediate repentance. In several instances, his conversation has made impressions which have terminated in an apparent conversion of the soul to God.

In Perkins' tour report sent to the American Board headquarters in Boston, their Amherst agent noted a loosening of Yankee pocketbooks when Obookiah spoke:

...and an awakening in the Christian public, a Foreign Missionary spirit....It is truly astonishing to see what effects are produced on the feelings of people by seeing Henry, and hearing him converse. It opens the hearts and hands even of enemies. Many have contributed generously who never contributed before.

Foreign Mission School Beginnings
The Heathen School at Morris Academy served as the start-up for an ingenious new type of school: an academy blended with a seminary where foreign students found residing in New England would be educated, trained to return as missionaries to their homelands in the company of American missionaries.

Back in Andover this missions-focused educational program was developed and given a simple, yet memorable name: the Foreign Mission School.

Obookiah's close friend and benefactor Samuel Mills championed opening the mission school along with the Rev. Elias Cornelius of Somers in Westchester County, New York. Cornelius, a graduate of Yale, was a candidate for the ministry. He studied one-on-one with Lyman Beecher while living at the parsonage in Litchfield town. This ministerial training was widely known as a School of the Prophets. Obookiah, Hopoo and Kanui often came by for a meal and fellowship with the Beecher family.

Cornelius saw the mission school concept as the solution for training Obookiah and friends to return to Hawai'i on an American Board mission.

Samuel Mills caught Cornelius' vision. He suggested opening a seminary based on the Theological Seminary at Andover, but geared in curriculum for foreign students, especially for Obookiah and his Hawaiian 'ohana. Vocational training would be added to biblical studies. American men set apart to go out on foreign missions would join the foreign students as an in-between step in acculturating them to living and ministering in foreign mission fields.

In December, 1815 Cornelius wrote to Joseph Harvey in Goshen, "I congratulate you on the animating prospects which God is giving us relative to our dear Hawaiians....I wish you would come and pay us a visit...."

In January 1816, Cornelius learned at a gathering of ministers that the plan for the Foreign Mission School was moving forward.

The American Board of Commissioners chartered through the Connecticut Legislature a "Foreign Mission School," and named agents tasked with developing the school and raising support for its building and operation. The list included Samuel Mills.

The Constitution of the school read:

...the education of heathen youth in such a manner, as that with future professional studies, they may be qualified to become Missionaries, schoolmasters, interpreters, physicians or surgeons, among the heathen nations, and to communicate such information in agriculture and the arts, as shall tend to promote Christianity and civilization.

Cornwall Selected

American Board agents selected picturesque rural South Cornwall village as the site for the Foreign Mission School. Cornwall is set in the floor of a valley almost cut off by the mountains circling it. There foreign students would be isolated from the streets of New Haven and Hartford where bad company and the distractions of the city might tempt them.

An unprecedented media campaign rolled out, preceding the opening of the Foreign Mission School. A forty-four page pamphlet sold for twenty-five cents and celebrated the Christian testimony and accomplishments of Henry Obookiah, Thomas Hopoo and their 'ohana. Rag-paper copies of the tract titled *A Narrative of Five Youth from the Sandwich Islands now receiving an Education in This Country* spread their heathen-to-Christian story across New England and beyond.

David W. Forbes, in his *Hawaiian National Bibliography*, notes that the publishing of *Narrative of Five Youths*, "...aroused all New England to the plight of the natives 'suffering in ignorance of Christianity,' was directly responsible for public support of the Foreign Mission School and ultimately the beginning of the movement that sent missionaries to Hawaii in 1819."

The *Narrative* came off the press in October 1816 and was distributed by Samuel Mills as he spoke in churches from New York to Washington.

The goal of the Foreign Mission School, the pamphlet stated, was to educate Obookiah and his 'ohana in preparation for sending them on a mission to Hawai'i:

The arrival in this country of several youth from the Sandwich Islands, and the leadings of Providence respecting them, have been viewed from the first, by those acquainted with the facts, as an indication of some important design, respecting the heathen of those Islands.

In distributing the *Narrative*, Samuel Mills, along with James Morris and Joseph Harvey, advocated for launching a mission to the Sandwich Islands, the common place name of Hawai'i in New England in the early nineteenth-century, one given by Captain Cook.

"May God hasten the time when the Board will see the way to open to establish a mission in the Sandwich Islands," Morris wrote in the *Panoplist*. Pointing to "glorious events" in "Otahiete" where the London Missionary Society was making great strides in Christianizing those islands, "...our hearts burn with desire and expectation of witnessing the same triumphs of the cross at Owhyhee and Woahoo."

Light to Lighten the Gentiles

In Cornwall, the townspeople committed to donating the "Academy," a 20-by-40 foot, two-story building with a first-floor classroom and second-floor boarding rooms. The barn-red academy, topped with a weather vane, was constructed in 1797.

Village farm lands were set aside to provide work to help foreign students pay their way. Acres of forest provided firewood for heating the academy building.

Promises of cash donations came from the Cornwall community, and plans were discussed on how to clothe, feed and provide bedding for the students.

Dozens of missionary societies formed across the United States in part to champion the Foreign Mission School. They gathered in local churches in towns large and small, from Maine to New York to Georgia, providing a steady flow of donations for American Board missionaries, and Foreign Mission School students.

The first foreign missions society of the American Board was chartered in Litchfield County. With the county's ties to its popular resident Native Hawaiians and other "heathen" students, Litchfield out-gave in per-congregation giving all the local missionary support chapters.

Donations from many sources flowed in and "innumerable societies sprang up for its assistance, with names diverse but single in purpose, each one standing for many interested souls...," for example, "...at Saybrook a Female Owyhean Society...."

Cornwall's people gave the use of ten acres of farm land and sent fourteen yoke of oxen to plow it. Rev. Timothy Stone, the pastor of the local Congregational church, asked the divine blessing on the field.

Stone published quarterly lists of donations to the students and school. A blind lady of ninety knit stockings for the pupils; a child sent sixty-four cents, a premium received in school; a plow came from Torrington; twenty-seven pairs of new pants; a load of hay and a gold ring from Cornwall; a prize ticket and a bill on a broken bank; thirty-four volumes of poems; a sword and gold epaulets; a peck of turnips.

The American Board named Edwin Dwight as the founding principal after candidates found more worthy were unable to take up the post. Dwight wrote to his mother:

> You will be surprised to hear from me at South Farms. I came here at the request of the Agent of the Heathen School to take charge at present of the Owyhee boys. Since I came on it has been ascertained that a Mr. Daggett whom I have been appointed as the permanent Instructor of the School cannot be released from his present engagement until next Spring.... and I am requested to continue at the School through this year...They propose to give me five hundred dollars and my board...about the same with the salary of the permanent instructor...except that he is to have the use of a house....
>
> I don't know how much you have heard concerning this Institution. It is established by the Board of Commissioners for Foreign Missions to be called "the Foreign Mission School."

Dwight described Obookiah in May, 1817, Henry was looked upon by the American Board as the star pupil at the Foreign Mission School:

> As Obookiah, at the time of his entrance into the school at Cornwall, had arrived at an age of considerable maturity, it may be proper that a more particular description should now be given of his person and character.
>
> He was considerably above the ordinary size; but little less than six feet in height, and in his limbs and body proportionally large. His form, which at sixteen was awkward and unshapen, had become erect, graceful, and dignified. His countenance had lost every mark of dullness; and was, in an unusual degree, sprightly and intelligent.

Foreign Mission School roll book with names of Owhyhee students displays the exceptional penmanship of student John Honoliʻi who compiled the names in a neat chart.

His features were strongly marked. They were expressive of a sound and penetrating mind. He had a piercing eye, a prominent Roman nose, and a projecting chin.

His complexion was olive, varied equally from the blackness of the African, and the redness of the Indian. His hair was black, worn short, and dressed after the manner of the Americans.

In his disposition he was amiable and affectionate. His temper was mild. Passion was not easily excited, nor long retained. Revenge, or resentment, it is presumed, was never known to be cherished in his heart.

In his understanding, Obookiah excelled ordinary young men. His mind was not of a common cast. It was such that, with proper culture, it might have become a mind of the first order. Its distinguishing traits were sound common sense, keen discernment, and an inquisitiveness or enterprize (sic) which disposed him to look as far as his mind could reach into every subject that was presented to his attention.

By his good sense he was accustomed to view subjects of every kind in their proper light; to see things as they are. He seldom misconceived or misjudged. By his companions his counsel was sought, and regarded as decisive. He had that clear sense of propriety with regard to his own conduct and the conduct of others, which always commands the respect or excites the fear of those who behold it. Had he been disposed to cultivate a talent for this purpose, he would have become one of the severest of critics upon the manners and conduct of those around him.

Few persons have a deeper insight into the characters of men, or have the power of forming a more just estimate of them, by their words and actions, than he had. Few are more capable of perceiving the exact import of language. or are less liable to be deceived as to its real meaning, by a designed ambiguity of terms....

His inquisitive mind was not satisfied with pursuing the usual round of study, but he was disposed to understand critically every branch of knowledge to which he attended. For this reason, his progress in his studies was not rapid-but as a scholar he was industrious, ingenious and thorough. His mind was also inventive.

In reading, writing, and spelling, he was perhaps as perfect as most young men of our own country, of the same age and with common opportunities. He wrote a legible manly hand, and had acquired the habit of writing with considerable rapidity. He had at this time studied the English Grammar so far as to be able to parse most sentences with readiness. He understood the important rules in common Arithmetic, and had obtained considerable knowledge of Geography. He had studied also one book of Euclid's Elements of Geometry....

The Foreign Mission School Comes to Life
Over the summer of 1817 the bonding of the pupils and teachers at the Foreign Mission School began, with bachelor principal Edwin Dwight boarding with his students. George Prince played the bass viol surprisingly well, his deep notes a graceful summer-evening sound track. Hopoo and Kanui walked Cornwall's country lanes, hoed cornfields and potato patches in the mission school fields, cut firewood for winter. No notice of any friction within the school was published; this may, or may not, have been the reality within school walls.

Students from another unique school paid visits. The girls from Miss Sarah Pierce's Academy in Litchfield attended the only all-female academy in New England. Miss Pierce was noted for providing a quality education for her young women.

Obookiah and Hopoo returned the visits. In a remembrance of studying at Miss Pierce's, published decades later, a now-elderly student thought back to the days when, "...two Hawaiian boys, 'Hoobokiah' and 'Hope' by name who were at the mission school at Cornwall. These youths were occasional visitors and were much petted and noticed."

William Dodge, then thirteen years old, the son of a shopkeeper living near New London, Connecticut, rallied his young friends in helping to support Obookiah. With no money on hand to contribute they planted a "missionary potato-patch" in a swampy field near their home. Dodge's biographer wrote:

> The boys took their spare time to get the soil into good condition, and their small stock of pocket-money to buy potatoes for planting. The season proved unusually dry, and most crops suffered; but their industrious tilling and damp soil produced a large return, and the boys increased their profits by delivering and storing away the potatoes with their own hands. The money they received was invested in sheeting (bedding) and other material, which the girls made up; and William was commissioned to carry the parcel to Cornwall....He was wont to say, "I never in my life felt more proud or happy. From the time of this missionary potato-patch everything I touched seemed to prosper."

The schooling at Cornwall flourished under Edwin Dwight. He applied his education, and his wit, drew upon his years of friendship and familiarity with Obookiah,

Memoirs of Thomas Patoo

Foreign Mission School student Thomas Patoo from Nu'uhiwa-Marquesas Islands prays in the woods in Cornwall, Connecticut. Patoo died in Cornwall, unable to adapt to the cold climate. He is buried near the Obookiah's gravesite in the Cornwall Cemetery.

---

gained insights no one else in New England could. He understood the likes and dislikes, problems and hopes of his Hawaiian students. Dwight patiently instructed them in penmanship, oration, English grammar, arithmetic.

The way Obookiah and his "Owhyee" 'ohana lived in rural Cornwall influenced the culture of the entire school. While practicing what they saw as Christian kapu behavior in abstaining from strong drink, from swearing as did sailors, by attending Sunday services and praying daily, the 'ohana formed a protective circle around themselves. They continued to embrace Hawaiian values while becoming practicing Christians. Henry served as the elder of the 'ohana, as their leader, just as older Hawaiian children looked after younger children back home. He and his friends cultivated the close-knit bonds formed at the Morris Academy, sharing whatever food, clothing, books and other goods came their way. In the farm fields and forests they worked as a team. In their rooms they continued to gab and gossip, met on Saturday nights for Obookiah to advise them and to pray, and comment about the town and their school; the English vocabulary only hinted at expressing what they were feeling and experiencing.

The daily routine of the students merged chores (cutting wood, feeding animals, ringing the school bell) to hours spent at their desks for lectures and assignments in the Academy. The level of academics taught at the Foreign Mission School rivals the curriculum of the best high schools found today. For example, George Prince was especially fond of astronomy, and ciphered complicated predictions of eclipses to occur during 1820 in the sky above his home in Waimea, Kaua'i.

Sunday was set aside for services at the Congregational Church of Cornwall. The congregation expected to be in church from morning into the early evening, and enjoy a meal in between.

Litchfield town, about twelve miles away, became the 'ohana's big city to explore.

Henry Obookiah's florid signature graced a letter to a friend he wrote in New England.

Lyman Beecher invited them to join his family for dinner, and the 'ohana returned to Cornwall with baskets filled with pies baked by the girls at Miss Pierce's Academy.

Captain Brintnall Returns to the Sandwich Islands

The ship *Zephyr* was spotted in sight of Cape Horn on June 11, 1816. Brintnall carefully timed the passage around the Horn to be in mid-summer in the southern hemisphere.

Once in the Pacific Brintnall's fear of finding lean sealing grounds came to pass. Coves and beaches on Más Afuera in the Juan Fernandezes, where once hundreds of thousands of fur seals beached, were now mostly stripped of the seal hunters' prey. He promised the crew they would find an abundant sealing ground, even if it meant sailing to the North Pole. Brintnall and his crew pressed on, searching the Galapagos, the Benitos Islands and Isla Guadalupe, where the *Triumph* crew had clubbed and skinned an abundance of fur seals. Brintnall even sailed the *Triumph* east around the south tip of Baja into the Gulf of California. Still, no seals.

In desperation, the New Haven captain set a course for Nootka Sound far to the north, up the Pacific coast. There New England sea captains, mostly from Boston and Salem, gathered valuable sea otter pelts using native hunters to spear the hard-to-catch mammals. New Haven ships were mostly in the fur seal trade carried on in the islands from Baja south and employed their own crews to hunt fur seals.

In the middle of the summer of 1816, the Year Without A Summer, a fierce storm, probably an early-season Baja hurricane, struck. The storm rolled in as the *Zephyr* was heading north into the waters of Alta California, on August 16, 1816. Unstable weather that season raked the northern hemisphere due to the explosion of the Tambora volcano in the Dutch East Indies. New Haven historian Thomas Trowbridge described the tempest off the California coast:

A few days only had the *Zephyr* been sailing toward the north when she encountered a tempest whose severity exceeded anything ever experienced by those on board. After a vain effort to make headway against the gale, the ship was placed before it; and for nearly twenty-four hours the fury of the storm increased....During the second night the gale continued to increase, and many of the crew gave themselves up for lost. To lighten the ship several of her guns, spars, and casks were thrown overboard. The vessel was under bare poles, and no one could live on deck unless lashed there. In that almost unknown sea, this New Haven ship lay reeling, plunging, and half submerged in the volumes of water that filled the decks....The storm then abated; the sea went down; the sun came forth; the wreck was partially cleared up; the fires in the galleys were relighted; jury masts were rigged; old sails were bent upon them, and in this forlorn, crippled condition (the voyage to the north having been abandoned), the *Zephyr* was headed for the Sandwich Islands.

Brintnall and his men limped along west-by-southwest, making a slow seventy-two day passage, to reach Kealakekua Bay for repairs. The *Zephyr* entered the bay with its sails and rigging in tatters, anchoring near where Captain Brintnall had dined with Obookiah aboard the *Triumph* in 1808. Kamehameha renewed his friendship with Brintnall, coming out in a royal canoe to leisurely dine aboard the *Zephyr*. Such palavers included negotiations between the Yankee sea captain and Kamehameha, now savvy in making profits from harbor fees and ship repairs. His stocks of supplies at Kealakekua included the ropes, yards, masts, and provisions needed to restart the *Zephyr* voyage.

A receipt list provided by Kamehameha for the repairs detailed a cost of over $4,000 in materials and labor, then a small fortune. The tally included pay for a linguist who conversed in Hawaiian and English, plus for harbor fees owed to Kamehameha following the major overhaul. The repairs took weeks to complete. All the while Brintnall pondered how he would fill his spacious cargo hold, which now months into the voyage held very little.

Kamehameha proposed a simple solution to Brintnall, one that would fill the cargo bay with *piculs* of fragrant sandalwood collected through great labor in the mountains of O'ahu. The king proposed placing the armed vessel *Zephyr* on patrol to check the danger of attack against O'ahu and his windward islands by Russians. He was on guard due to the shady dealings of a Russian American Company physician and company officer, a German named Georg Anton Schaffer. Kamehameha had booted Schaffer and his men from Kou at Honolulu Harbor after he discovered the Russians were building a fort in his capital. Now Schaffer was stationed on the leeward side of Kaua'i, at Waimea, aligned with the island's king, Kamumuali'i.

Kaumuali'i built a fort in cooperation with Schaffer on the east side of the river entrance at Waimea. He had already signed a pact drawn up by Schaffer in May 1816, that falsely claimed Kaua'i had been put under the protection of Czar Alexandar of Russia. The leeward island was still under the control of Kaumuali'i, though the king had in 1810 promised to cede the island to Kamehameha. Despite the deal, Kaumuali'i had ordered his own ship built, one capable of carrying warriors to attack O'ahu or other windward islands within Kamehameha's kingdom.

Kamehameha offered the sandalwood to Brintnall if he would employ the *Zephyr* in patrolling Hawaiian waters, across the Kaua'i Channel and elsewhere, to contain any threat to his kingdom from Russians in the Leeward Islands. Brintnall agreed and Kamehameha commissioned him into his navy, bestowing upon the New Haven sea captain and trader the grand rank of "Admiral of the Sandwich Islands."

Brintnall took up the post, hoping he had found a way to reclaim success for the so-far disastrous voyage of the *Zephyr*. Here Brintnall again, as had happened in 1808 with the death of Elihu Mix, set himself up for a loss in the enigmatic world where western traders crossed paths with Kamehameha and his Kingdom.

Acclaim for the School

Edwin hoped for a good performance by his students at their first examination day, set for September, 1817. The American Board's select Foreign Mission School oversight committee sat front and center. The prestigious board was there to gauge the success of their mission's training experiment, and to underscore their support for the school. "An interesting occasion," James Morris commented.

Preceding the examination, Morris reported to the American Board in a brief dated September 2, 1817. "The...school meets with universal approbation; and the conduct of the students has been so regular and respectable as to gain the confidence and affection not only of the people of Cornwall, but of all the surrounding towns. Hitherto the Lord hath helped us...."

The students orated confidently before an audience of interested observers drawn to Cornwall from other Litchfield County towns, and across Connecticut.

Dwight knew it would be a notable day. Obookiah took the lead as the star pupil, his celebrity growing among the New England churches thanks to accounts in the press and his missions fund-raising. Hopoo and Kanui, and Honoliʻi displayed their knowledge of English grammar, arithmetic, and reading. Weeks earlier Hopoo had been accepted as a member of the Cornwall church, and professed being a Christian. Morris noted, "...(Hopoo) has the zeal of an apostle, and ardently longs for the time, when it shall be thought his duty to return to his countrymen with the message of Jesus."

In his history of Cornwall, E. C. Starr wrote of the acclaim the Foreign Mission School drew from throughout the world to rural Cornwall. "It was reckoned with Yale College and the Deaf and Dumb Institution in Hartford as one of the three noteworthy things in (Connecticut) to be visited by intelligent travelers."

Joining the Foreign Mission School to prepare to depart on a mission to the Sandwich Islands were two students raised in Connecticut churches: Samuel Ruggles of Brookfield and James Ely of Lyme. They possessed more faith than finances. Both applied with hopes of being sent to perform "missionary labor among the heathen." Ruggles previously studied at the Morris Academy.

Within a few months, Ruggles and Ely proved their worth. "Having gained the entire confidence of the foreign boys, they keep them from desiring other company, and maintain a kind of influence, which greatly assists the instructor, and promotes the harmony of the school. They are also fast catching the language of the youths... and will soon be able to converse in the language of Owhyee."

Going into the year 1818 the success of the Foreign Mission School was all but assured, according to reports printed in the evangelical publications. These reports spread, reprinted in newspapers in cities and towns across New England. Obookiah continued to prepare his Hawaiian grammar, grew as a Bible scholar and his lead was followed by Foreign Mission School students, both in and out of the classroom.

CHAPTER FIFTEEN
ALLOAH O'E – MY LOVE BE WITH YOU

Memoirs of Thomas Patoo

Thomas Patoo, a Marquesan, wearing cold-weather overcoat and boots is joined by other Foreign Mission School students at the grave of Obookiah in Cornwall Cemetery c. 1820.

A REVIEW OF THE LIFE OF OBOOKIAH published in the *Missionary Herald* described his growth as a Christian coming into the New Year of 1818:

> We deem it highly important that the christian public should be informed what God has done for the soul of a heathen stranger, who sought a refuge in this land from the pagan cruelties of his own. (Obookiah is)...."heavenly-minded,"..."much employed in secret prayer,"..."felt his dependence on God for those supplies of grace which he needed at every successive step of his christian course,"..."delighted in social prayer with his pious friends,"..."experimentally acquainted with the Christian (spiritual) warfare,"..."employed in devout meditations,"..."anxious for the salvation of sinners," "the conversion of sinners afforded him unspeakable joy."

However, overshadowing his Christian growth was an immediate and serious concern. Early in the New Year of 1818 a gloom hung over the Foreign Mission School. Obookiah lay seriously ill, near death, being nursed in an upstairs bedroom in the white clapboard home of pastor Timothy Stone in Cornwall. Just weeks earlier, Obookiah spoke enthusiastically of returning to Hawai'i with Samuel Mills, his adoptive brother. Together they were to lead the mission to the Sandwich Islands. Surely, his illness wasn't in God's plan. Or was it?

Edwin Dwight expressed concern over Henry's illness, and hope for his recovery:

> Obookiah became seriously indisposed, and was obliged wholly to abandon his studies. A physician was called, and speedy attention paid to his complaints. It was

soon found that his disease was the typhus fever; and a thorough course of medicine was commenced, which after one or two weeks appeared to check the progress of the disorder, and confident expectations were entertained of his recovery.

Obookiah desired to bring the Gospel to Hawai'i. He and Samuel would sail together to Hawai'i to colead a mission. Preparations for their departure awaited Mills' return from his first foreign mission, a voyage to West Africa as a representative of the American Colonization Society. The Society formed as a Second Great Awakening attempt at social reform based on an idealized plan to send freed slaves from the United States to settle a colony in Africa. Once settled, the African-American Christians would spread out in glory to evangelize the African continent.

In 1810 New Bedford Quaker Paul Cuffe, a man of Native American and African-American heritage, led and underwrote a voyage to Sierra Leone, the freed-slave British colony. Cuffe and Mills became close friends, drawn together in their efforts to help free slaves.

Mills at age thirty-three sailed from Philadelphia to London in 1817 with Providence College graduate the Rev. Ebenezer Burgess, a man about Samuel's age, to meet with anti-slavery advocate William Wilberforce, and to receive permission from Great Britain to enter Sierra Leone. Mills and Burgess acquired the proper permits and found passage on a British ship sailing to West Africa. Their American Colonization Society mission was to locate and survey lands south of the British colony. They were to seek a homeland for freed American slaves.

Hawai'i was to be Mills' next and final mission. He planned to make his home in the Islands in concert with Obookiah's 'ohana, just as the Mills family and the churches in Litchfield had adopted and supported Obookiah.

But now, those plans were in jeopardy. Mary Stone, the wife of Cornwall pastor Timothy Stone, nursed Obookiah, and physician Dr. John Calhoun cared for him. Calhoun diagnosed his condition as a typhus affliction. Henry's resistance was low to the deadly disease, he became feverish and showed signs he might not recover.

Year Without A Summer

Cases of typhus fever, once an uncommon malady in the United States, spread into an epidemic across the young nation in 1816 and 1817. Field rats invaded homes, barns and out-buildings due to a lack of abundant fodder in farm fields due to crop failures. The typhus-carrying fleas spread from rats to domestic animals to humans. Once infected, the typhus bacteria remains permanently in the human bloodstream.

The cause of the three-year-long typhus outbreak was "The Year Without A Summer" of 1816. That summer bitter freezes and snowfall led to crop failures and alarmed the people of New England. Some worried the summertime frosts and snows were a permanent curse on farmlands, fisheries and Puritan society.

No one in America then knew the source of the remarkably cold summer, for it lay 10,000 miles away, on the island of Sumbawa in the Dutch East Indies. There about three-thousand feet of the summit of Mount Tambora blew sky-high in April, 1815. Tambora is one of the tallest peaks between Asia and New Guinea. From its crater more than fifty cubic kilometers of magma cooled into rocks, dust and ash shot twenty-seven miles into the sky. The Tambora eruption is cited at the most massive volcanic eruption in history. The blast could be heard up to 1,000 miles away, in Sumatra to the west, and to the Portuguese Moluccas (Spice Islands) to the east. The eruption obliterated the ancient Tamboran culture and language.

By the summer of 1816, the Tambora ash collected in the atmosphere, circling the globe. The ash shadowed the atmosphere above New England, acting as a veil between earth and sun, filtering out about one-fifth of the sun's rays, bringing cold weather to usually warm summer months. This brought on the Year Without A Summer in New England and the British Isles, and in Europe. In Europe, a famine resulted, leading to the deaths of hundreds of thousands of Europeans. In New England, crop failures brought hunger and spiked out-migration to the rich soil of the Ohio Valley and points west.

Year Without A Summer-caused outbreaks of typhus were reported in the August 10, 1816 issue of the *Niles' Weekly* national newspaper.

> With regard to the effects upon the human system that have resulted from the changes we have noticed, it is to be observed that the low nervous fever (Typhus miter, or *febris inerritativa*) a disease hardly known in former years, has now become common amongst us; and not only so, but almost every disease is now liable, to assume a typhus cast—a depression of pulse and prostration of power often taking place in cases that had never heretofore been thought liable to such symptoms. We cannot conceive a more complete proof of the change of climate....

Deathwatch

Edwin Dwight stood by Obookiah's bed. He still served as principal of the Foreign Mission School, and fondly remembered his time tutoring Obookiah at Yale in 1809.

> Hope continued to be cherished until it became evident that his strength was wasting, and that his constitution, naturally strong, was giving way to the violence of the disease, which had taken fast hold of him, and had not been essentially removed. Notwithstanding the unremitted care and the skill of his attending physician, and the counsel of others called to consult with him, the kindest and most judicious attentions of the family into which he had fallen, and the universal solicitude of his surrounding friends, he continued to decline....

Hopoo and the Foreign Mission School 'ohana kept watch with the Stones, Edwin and Dr. Calhoun. Another observer, an unnamed young lady visiting Cornwall, joined them and wrote an account of Obookiah's affliction for the *Boston Recorder* newspaper:

> He addressed a great deal of conversation to his Brethren; and took leave of them all with the greatest affection and composure. Thomas was his bosom companion. They expected to go home together. They were continually praying and weeping together, and felt as though they could not be separated. "You will not go with me to Owhyhee now," said Thomas to him, "and I cannot go alone." Henry put his hand before his eyes, and appeared in prayer: he then looked at Thomas, and both burst into tears. When he was dying, the other Youths hung on one another's

necks, overwhelmed with grief; but, at that moment, Thomas was raised above sorrow, and did not shed a tear: he seemed transported with heavenly views.

Edwin noticed a struggle within Obookiah's spirit as Henry lay on his death bed. His longing to go home to Hawai'i conflicted with his faith in the providence of God in the timing of his dying. This struggle of the soul mirrored the Calvinistic tenet of pre-destination of human life, a central truth taught to Obookiah.

He said to one of his countrymen, who had been a faithful nurse to him, "I must eat or I can't live"-and then enquired of him with anxiety, "Have you eat breakfast, W (William Kanui)-? How thankful you ought to be that you have strength, and can eat." Soon he raised his hands and said, "Oh! how I want to see Owhyhee! But I think I never shall-God will do right-he knows what is best"—and burst into a flood of tears.

Obookiah asked his 'ohana to carry a message from him back to his family and friends in Kealakekua: "W-, if you live to go home, remember me to my uncle." Hopoo, Kanui and the others continued their vigil as Obookiah weakened.

He appeared very affectionate to all, especially his countrymen. He insisted on some one of them being with him continually; would call very earnestly for them if they were out of his sight; and would be satisfied only with this, that they were gone to eat or to rest....

Henry wrote out a note on Sunday morning, February 15 and sent it to the Cornwall Congregational Church, seeking prayers that he might live, and be able to return to Hawai'i, "to preach the gospel to his countrymen."
He spoke an affecting message in Hawaiian to his 'ohana, pleading with them to stick to their Christian ways in the alien land in which they found themselves, to trust in Christ, not on him, as their leader.

My dear countrymen, I wish to say something to you all-you have been very kind to me-I feel my obligation to you-I thank you, And now, my dear friends, I must beseech you to remember that you have got to follow me. Above all things, make your peace with God-you must make Christ your friend-you are in a strange land-you have no father-no mother to take care of you when you are sick-but God will be your friend if you put your trust in him-He has raised up friends here, for you and for me-I have strong faith in God-I am willing to die when the voice of my Saviour call me hence-I am willing, if God design to take me. But I cannot leave you without calling upon the mercy of God to sanctify your souls and fit you for Heaven....

The young son of the Rev. Stone, who had been befriended by Henry, came to his death bed. "...after looking at him, was about to withdraw, he said, 'Wait-wait-I wish to speak to you. You have got to be a great boy-you have been to school a great deal. Remember you will be examined at the Day of judgment, for your improvement.' To a friend, he said, 'My faith holds out.' To another, 'How soon shall I be taken away,' It

The Henry Obookiah grave site in the Cornwall Cemetery. Henry's Hawai'i family placed a plaque at the foot of the grave to commemorate the return of his remains to Hawai'i Island in July, 1993, inscribed with Henry's plea "Oh! How I long to see Hawai'i." The people of Cornwall in 1818 subscribed $28 to pay for Henry's tomb, field stones supporting a granite slab with an inscription. Some residents argued that the funds should have gone to supporting missionaries. For almost 200 years Henry's gravesite and the story of his life have inspired the people of Hawai'i and Cornwall, and influenced Christians to depart on foreign missions.

was answered, 'Pretty soon.'"

Father Mills traveled from Torringford to comfort Obookiah the evening before his death.

> ...Father Mills, whom he always called Father, came in to see him. He looked at him very wishfully, and said, "Will you pray, Sir, before we part?" He listened to the prayer with fixed attention, and when it was closed, said, as he had done in every instance before, "I thank you. Sir-"-and this with a sweetness of voice, and an expression of countenance, which none can conceive but those who witnessed.

On Tuesday, February 17 Obookiah fell gravely ill, displaying typhus symptoms.

> As death seemed to approach, Mrs. S(tone). said to him, "Henry, do you think you are dying?" He answered, "Yes ma'am"-and then said, "Mrs. S. I thank you for your kindness." She said, "I wish we might meet hereafter." He replied, "I hope we shall"-and taking her hand, affectionately bid her farewell. Another friend taking his hand, told him that he "must die soon." He heard it without emotion, and with a heavenly smile bade him his last adieu.
>
> He shook hands with all his companions present, and with perfect composure addressed to them the parting salutation of his native language, "Alloah o'e.'-My

love be with you."

...But a few minutes before he breathed his last, his physician said to him, "How do you feel now Henry?" He answered, "Very well-I am not sick-I have no pain-I feel well." The expression of his countenance was that of perfect peace. He now seemed a little revived, and lay in a composed and quiet state for several minutes. Most of those who were present, not apprehending an immediate change, had seated themselves by the fire. No alarm was given, until one of his countrymen who was standing by his bed-side, exclaimed, "Obookiah's gone." All sprang to the bed. The spirit had departed-but a smile, such as none present had ever beheld-an expression of the final triumph of his soul, remained upon his countenance.

The young lady, writing for the *Boston Recorder,* spoke with Hopoo. "I told Thomas he must not be discouraged, for perhaps God meant to do all that by him which we expected of Henry. 'Yes, (said he,) I wish to stay and do God's work; but I shall not see Henry in these streets again; there he walks in the streets of the New Jerusalem!'" Hopoo told her that God was with him and that he would return to Hawai'i to do both his work and Henry's.

His Death Will Give Notoriety to This Institution

Obookiah's coffin lay in state at the Cornwall meeting house. Word of his passing spread quickly to towns nearby in Litchfield County. The Rev. Lyman Beecher traveled up from Litchfield the next day to preach the funeral sermon alongside Obookiah's coffin. Beecher described Obookiah's noble death to an overflowing crowd that filled the chilly, winter-season, flowerless church. At the head pews in the sanctuary sat Hopoo and the students of the Foreign Mission School. A crowd from the Cornwall church, and from out of town, joined the students, the mourners bundled up in the unheated church.

In his sermon, Beecher spoke about the meaning of the life of Obookiah to the people of Hawai'i.

> By means of his conversion, numbers of his brethren, wandering like lost sheep in our land, have been brought also to the knowledge of his truth, and by the remote instrumentality of the same event, this Institution, the hope of Owhyhee, and other heathen lands, has been established....His death will give notoriety to this institution–will awaken a tender sympathy for Owhyhee, and give it an interest in the prayers and charities of thousands who otherwise had not heard of this establishment, or been interested in its prosperity.

Beecher concluded, turned to the mournful congregation and walked to the vestry to lead them in a procession to a grave site located in the town cemetery, out on the edge of the village. The mourners shuffled behind the coffin for about a third of a mile to an open grave dug in the hillside Cornwall Cemetery. The Foreign Mission School weather vane could be seen in the distance through the leafless forest between town and graveyard. Dozens of mourners circled the newly-dug grave in the February highland Litchfield freeze. Girls and their instructors from Miss Pierce's Academy stood shoulder-to-shoulder with Henry's 'ohana and other students from the Foreign Mission School. The young lady noted in the *Boston Recorder*:

> On entering the burying-ground, the Anthem (from the Book of Revelation) was sung, "Blessed are the dead which die in the Lord." Mr. Dwight made a short Address at the grave. Mr. Beecher preached on the occasion...Some memoranda of Henry's conversation were read, and the whole scene was one of the most affecting which a people are ever called to witness. Mr. Beecher remarked, that if the Churches of New-England had chartered a ship to go to Owhyhee, and bring Obookiah that he might be converted and die as he has, they would be amply recompensed....

Accompanying Obookiah in his coffin was a head cushion, perhaps crafted by the girls from Miss Pierce's school, decorated with brass carpet tacks spelling out H O 26 (Henry Obookiah, age 26).

Samuel is Dead

In Torringford, on a summer day in 1818, about six months after Obookiah's passing, a messenger on horseback reared up unexpect-

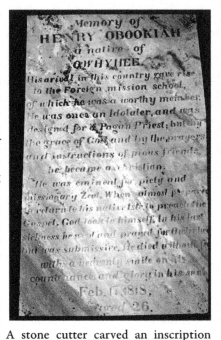

A stone cutter carved an inscription likely composed by Edwin Dwight atop the gravesite of Henry Obookiah in the Cornwall Cemetery. Soon after his death in February, 1818 friends in Cornwall raised the funds for the memorial stone.

edly alongside Father Mills. The rider delivered a shocking message from the American Colonization Society. A fellow minister, who that day happened to be visiting Torringford, wrote of the poignant moment:

> About to leave his neighborhood after a visit in it, I was standing with him, on the broad street; a horseman rode up and handed him a letter. He broke the seal and read a few lines; stopped, and with the letter in one hand, spectacles in the other, his face filled with astonishment and consternation, he said, "Samuel is dead; this beats all; when Obookiah died, I thought that beat everything, but this beats that." At this instant the rider took out a watch, and handed it to him, saying, "This was his watch." The patron of missions gave place to the father. He took the watch, and with streaming tears, and a voice choked with grief, his lament burst forth, "Samuel is dead; I shall never see Samuel again; he is in the bottom of the sea."

Samuel Mills died in May 1818 off the coast of West Africa, about three months after the passing of Obookiah. Contemporary reports list consumption (tuberculosis) as the cause of Samuel's death. Consumption was then plaguing the United States, accounting for one death in seven. Samuel was on a voyage back to England following his scouting tour of lands south of British-run Sierra Leone for the American Colonization Society. The exploratory trip surveyed the lands that would within a few years become the home of freed American slaves, a nation the Society named Liberia.

Ebenezer recalled the hope for Hawai'i held by his close friend and fellow traveler:

> Our progress on the voyage was slow, when six days out, leaning on the taffarel in the evening twilight, and looking towards the Continent behind he said, "I have now transcribed the brief journal of my visit to the coast of Africa, and turned my face towards home. If it please God that I may arrive safely, as I may reasonably hope, I think that I shall take Obookiah and go to the Sandwich Islands and there I shall end my life." Within a week, saying little, taking medicine at his own discretion, sitting at the table and walking on deck to the last day, and with no apparent suffering, he fell asleep with a most benignant smile on his face. I closed his eyes and said, "My Brother." His remains were decently enveloped, and committed to an ocean grave.
>
> On my return to the United States...I found that he (Obookiah) died some months before his patron, which intelligence no angel-bird had borne to the mortal ear. What was his surprise on entering Heaven, to find Obookiah there, ready to congratulate him on his safe arrival.

The Small Book That Launched the Sandwich Islands Mission

Soon after the funeral of Obookiah, an obituary written by Edwin Dwight appeared in newspapers across the United States, likely distributed by the American Board. Edwin added a note, soliciting unpublished letters and anecdotes of Obookiah's life in New England, to be sent to the Foreign Mission School in Cornwall.

Edwin's unique vantage point to Obookiah's odyssey in New England, from his first days to his last, made him the absolute best choice to be the author and editor of the *Memoirs*. Soon Edwin went to work compiling the small, slim memorial volume tentatively titled the *Life of Obookiah*.

Edwin collected Obookiah's papers scattered about in his room at the Foreign Mission School. He filed Henry's letters, notes on Hawaiian grammar and word lists. Critical to the Hawaiian side of the book was the history of his life written by Obookiah in 1815 as suggested by the Rev. Prentice in South Canaan. Obookiah also kept a journal he began writing in March, 1816. A request for copies of letters from the extensive correspondence sent out by Obookiah drew reminiscences of ministers and friends from churches and homes across New England. Today the whereabouts of most of this trove of materials is unknown.

The palm-size book—about three inches wide and five inches high—came off the *Religious Intelligencer* press in New Haven in September, 1818. "Slender and simple as it was this book shaped the future of Hawai'i," wrote author Albertine Loomis in the mid-twentieth-century.

The *Memoirs of Henry Obookiah* spread the story of his pilgrimage to faith across the United States and across the Atlantic to the British Isles. Released simply as a fund-raiser for the Foreign Mission School, the *Memoirs* became a publishing sensation. The biography of an orphan heathen priest from Hawai'i turned evangelical, scholar and preacher in New England became a best-seller. In turn, the *Memoirs*

attracted great interest among the churches and public
in supporting a mission to Hawai'i.

The Foreign Missionary Society in Litchfield sent
Kanui out on a tour of churches to sell copies of the
Memoirs to promote and support the Foreign Mission
School, and to raise interest in the mission to Hawai'i.
Kanui traveled to "many of the principal towns of
Massachusetts and dispose of the books, with the
hope of exciting an interest in the contemplated mis-
sion to the Sandwich Islands." The Foreign Mission
School student made appearances in Springfield,
Northampton, Amherst, and many other places.

Beyond all expectations, booksellers from Boston
to Savannah found the little book outsold even the al-
manacs purchased each year by most households.

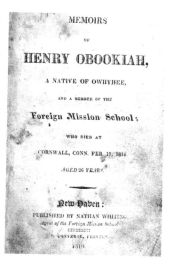

MEMOIRS
OF
HENRY OBOOKIAH,
A NATIVE OF OWHYHEE,
AND A MEMBER OF THE
Foreign Mission School;
WHO DIED AT
CORNWALL, CONN. FEB. 17, 1818
AGED 26 YEARS.

New-Haven:
PUBLISHED BY NATHAN WHITING,
Agent of the Foreign Mission School.
CONVERSE, PRINTER.
1819.

The Memoirs *and the Sandwich Islands Mission*

A new printing of the *Religious Intelligencer* first edition was advertised in November, 1819, released to tie-in with the departure from Boston of the Sandwich
Islands Mission aboard the brig *Thaddeus*.

In the early editions, there is no mention in the credits of the name Edwin Welles
Dwight. Edwin did provide a credited introduction to the *Memoirs*, in the American
Tract Society edition published in 1832. He recalled, "At this distance of time, we
have opportunity to see to great advantage the design of God in calling Obookiah,
like Abraham, from his own country, as well as in taking him away so early in life; and
we cannot but be led to consider how surely and rapidly the benevolent purposes of
God go on to their accomplishment, though to us there may seem to be occasional
and affective interruptions."

Mark Twain *and Obookiah*

Beginning in the 1830s, Obookiah became an evangelical heathen-turned-saint
to young readers through the American Tract Society's Sunday school edition. His inspirational life story had a far-reaching influence. Henry's life inspired Narcissa Whitman, wife of American Board missionary Marcus Whitman, to leave a comfortable
life in rural Prattsburg, New York, for a mission to Indian tribes in the wilds of the
Oregon Country. In the end, this resulted in the couple's martyrdom, and the opening
up of the Pacific Northwest to pioneers traveling across the Oregon Trail.

The Sunday school version found its way into churches across the lands west of
the Alleghenies surveyed by Samuel Mills, even to the Mississippi River steamboat-
stop town of Hannibal, Missouri.

Curious Hannibal boy Samuel Clemens discovered the life of Henry Obookiah
when borrowing American Sunday School Union books he picked out in the library
of the Old Ship of Zion Methodist Church in Hannibal, in the mid-1840s.

Leaving behind his steamboat piloting days on the Mississippi in the 1860s, Clemens turned to journalism. In 1866 he found himself on the cusp of fame in Hawai'i,
a roving reporter for the *Sacramento Union* newspaper. Traveling by sea and horse

around Hawai'i Island, Clemens made a point of touring the Hikiau Heiau at Napo'opo'o to see the home site of his Sunday school hero, Obookiah.

In writing his travelogue book *Roughing It*, Twain described his adventures on Hawai'i Island seeking the temple of his childhood hero:

> Obookia was a young native of fine mind...taken to New England...during the reign of Kamehameha I...attracting the attention of the religious world.... This resulted in the sending of missionaries there. And this Obookia was the very same sensitive savage who sat down on the church steps and wept because his people did not have the Bible. That incident has been very elaborately painted in many a charming Sunday School book—aye, and told so plaintively and so tenderly that I have cried over it in Sunday School myself, on general principle, although at a time when I did not know much and could not understand why the people of the Sandwich Islands needed to worry so much about it as long as they did not know there was a Bible at all.

Courtesy Norman Rockwell Museum Archives, Dwight Collection
Edward Welles Dwight portrait painted by J.P. Rosseter in 1809, water color on paper.

With a boost from the popularity of the *Memoirs of Henry Obookiah* driving public opinion, in mid-1819 the Prudential Committee of the American Board voted to support the organization and to sending out the Sandwich Islands Mission. With Henry and Samuel Mills deceased, two new leaders needed to be recruited to lead the party aboard a fur trade ship bound for Hawai'i.

In his funeral sermon, Lyman Beecher pictured the influence of the Foreign Mission School on the future of Hawai'i as an extension of the providence of Obookiah and his 'ohana landing in New England:

> By means of his conversion, numbers of his brethren, wandering like lost sheep in our land, have been brought also to the knowledge of his truth, and by the remote instrumentality of the same event, this Institution, the hope of Owhyhee and other heathen lands, has been established. Nor are we compelled to believe, that his usefulness will terminate with his life, or that the immediate consequences of his death, will be calamitous. His death will give notoriety to this institution—will awaken a tender sympathy for Owhyhee, and give it an interest in the prayers and charities of thousands who otherwise had not heard of this establishment, or been interested in its prosperity.

Obookiah's obituary appeared in publications throughout the United States and Great Britain. As his celebrity grew, and the wide-spread view of him as a saintly man from a pagan nation spread, so did pious accounts of his close companion Thomas Hopoo.

CHAPTER SIXTEEN
HOPOO AND THE FOREIGN MISSION SCHOOL

ACCOUNTS OF AMERICAN AND BRITISH TRAVELERS touring New England in the late 1810s list as must-sees the Foreign Mission School in Cornwall, and Thomas Gallaudet's Asylum for the Instruction of the Deaf and Dumb in Hartford.

At Cornwall young foreign students from around the globe attended a Christian mission academy; at the Asylum in Hartford for the first time in America deaf students were offered a proper education and hope for a meaningful future. The schools shared a common bond: both were inspired by the mission spirit of the Brethren.

While a graduate seminary student at Andover (following graduation from Yale College in 1808) Professor Gallaudet desired to go out on a foreign mission. But the tall, lean, young Huguenot descendant from Hartford knew he was too frail. He knew he wouldn't survive the hardships of serving at a foreign mission station.

Soon after he graduated in September, 1814 Gallaudet sought ordination as a minister, and to find his most suitable field of ministry. He found his calling through a chance meeting with Alice Cogswell, the deaf daughter of a neighbor of his parents in Hartford, whom he later married.

Thomas Hopkins Gallaudet

Alice's family asked Gallaudet to travel to England, Scotland, and Paris for training at pioneering schools for educating the deaf. Their goal was to have him return and open a similar school in Hartford.

Gallaudet opened his Asylum in West Hartford in 1817, concurrent with the opening of the Foreign Mission School. Gallaudet saw his work with the deaf as evangelical, as a Christian mission to save his students' souls as well as help them succeed in the hearing world. The Hartford Asylum was the first school in the United States devoted to educating deaf children. Congress granted 23,000 acres of undeveloped land to be sold to raise funds for the Asylum.

A Conversation Merely By Signs and Gestures

At a springtime Foreign Mission School examination, held at the Cornwall church, Gallaudet sought to learn the Hawaiian sign language from Hopoo. Gallaudet was familiar with his 'ohana at Cornwall. At Andover he met Obookiah, asking Henry how he imagined the world was created. Gallaudet probed the minds of foreign students regarding their concept of God for clues on how to reach into the minds of his deaf students; he observed the deaf youth perceived God in a manner different than those able to hear, in a sense he saw they lived in a different world. Obookiah's providing a Native Hawaiian perspective on creation and God would aid him in communicating abstract biblical concepts to the students.

Gallaudet wrote in 1826: "I recollect once asking Obookiah what he thought, when a youth in his native country, of the sun, moon, and stars, and in what manner they were formed. His reply was; 'always so.'"

John Warner Barber *Connecticut Historical Collections*
Thomas Gallaudet's Hartford Asylum located on a hillside overlooking Hartford c. 1830.

At Gallaudet's invitation, Thomas rode about forty miles in a coach, from Cornwall to Hartford, Connecticut's capital located along the west bank of the Connecticut River. The Asylum stood on a hilltop to the west, overlooking downtown Hartford.

Gallaudet theorized that deaf people throughout the world used the same basic hand signs to communicate. The professor had worked up a standardized signing system known as "natural signs." Codified, his system became the core of the American Sign Language.

Gallaudet became encouraged in the summer of 1818 by a report of a young non-English-speaking Chinese man being found passing through Hartford. Signing with Gallaudet's system, an Asylum aide communicated back and forth with the Chinese visitor, quickly learning about twenty Chinese words. This novel discovery led Gallaudet to visit the Foreign Mission School for an applied test of his sign language with the foreign students.

Hopoo (along with other Hawaiian students and a Tahitian student) told Gallaudet that a number of the signs he "employed in the instruction of the deaf and dumb, are precisely the same" to signs used in their own Polynesian sign languages. Gallaudet wrote:

> Thomas Hooper (Hopu), a native of Owhyhee, was asked if his parents were living; how many brothers and sisters he had; when he left his native shores; whether his countrymen worshipped idols and sacrificed human victims; how the women were treated by the men; what was the climate of his country; what its production; with many inquiries of a similar nature, all of which he comprehended, and to many of which he replied with signs.

At Hartford, Gallaudet requested Hopoo to communicate with his deaf students using just his Hawaiian signs.

...he attempted by natural language of signs, such as his own feelings and conceptions of the time dictate, to give a circle of pupils around him a sketch of his history. In doing this, he occupied a half an hour or more, and secured the fixed attention and interest of the pupils. It was surprising to see the ingenuity and readiness with which he employed this language of signs and gestures...a very considerable part of what he said, certainly more than half of it, was fully understood by those to whom it was addressed.

Hopoo livened up the discussion by describing the rites of the heiau as practiced in Hawai'i.

As a proof that they understood each other perfectly, I was told that Thomas undertook to describe the idolatrous rites & wretched superstitions of his countrymen....(They) looked on with intense interest, and at length a large number burst into tears of compassion for their fellow creatures involved in such deplorable ignorance.

Hopoo Rising

In 1818, a few months after the death of Obookiah, Hopoo rose up to become the star pupil at the Foreign Mission School's public examination. At the school event Edwin Dwight delivered a farewell address, he was leaving, no longer to be the principal at the Foreign Mission School. Edwin would be working on Henry's biography.

The Rev. Chauncey Lee wrote a first-hand account of the public speaking skill Thomas displayed before the examiners:

...A dialogue was then spoken in the Owhyee language, by four of the Owhyhee youths, with animation and propriety. Thomas Hopoo, who had a part in the dialogue, closed the performance with an address to the audience: It was introduced in the most striking manner. After two of his companions had sung one of the rude, barbarous songs of Owhyhee, of which I can give you no adequate description, Hopoo, who is a professor of religion, broke out in the following tender and animated apostrophe to the audience. "Such," (pointing to the two singers), "my dear Christian friends, are the highest amusements of Owhyhee:—these are the sublimest joys my poor ignorant countrymen can boast. They know nothing of that God who made the world, nor of that Saviour who died to redeem it; They worship dumb idols, and chant their stupid hosannas to gods of wood and stone. O pity them—pray for them and send them the gospel. They are daily perishing for the want of those blessings you enjoy. Divine Providence has cast us upon your shores, and upon the arms of charity. The fruits of your benevolence we have richly shared, and we humbly thank you. Our bodily wants have been bountifully supplied by your liberality, and by your kind instruction and prayers, we are made acquainted with the Saviour, and our souls have been fed with the bread of life which came down from heaven. We burn with desire in due time to return and impart it to our poor ignorant countrymen." In this pathetic strain, and tenderly noticing the late lamented death of their beloved and pious Obookiah, he continued his address about 15 minutes. Every heart beat high with sympathetic emotions, and every eye was streaming. The impression was altogether irresistible.—The exercise closed with a liberal contribution for the school.

Attorney's Repentance

Foreign Mission School steward John Northrup (the man who oversaw the buildings, the food supplies and preparation, the farm and timber lands) brought Hopoo with him to New Jersey, perhaps on a fund-raising trip for the school. They boarded in the home of a minister residing near the Delaware River. Northrup soon departed on a side-trip, telling Hopoo he would be staying behind, cared for by the minister.

The Jersey minister coaxed Thomas into going to a party hosted by a powerful attorney at law, a man whom, he was warned, "...imbibed strong prejudices against religion...." At the party fashionable guests joined the lawyer. Thomas, wearing clothes culled from a missionary barrel, felt uncomfortable and "...embarrassed, and sighed in his soul for retirement," having never been in such company. The attorney began to condescend towards Hopoo, mocking him by asking him intricate questions. The minister attempted to divert the attorney's scorn, but to no avail.

Thomas, displaying his stoic Hawaiian spirit, "manifested no impatience under this abuse, but exhibited the meekness and gentleness of the lamb, and continued to reply amidst a jovial company, 'Your question too hard for poor heathen.'"

Finally, Thomas could stand the mocking no more. He spoke up in a firm voice:

You, sir, have asked me a great many questions I cannot answer, for poor heathen are in the dark: but there be some questions I think I can answer. When Lord Jesus comes down to judgment, I suppose he ask great many questions to poor heathen, and to Christian people; and if he say, Thomas Hopoo, do you love Jesus Christ? I think I can say, "Yes, Lord, I love you." And if he say to you, do you love Lord Jesus? What will you say? The shock was instantaneous, deep, and universal in the room, and the soul of the clergyman went up, for God to descend and seal a blessing upon them. Solemnity now took the place of merriment, and the gentleman was heard to answer in his turn, to the question of Thomas so directly put, "I do not know."

Deep conviction of his sin fastened upon the heart and conscience of the host and his guests, and before the party broke up, this gentleman asked Thomas if he would pray with them, and particularly for him? They all fell upon their knees, whilst Thomas poured forth his soul in humble and fervent supplication at the throne of grace for them, and when he came to pray that those men in Christian lands, who knew so much more than the poor heathens, might love and serve Christ, this gentlemen wept and sobbed aloud.

The attorney's repentance sparked a revival. Steward Northrup returned after two weeks to find forty people (including the attorney and fifteen guests) turned to Christ thanks to Hopoo's godly retort to the attorney. A revival followed in the town, and drew one hundred conversions. Seeing the genuineness of Hopoo's conversion, the village raised a sizable donation of money and clothing and sent it to the Foreign Mission School.

Northrup's daughter Sarah in 1824 married Foreign Mission School student John Ridge, a student from the Cherokee nation. The marriage of a Native American student and a white woman from the Cornwall village angered some in the community. Ridge returned with his wife to the Cherokee nation in Georgia, where John became a leader of his people.

Farewell Address

In May, 1819, with great anticipation over being chosen to depart from Boston in the fall on a mission to Hawai'i, Hopoo and George Prince Tamorree presented superlative orations at another springtime Foreign Mission School examination. Brethren member and Andover theological student Hiram Bingham attended the event. Bingham was being considered for ordination as a missionary to the Sandwich Islands. An American Board report read:

> The piece spoken by Hopoo was composed by himself, as a farewell address to the scholars, in contemplation of the separation, which would take place, should he first visit the land of his fathers, to bear the message of salvation....Towards the close he alluded to the death of Obookiah, and of his friend and benefactor, Mr. Mills, in the tenderest manner.
>
> Hopoo went through a course of theological questions, and the readiness with which they gave satisfactory answers to all the questions, and recapitulated the arguments and proofs in support of the answers, and especially their readiness in repeating and applying passages of scripture, were truly astonishing to every one present....Hopoo pronounced a part of the first chapter of Genesis in Hebrew. There were now six Hawaiian students and two from Tahiti, and fifteen Indians.

Several months later excitement among the Foreign Mission School 'ohana grew as the ordination neared of Hiram Bingham and Asa Thurston as coleaders of the Sandwich Islands Mission. The students were invited to attend the day-long service in the nearby village of Goshen. A new chapter in their lives lay ahead. Four of the six Hawaiian students studying at Cornwall had been chosen to sail back home to Hawai'i with Bingham and Thurston.

CHAPTER SEVENTEEN
MANTLE OF OBOOKIAH AND SAMUEL

Barber's Views of Connecticut
The Sandwich Islands Mission ordination took place in the Congregational Church of Goshen, pictured right center. The church stands at a crossroads in the rural Litchfield town.

THE SANDWICH ISLANDS MISSION came to life in the summer and fall of 1819 in the rural Litchfield towns of Goshen and Cornwall.

The roots of the mission went back ten years, to the chance encounter of Samuel Mills and Henry Obookiah in the Yale room of Edwin Welles Dwight. In his December 1809 letter Mills wrote to fellow Brethren member Gordon Hall:

> What does this mean! Brother Hall, do you understand it? Shall he be sent back unsupported, to attempt to reclaim his countrymen? Shall we not rather consider these southern islands a proper place for the establishment of a Mission?...I trust we shall be able to establish more than one Mission in a short time, at least in a few years; and that God will enable us to extend our views and labors further than we have before contemplated.

The Sandwich Islands was first proposed as a foreign mission field in 1798, by the London Missionary Society. That year the Society sent out the ship *Duff*, carrying a missionary party of seventeen to the Society Islands, then known to western sea captains as Otahiete. A mission to the fur trading region of the Pacific Northwest was also proposed by the Society. Interest waned in sending missions to Hawai'i and the Northwest, perhaps due to the high cost of posting missionaries to Tahiti and the near failure of the mission in its early days. The onslaught of the Napoleonic Wars in those years taxed the finances of Great Britain.

During Obookiah's two years at Andover and Bradford, he drew interest in a mission to Hawai'i by mingling with Brethren students at the Seminary.

By 1815, Obookiah had moved along on his path back home, maturing as a Christian, joining the Torringford Church and being baptized by Father Mills. The Rev. Joseph Harvey of Goshen sent a request to the American Board of Commissioners for Foreign Missions, seeking consideration for sending a mission to Hawai'i. Harvey's associate pastor was Amos Bingham from Bennington, Vermont, the brother of Middlebury College student Hiram Bingham. Amos held out an invitation in early 1816 for Hiram to seek a post in a Sandwich Islands mission.

Hiram vacillated over whether to stay in New England to become a pastor of a Congregational church, or whether to commit his life to a foreign mission. After graduation from Middlebury, Hiram chose to study at Andover. There he joined the Brethren.

Inspired by the enthusiasm of the Brethren, at the end of his first semester at Andover Hiram revisited his brother at Goshen. Amos urged Hiram, then in his late twenties, to join the Foreign Mission School to acculturate himself with the Hawaiian culture through studying with Obookiah and Hopoo.

Hiram recalled, "(This)...drew my attention to the work of training these youths for missionary service and conducting them to the Hawaiian field. But not having finished my collegiate course of study, and wishing to prosecute uninterruptedly, a three years' theological course, I declined the service which they commended to me."

At the annual American Board of Commissioners meeting, held at Yale in September, 1818, it was proposed that the American Board send an agent to the Sandwich Islands in advance of sending a missionary party. The proposal was rejected.

By the end of 1818, the deaths of Henry Obookiah and Samuel Mills left the nascent Sandwich Islands Mission without leaders. This left the position open for Bingham. He applied in the summer of 1819, soon after graduating from the Theological Seminary, and was accepted.

In May 1819 Hiram walked thirteen miles from Litchfield through Goshen to Cornwall. Bingham later recalled:

> Visiting the Foreign Mission school, during a vacation of the Theological Seminary, at Andover, and feeling a new impulse to become a pioneer in the enterprise of spreading the Gospel in that dark portion of the Pacific Isles, I freely offered myself to the American Board for that purpose, and was accepted by their Prudential Committee, in the summer of 1819; and soon after, Mr. (Asa) Thurston, my classmate, offered himself for the same work, and was likewise readily accepted. We completed our course of Theological studies...in September, 1819. On the 29th of the same month, we were, at the request of the Prudential Committee, solemnly set apart, at Goshen, Connecticut, for the work of this ministry.

Ordination at Goshen

Bingham and Thurston traveled to Goshen in late September for their ordination as missionaries. They were to be the leaders of the mission as ordained ministers trained at Andover; the other men departing with them would be given the title of missionary assistant. In gauging the revival spirit of the Second Great Awakening of the rural Litchfield County town, Goshen was selected as the site for the ordination. At Goshen Obookiah had lived in the home of pastor Joseph Harvey; here Harvey and James Morris and the executive committee of the Foreign Mission Society of Litchfield first formally proposed the mission to the Sandwich Islands.

After years of waiting, once the plan was put into action, the chain of events leading to the departure of the Sandwich Islands Mission played out quickly. A tentative sailing date was scheduled for mid-October, 1819, set for just two weeks after the ordination of bachelors Bingham and Thurston. The week prior to sailing the mission party was to gather at the Park Street Church in Boston to prepare for a long weekend of departure services. Awaiting the missionaries at the Long Wharf in Boston was the Northwest fur trade brig *Thaddeus*, a vessel just eighty-five feet in length. The missionary party faced being at sea for about six months, to set off on a sail of some 18,000 miles 'round the Horn to Hawai'i.

Missionary Ordination

The ordination of Hiram Bingham and Asa Thurston as missionaries to the Sandwich Islands was celebrated at the steepled, white clapboard Congregational church set at a crossroads in Goshen on Wednesday, September 29. The unique service drew American Board dignitaries along with the people of Goshen and nearby communities, and the students of the Foreign Mission School.

> Providence smiled noticeably in all circumstances of the ordination. The day was singularly clear, and the air unusually exhilarating, never did the sun look down more brilliantly on our ample woodlands and our little lakes. The very brooks seemed to leap and foam in special excitement. Mohawk and Ivy Mountains, retouched with autumnal splendors, rose more majestic than ever. The hills clapped their hands. A larger assembly than had ever congregated here thronged the old meeting-house.

> Many ordination guests boarded with families living in Goshen village, and in outlying farmhouses.

Nearly all the Foreign Mission School students traveled over from Cornwall. Several Brethren students from the Andover seminary traveled far to join them, hoping their own ordinations and send-offs to foreign lands would be as memorable.

Father Mills, over from Torringford, opened the service in prayer. The Rev. Heman Humphrey, pastor of the Congregational church in Pittsfield, Massachusetts, delivered the sermon "The Promised Land." Humphrey, a Yale graduate and theology student of Timothy Dwight, studied to become a minister under the Rev. Asahel Hooker in Goshen in 1806. He was licensed to preach by the Litchfield North Association, and preached his first sermon in the pulpit of Rev. Stone at Cornwall. In his sermon, Humphrey called the *Memoirs of Obookiah*, "...that little volume, which has given birth to so many prayers, and brought in such large contributions to the missionary fund." Focusing on Obookiah being the seed of the mission, he added:

> Who could have anticipated, that an important Christian mission would ever spring from a savage massacre in a far distant isle? Yet, but for that heart-rending tragedy, Obookiah might never been heard of by the American Church; might now have been a pagan priest, bowing before an idol, instead of a 'king and a priest unto God,' in his heavenly temple... He however speaks from the grave to the American church in just such a voice as was need to rouse her energies....

"...And there remaineth yet very much land to be possessed," Humphrey preached from Joshua 8:1, and told of spreading the blessings of Christian society in New England to Hawai'i, to make the people of the Islands "...acquainted with the arts and improvements of civilized nations, to pour upon their benighted minds the light of science and literature, to multiply among them the sources of enjoyment in this life, and above all, to prepare them for endless happiness in the world to come."

Speaking directly to Bingham and Thurston, Humphrey recalled the ties between Obookiah and Samuel Mills: "Our hearts, and desire and prayer to God for you, dear Brethren, is, that the mantle of our ascended Samuel (the late lamented Rev. S. J. Mills) may fall upon you."

For effect, a large Bible sitting on the Goshen pulpit was held out to Bingham and Thurston to lay their hands on. The men in turn committed to a long list of duties detailed in the charge delivered at the service: to lead and serve, to plant a church, to bring Christ and civilization to Hawai'i.

Speakers weaved references to Hawai'i into the ordination service. Listening intently were Thomas Hopoo and his 'ohana from the Foreign Mission School. Seated in pews near the front of the sanctuary, they perused Bingham and Thurston and wondered what the future held for them after long years away from home.

In a novel move, Bingham and Thurston, men of medium height and athletic builds, dressed in waistcoats, "without previous intimation" stopped the solemn service in its tracks by stepping into the broad aisle of the Goshen sanctuary. In clear, strong, ringing voices (Thurston, tenor, Bingham, bass) the duo sang out the hymn "Head of the Church Triumphant" to the tune "Melton Mowbray."

> The effect was electrical. Those young missionaries were looked upon as martyrs. Some pictured them as finding their graves in the bottom of the ocean; some as meeting with death at the hands of savages; some as the welcomed heralds of glad tidings to isles waiting for God's law, and for the gospel of our Lord Jesus Christ.... The whole occasion is spoken of, by those now living who were present, as one of thrilling interest.

Shadow of Captain Brintnall

The shadow of Captain Caleb Brintnall cast itself across the ordination, at least over the pew where the American Board commissioners sat. Brintnall referred young foreign sailors arriving in Providence, Rhode Island to the Foreign Mission School. At the time of the ordination, he was at sea on an outward bound voyage, possibly heading to Hawai'i to avenge a grievous financial loss.

Back in 1816, Kamehameha had offered to fill the hull of the *Zephyr* with sandalwood if Brintnall put the ship in the service of the Kingdom of Hawai'i. Kamehameha feared an attack by Russian ships sent by the Czar in collusion with the Russian American Company outpost at Waimea, Kaua'i and Kaua'i's ruler Kaumuali'i. Brintnall agreed. Kamehameha commissioned him as an "Admiral of the Sandwich Islands."

Brintnall took up the post, hoping he had found a way to reclaim success for the so-far disastrous voyage of the *Zephyr*. Here Brintnall again (as had happened in 1808 leading to the death of Elihu Mix) set himself up for a loss in Hawai'i where the West crossed paths with Kamehameha and his Kingdom.

In Honolulu Brintnall met James Hunnewell, a ship's officer from Charlestown, Massachusetts. Hunnewell then served as first mate aboard the hermaphrodite-rigged brig *Bordeaux Packet*. Under Captain Andrew Blanchard, Hunnewell had sailed out of Boston Harbor in November 1816. Blanchard planned to trade for sandalwood in the Sandwich Islands and to sell New England wares at Spanish ports on the California coast. On March 30, 1817 the *Zephyr* anchored off of Kailua Bay on the leeward side of Hawai'i Island. Brintnall and Blanchard left

Dodds Family Collection

The speedy *Zephyr* built in 1815 in a Middletown, Connecticut shipyard. A hurricane driven by Year Without A Summer weather almost sank the ship with Captain Caleb Brintnall aboard off the coast of Southern California in 1816.

the bay, sailing together in convoy to Maui, facing a stiff gale in their crossing of the 'Alenuihāhā Channel. In June, 1817 the 12-gun *Zephyr* was in Kaua'i waters, anchored in Hanalei Bay to enforce the removal of Schaffer and his men from Kaua'i immediately and forever. The Russian party sailed to Honolulu Harbor in a leaky ship, gave up their arms, and departed the Islands, ending any threat against Kamehameha.

With the crisis resolved without armed conflict after Brintnall had been on patrol for fourteen months, Kamehameha reneged on the sandalwood payment. Edward Mix, the son of Elihu Mix, who at age thirteen sailed with Brintnall aboard the *Zephyr*, years later recalled that Kamehameha felt justified in shorting Brintnall. The ali'i linked him to a deal gone bad with a hard-bargaining Yankee sea captain. Brintnall received only six and a half tons of sandalwood, enough to fill but a corner of his spacious cargo hold.

A frustrated and angry Brintnall gave up on negotiating with Kamehameha and sailed for Canton, trans-shipping sandalwood for James Hunnewell. Once in Canton, Brintnall traded his short cargo of sandalwood for China goods. Resigned to his misfortune, Brintnall loaded a cargo heading to Europe for a hauling fee, earning a fraction of what a full cargo of tea, silk, and chinaware could bring in New York.

After a sail home of over 170 days from Canton, and over three years at sea, due to the financial failure of the voyage Edward Mix left the ship empty handed. He walked away from the *Zephyr* without paying a $5 debt he owed to the ship's store. Brintnall and his investors lost a small fortune, and the New Haven captain arrived home to a distraught family, his wife Lois having died from her ailment months earlier.

Just prior to the Goshen ordination, a rumor had Brintnall seeking revenge against Kamehameha on a new voyage. The American Board commissioners heard the New Haven captain might stir up a conflict with Kamehameha over his deal gone bad in Honolulu. Brintnall, some feared, might poison the king's relationship with the United States ahead of the arrival of the Sandwich Islands Mission. The Rev. Paul

Couch of Newburyport, Massachusetts wrote:

> I recollect that Dr. Worcester and Mr. Evarts spent a night at my house, after having attended the ordination, at Goshen, of the first missionaries who went out to the Sandwich Islands. A report was abroad that a Captain Brintnall, I think of New Haven, who had received some indignity or injury from the natives not long before, had determined to return to the Islands, and punish the wrong he had suffered. It was apprehended he might arrive there about the time the missionaries would; and if he carried out his threats, disastrous consequences, it was feared, would follow to the mission. I remember well the remark made by Dr. Worcester, in the course of the conversation on the subject. In his own meek and confidential manner, he said: "The Lord will take care of Capt. Brintnall." And so he did; for he either never returned to the Islands, or, if he did, he was not suffered to do any harm.

Seeking Pious Wives

In September, 1819 following their ordination Hiram Bingham and Asa Thurston faced a seemingly impossible task: finding a bride willing to leave home and country likely forever for faraway pagan Hawai'i–and be able to depart within a few weeks. Without a spouse the men were uncertain of securing a berth on the *Thaddeus*. Along with packing clothing, books, tools and all that was needed to launch the mission once in Hawai'i, they needed to immediately find pious wives as commanded by the American Board. The candidate for marriage must be ready to depart on a life-long mission to Polynesian islands located in the Pacific Ocean half a world away from home and family. And wed a man they had just met.

Hiram's first choice to be his bride, the daughter of a minister, spurned his offer after her father refused to let her marry him. Sarah Shepard told him, "Is not this a plain intimation, that providence desires to employ another and not me in the good work in Owhyee?"

Bingham notified Jeremiah Everts of the American Board that he might have to "go it alone." That never happened thanks to a providential meeting at Goshen. Bingham recalled:

> I was quartered at the Rev. Mr. Harvey's. He and others attended, in the evening, a Bible Society meeting; but fatigued with closing all up at Andover, my journey and examination, I chose to stay quietly at the house of Mr. Harvey....Rev. Mr. Brown, called and asked for lodgings for himself and a young lady, whom he had brought with him from the valley of the Connecticut....Mr. Brown went to the public house, and brought out the young lady, introduced her to me, and took us into his vehicle, and, at my direction, drove to Deacon Thompson's. I had taken cold by a night's ride over the mountains, and I wrapped a handkerchief about my neck, chin, and mouth, that cold evening, and this awakened ready sympathy in the sensitive heart of the young lady, who had for years been warmly interested in the missionary cause. Mr. Brown had introduced her as Miss Moseley, the name of a lady teacher at Canandaigua, N. Y., whom Rev. Levi Parsons had mentioned to me as a most amiable, and thoroughly qualified companion for a missionary. During the whole interview, the ride, and the call at your father's, my mind was intently querying whether this

could be the very same....seated by a hospitable fire, we sat and conversed for a few minutes. I measured the lines of her face and the expression of her features with more than an artist's carefulness, and soon took leave of her, and Mr. Brown, and the family, receiving some very generous cautions from her respecting my cold. The next day I learned that she was the young lady of whom Brother Parsons had spoken so highly. I saw her in the course of the next day most intensely interested in the missionary cause....A prayer-meeting was arranged at Mr. Harvey's while I authorized Dr. Worcester to ascertain from her whether a private and special interview with me would be allowed. He saw her while prayers were offered for Divine guidance. He stated my case, held up the great work at the Islands with which her soul was already filled, and left her with the words, "Rebecca said, 'I will go.'"

A portrait of Hiram and Sybil Bingham painted by Samuel F. B. Morse days prior to the couple's departure for Hawai'i in October, 1819.

Sybil Moseley had overnight to weigh Hiram's proposal. She sat by the fire at the home in Goshen, and did "continue all night in prayer." She knew a "yes" would be "severely criticized in many quarters." Levi Parsons had told Hiram that Sybil would be his choice for a wife, if he had been allowed to take one to Palestine. Hiram wrote years later:

Returning to Mr. Harvey's, he told me I could see her. I gave her some account of myself, put into her hands a copy of my statement to the Prudential Committee, in offering myself to the work, asked her to unite with me in it, and left her to consider till the next day whether she could give me encouragement, or not. The next day she said she would go with me to her friends, and, if they did not object, she thought she should not. It was arranged for us to ride in a chaise to Hartford. The result you know.

The Life of Sybil

Hardship marked Sybil Moseley's life. She personified the humble roots of many American Board missionary wives, much more so than the fictional life of missionary wife Jerusha Hale, as presented in James Michener's novel *Hawaii*. Michener pictured the leader of a Sandwich Islands mission as a bumbling, overly-zealous and too-pious missionary he named Abner Hale, Jerusha's second-choice husband. Unlike Jerusha, who lived in a privileged home with wealthy parents, Sybil's mother and father both died before she was twenty. She was the eldest of three sisters. To support her sisters she went to work as a school teacher, and boarded them with relatives.

Sybil joined the Congregational church in Westfield, Massachusetts in 1812. While teaching in Westfield she conceived the idea of becoming a missionary like Ann Hasseltine Judson. Ann departed that year on the first foreign Protestant mission sent out from America with her husband Adoniram, ending up in Burma.

Sybil was teaching in a school in the frontier town of Candadaigua, New York around the time of the Goshen ordination. Sybil's daughter, Lydia Bingham Coan, the wife of Hawai'i missionary Titus Coan, wrote of her mother, "She was a remarkably mild and gentle person in her manners; in fact, her portrait, taken at the time of her marriage, reveals the character of her mind and heart."

Reuben Clapp, Sybil's first love, died in 1815 while studying at Yale. Later she became engaged to Theological Seminary student and Brethren member Levi Parsons. But in 1818 Parsons was chosen to go out to Turkey, Egypt and Palestine on the American Board's Palestine Mission. Parsons broke the engagement. American Board secretaries concluded going out to the Levant, then under the control of the Caliphate in Turkey, posed too much danger for wives to safely accompany missionary husbands. Her setbacks only made Sybil more committed to missions.

A Hasty Wedding

Daughter Lydia wrote of the marriage of her parents: "The announcement of so sudden an arrangement, was, of course, a great matter of surprise to all the people here...The occasion was one of great interest. It was sudden. It was a new thing."

Hiram and Sybil wed at the landmark Brick Church in downtown Hartford on October 11, 1819. A Hartford minister performed the brief ceremony in the middle of a Sunday morning service. Thomas Gallaudet delivered the sermon, one on missions. An account of the wedding printed in the evangelical newspapers read:

> The occasion on which this address was made was one of unusual and even romantic interest...We have on no occasion witnessed in this city so large an audience assembled for Divine Worship. After singing an appropriate Psalm and prayer... (the couple)...presented themselves in the broad aisle and were married by the Rev. Mr. Hawes...We have seldom witnessed more solemn exercises and never a more attentive audience....
>
> ...God in his mysterious providence may appoint you both a watery grave; or one of you, like the afflicted (missionary wife Harriet) Newell, may be left to mourn the departure of the other to a better world and to dress the sods of an early grave in Owhyhee. Be prepared to meet such afflictions, and if called to endure them may your Heavenly Father succour and sustain you. Perhaps, too, like your brethren and sisters at Otahiete, you may have to encounter innumerable trials and difficulties in the prosecution of your work from the perverseness or hatred of the very savages whom you go to enlighten and to save...
>
> ...Next to God rely on the support of your Christian Countrymen.—From thousands of hearts will intercessions for you ascend daily to the throne of grace. Be faithful unto death. And may the mantle of Obookiah descend and rest upon you—FAREWELL!

In Sybil's journal entry for her wedding day in Hartford, she noted, "I pen this date, and pause. Happy day! that joined me to the worthiest of husbands–that opened the way, plain & wide, into missionary work."

CHAPTER EIGHTEEN
MAYFLOWER OF THE PACIFIC

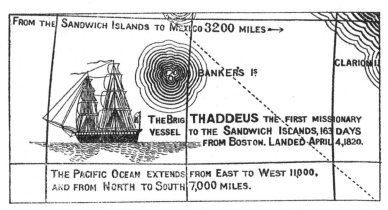

A History of C. Brewer & Company Limited
An illustration of the *Thaddeus* taken from a missionary map found in a New England inn.

THE LIVES OF THE SANDWICH ISLANDS MISSION party were joined together in Boston in October 1819. Their private young lives became complex public ones in the space of a few weeks. They faced the likelihood of never again seeing their loved ones with fulfilling their call from God; the discomforts of sailing to Hawai'i aboard a ship the size of a large home; the dangers of a passage through the huge seas and gales of Cape Horn; of entering what they saw as a pagan kingdom armed only in the spirit.

Half a world away from Hawai'i–from within the safety of the Christian demimonde of New England–they dreamt glorious dreams of launching a mission to the "far distant land of Obookiah." They would be in the vanguard in preparing Hawai'i for the arrival of the New Millennium, the global return of Christ, and the ushering in of a new Kingdom, one to supersede all worldly kingdoms.

Captain Andrew Blanchard, master of the 85-foot-long, two-masted brig *Thaddeus,* knew the dangers that lay ahead at sea outside of calm Boston Harbor. He and his first mate James Hunnewell of Charlestown had arrived home just months earlier from Hawai'i, completing a voyage made aboard the 180-ton brig *Bordeaux Packet.*

Blanchard and Hunnewell prepared the scant space available on the *Thaddeus* for the lands-men missionaries, their wives and children. The ship's manifest called for cramming into the cabins seven couples, plus the five children of the Chamberlain family. The couples were: Hiram and Sybil Moseley Bingham, Asa and Lucy Goodale Thurston, Samuel and Mercy Partridge Whitney, Samuel and Mary Welles Ruggles, Daniel and Jerusha Burnap Chamberlain, Elisha and Maria Sartwell Loomis, Dr. Thomas Holman and Lucia Ruggles Holman. Ship carpenters hammered, nailed and sawed aboard ship, dividing up already small cabins into tiny cubicles.

Blanchard issued the Foreign Mission School 'ohana their own cramped space: Thomas Hopoo, John Honoli'i, William Kanui, and George Prince Kaumuali'i would sleep in two-up bunks in a cabin barely long enough for the men to stretch out in.

The tight spaces reflected the bargain price of passage. The American Board of Commissioners paid $2,500 for the one-way voyage of the mission party and their belongings to the Sandwich Islands, about $100 per person to travel 18,000 miles by sea.

As the *Triumph* was captained by church-going Captain Brintnall, so was the *Thaddeus* guided by a believer, first officer James Hunnewell whose pastor Rev. Jedidiah Morse had lifted George Prince from his destitution at the Charlestown Navy Yard. The *Thaddeus* may have been chartered through the Hunnewell-Morse connection. Blanchard hailed from Medford, a shipbuilding town located along the Mystic River, just a few miles northwest of Charlestown.

On land, in downtown Boston, the American Board's Prudential Committee reassured the pioneer Sandwich Islands Mission party of a long-term supply of financial, material and spiritual support from half a world away. Baskets and boxes of savory foods and other comforts piled up on the deck of the *Thaddeus*, sent by family and friends.

The Park Street Church posted notice of a grand send-off, a long weekend of church services. The landmark church was located along the grassy Boston Commons at Brimstone Corner, the site of a War of 1812 gun powder magazine.

Asa Thurston's young bride Lucy Goodale Thurston felt the presence of Obookiah amidst all the excitement:

Six marriages were solemnized; two missionaries ordained; a band was gathered from four different States, and a dozen different churches, to go forth as messengers of the churches, to the far distant land of Obookiah, having hold of the strong cable, of leaving the church on her knees. Obookiah from on high saw that day. He saw the darkness fleeing away from Hawaii, and that that mission family, so hastily fitted out, was going forth to carry the Bible to a nation without a God.

Your Views Are Not To Be Limited
On Friday, October 15, for the first time, all the disparate personalities of the Sandwich Islands Mission gathered in the vestry of the Park Street Church, to be formed into a missionary church led by Bingham and Thurston. One observer remembered, "...the whole scene, with its many associations, was more interesting than can well be conceived."

The mission party entered into a covenant of support and sacrifice for one another. Their hand-written compact read much like the Pilgrim fathers' Mayflower Compact attested to two hundred years earlier, prior to landing in New England.

That evening (following a sermon by Hiram Bingham) the Secretary of the American Board of Commissioners, the Rev. Samuel Worcester, exhorted the mission party to establish in Hawai'i a Puritan Christian society as a necessary step in ushering in the New Millennium in the Islands:

Your views are not to be limited to a low or narrow scale; but you are to open your hearts wide, and set your mark high. You are to aim at nothing short of covering these islands with fruitful fields and pleasant dwellings, and schools and churches; of raising up the whole people to an elevated state of Christian civilization.

A Saturday morning service followed, drawing an overflowing congregation to the Park Street Church. Asa Thurston delivered the sermon, and Thomas Hopoo a benediction spoken in the Hawaiian language. "It was a most affecting spectacle to see a native of Owhyhee preaching the gospel to the citizens of Boston," the *Boston Recorder* newspaper reported. The *Missionary Herald* published an in-depth report of the service:

> ...at 10 o'clock in the spacious white walled sanctuary of Park Street Church at a crowded service, an address was delivered, in behalf of the mission, by Mr. Thurston in which he bade farewell to the personal friends of himself and his associates, to the friends of missions, and to his native land. Hopoo then ascended the pulpit and made an extempory address to the audience. His manner was grave, dignified, and highly becoming the house of God; his observations indicated good sense and piety; and his delivery was free from any embarrassment, except what arose from his want of readiness in the use of our language....The choir of Park Street Church, at the request of the missionaries, joined them in singing an anthem (the one Thurston and Bingham sang at Goshen), "Head of the Church Triumphant!" and which was performed in a very superior style. The introductory prayer to these services was offered by Hiram Bingham, and the concluding prayer by Brethren member and Palestine Mission missionary Pliny Fisk.

Heading to the Holy Land

Sending a mission to the Sandwich Islands fit into the promotional plans of the American Board of Commissioners, too. In the fall of 1819 the American Board launched not just one, but two missions to distant lands. Together the missions aimed at engaging the Christian church in America in fulfiilling the major New Millenium goals of the Second Great Awakening, both enabled by America's global maritime trade. The young men and women of the missionary parties would bring the Gospel west to the Isles of the Sea, and east, back to the Source, to the biblical cities of Asia Minor, and to Jerusalem, thus playing key roles in bringing about Christ's kingdom on the earth.

The missions would be led by Andover seminary graduates whose names were listed in the same Brethren roll book as Samuel Mills and Adoniram Judson.

Pliny Fisk and Levi Parsons of the Palestine Mission were to board a trans-Atlantic packet, heading out into the stormy North Atlantic, destination the island of Malta. Departure was scheduled for about one week after the *Thaddeus* sailed.

Many formal and personal ties bound together the two missions. Both were idealistic ventures, of high interest to the American public which in 1819 avidly read accounts sent back by youthful American and British foreign missionaries. Foreign missions then was a new, exciting facet of New England life, one the Christian public saw as confirming their belief in the soon return of Christ.

Few in the congregation at the services knew of Sybil's past engagement to Levi Parsons. A belief in a godly providence driving the Sandwich Islands Mission was now all-important to her. She overcame the perplexing vision of seeing Levi, once the love of her life, standing with Hiram, a man she met just a few weeks earlier who was now her husband–and all of them actually departing for faraway foreign shores after years of preparing for this moment.

The American Board's missions strategy recognized that the Holy Land and

Hawai'i were places well known to the public in New England. Palestine for its wondrous ties to the life of Jesus and the Bible; "Owhyee" due to the American fur traders and sea captains and crews who had stopped there for provisioning and rest in their China trade voyages, returning home with tales of a paradise. Earlier missions to India, Burma, Ceylon were sent to ports beyond the trade routes of most American sea captains; nations unconnected to the lives and times of most Americans.

Courtesy American Bible Society, New York

George Prince Tammoree (Humehume) request to the American Bible Society for a Bible for his father Kaumuali'i.

Multitude of Spectators

About 600 people joined the missionary party in taking communion on Sunday afternoon, October 17 at the Park Street Church, "...the multitude of spectators was very great. The occasion was one of the most interesting and solemn, which can ever exist in this world. The impression which it made on many minds will not soon be erased."

Contrary winds held up the mission departure until the next weekend. The mission party gathered at the Long Wharf in Boston on Saturday, October 23, 1819. They knew of Captain Blanchard's course heading south for Cape Horn, then north to the Sandwich Islands. Once the missionaries and their goods were landed, Blanchard would sail the *Thaddeus* to the Northwest Coast for fur trading.

Along with the stony ballast in the hull of the *Thaddeus* lay wooden crates filled with Bibles supplied by the American Bible Society. One of the Bibles–a large, fancy, leather bound copy–bore in gilt gold the name Tamehameha, another Tamorree, sent as gifts to the ali'i nui. Once word reached the Foreign Mission School that Kamehameha would be sent his own Bible, the school contacted the American Bible Society, headquartered in Manhattan. A handwritten request was sent from George Prince for an identical deluxe Bible for his father, Kaumuali'i. The Society, fearing a slight of a Hawaiian king, granted George Prince's request. The Kaua'i king's Bible was added to the *Thaddeus* shipment of hundreds of inexpensive copies of English-language King James Bibles.

Lucy Thurston's cousin William Goodell traveled to Boston see off Lucy and to boost his hopes of being chosen to depart on a foreign mission. The American Board later stationed Goodell in the Turkish Empire. An account of the Sandwich Islands Mission departure appears in Goodell's biography:

> A fervent and affectionate prayer was offered by the Rev. Dr. Worcester; a closing address was made by Hopoo, a young convert from the Sandwich Islands...A fourteen-oared barge, politely offered by the commanding officer of the Independence 74, was in waiting; the members of the mission took leave of their weeping friends, and were speedily conveyed on board the brig "*Thaddeus*." They were accompanied by the committee and

other particular friends. In a short time the vessel weighed anchor, and dropped into the lower harbor, and the next day, the wind and tide favoring, put to sea....

Sunday, October 24 found the Sandwich Islands Mission about ten miles out of Boston Harbor, awaiting favorable winds to power the ship south.

Advancing Ye Kingdom of Christ

In New England the brig *Thaddeus* became known as the Mayflower of the Pacific. The missionary voyage to the Sandwich Islands would sail into Hawaiian waters during the 200th anniversary year of the arrival in America of the ship *Mayflower*, the Pilgrims landing on Cape Cod in 1620.

Pilgrim leader William Bradford, in his book *History of Plymouth Plantation*, the first book written in New England, quoted Pilgrim pastor John Robinson. Bradford, rather than seeing the Pilgrims as fleeing the Old World for religious freedom, portrayed Robinson as sending off the Pilgrims as missionaries. Bradford quoted Robinson:

(They had) a great hope & inward zeal they had of laying some good foundation, or at least to make some way thereunto, for ye propagating & advancing ye gospel of ye kingdom of Christ in these remote parts of ye world; yea, though they should be but as stepping-stones unto others for ye performing of so great a work.

Hawaiian Studies at Sea

Once acclimated to the constant sea swells rolling the *Thaddeus*, the mission party gathered mornings for an exercise in the Hawaiian language. They read a hand-written collection of Hawaiian language materials including Obookiah's grammar notes and word list of the "language of Owhyhee." Foreign Mission School students James Ely and Samuel Ruggles had collected Obookiah's Hawaiian language papers.

In September, 1819 Herman Daggett, who replaced Edwin Dwight as principal at the Foreign Mission School, began compiling this basic guide book to the Sandwich Islands. The hand-bound book served as a Hawaiian language primer passed around for study. Daggett, assisted by Hopoo, added a "Short Account of Creation," featuring scripture passages from the first chapter the *Book of Genesis* that Obookiah translated from Hebrew into the Hawaiian language. "An Account of Obookiah" was added, pressed together with Hawaiian language versions of The Ten Commandments, the Parable of the Prodigal Son, the Lord's Prayer. A sheet listing Hawaiian numbers from one to one-thousand was slipped in too.

An unforeseen danger threatened the mission party six weeks out of Boston, on December 9, while crossing the equator. Assistant missionary Samuel Whitney wrote in his journal of a shipment of gunpowder, likely accompanying firearms, to be traded for furs procured from Indian tribes along the Pacific Northwest coast:

Kind providence has this day interposed in delivering us from an awful death. The lightnings of Heaven have placed about us for several hours, accompanied by the most tremendous peals of thunder. One flash struck the main topmast, but without any injury; had it found way to the magazine, which contains upwards of five-thousand pounds of (gun) powder, more than forty souls must have instantly gone to the world of Spirits.

CHAPTER NINETEEN
ARRIVAL IN HAWAI'I

The landing at Kawaihae Bay circa 1820. Puʻukoholā Heiau is pictured mauka, upon a rise.

THREE MONTHS OUT FROM BOSTON the Sandwich Islands Mission party for the first time at sea heard the cry of "Land ho!" at mid-day on January 25, 1820. Though mid-summer, in the Southern Hemisphere, it was chilly as the treeless, northeast coast of the Tierra Del Fuego archipelago loomed up on the horizon.

Captain Blanchard chose to lie-to overnight on January 26, halting the voyage to avoid going adrift in the Strait of Le Maire; the Tierra Del Fuego coastline lay to the west, and the rocky edge of Staten Island to the east.

On January 27-28 rough seas and a strong westerly current caused the *Thaddeus* to lose ground as the ship fought to sail west. On January 29 favorable winds blew and Cape Horn, the southern most headland of Tierra Del Fuego, came into view.

On Sunday, January 30 the *Thaddeus* rounded Cape Horn, passing beyond the notorious landmark, heading southwest towards the Antarctic Sea. A scribe noted in the *Thaddeus Journal*, "No Sabbath, perhaps, since our embarkation has been more interesting or happy than this, or deserves a more grateful remembrance. This day we double Cape Horn, and write upon it 'Ebenezer.'"

By Monday, February 8, the mission party realized they had skirted Cape Horn, escaped the threat of huge swells and high winds shipwrecking the *Thaddeus*. Captain Blanchard had chosen to sail south, deeper into Antarctic waters. But now he edged the *Thaddeus* north. All aboard welcomed being at last headed towards Hawaiʻi, the ship making good time sliding steadily up and down in the long fetches and steady swells of the far South Pacific.

Passage to Hawai'i

The passage to Hawai'i sped up once the ship entered the northeast trades above the equator. The mission party had now passed six months at sea without going ashore.

Nearing Hawai'i, fear of a savage welcome swirled in their minds, a train of thought impressed on them by so many at home. But there was an out. The contract between the American Board and Captain Blanchard stipulated immediate passage away from Hawai'i for the mission party should landing prove dangerous. American Board Secretary Samuel Worcester wrote Bingham and Thurston on August 22, 1819:

> If...in the sovereign wisdom of Providence, things be found in such a state as to render an attempt for establishing the Mission in the Sandwich Islands, or either of them, impracticable or extremely hazardous, you will make the best arrangements in your power, conformably to the articles of agreement between the Prudential Committee and the owners and captain of the Thaddeus, for getting to the Society Islands, and will act according to your best information and judgment in regard to settling there or going to some other of the dark places of the earth.

About two weeks south of Hawai'i Island, James Hunnewell armed the ship and its crew. Hunnewell noted in his journal, "Large guns were hoisted on deck," and on March 20 that defensive precautions were being taken, "the armorer getting up his forge, the carpenter making gun carriages, others putting up quarter-nettings, etc."

On March 30 the peaks of snow-capped volcanic mountains Mauna Kea and Mauna Loa appeared in the dim light of late evening, visible in the starlight on the horizon to the northwest. Word of the sighting of Obookiah's home island spread below deck and the entire mission party awoke. They stumbled upon deck in midnight for a first glimpse of the Islands.

In his journal missionary printer Elisha Loomis remembered this auspicious moment. He noted the remarkable events of his first day in Hawaiian waters as the day unfolded.

> (11 o'clock a.m.). We are now coasting along the northeast part of the Island so near the shore as to see the numerous habitations, cultivated fields, rising smoke... Hopoo has designated the spot in a little valley where he was born. He and his native companions are much animated with a view of their native shores. Near the northern extremity the walls of an ancient heiau appears....
> (4 o'clock p.m.). As we double the northern extremity of Owhyhee (Hawai'i) the lofty heights of Maui are on our right. As no canoes approach us it is thought that it is a time of special taboo and all the people are employed in its observance. Captain Blanchard has concluded to send a boat to make inquiries respecting the king and the state of the islands. Mr. Hunnewell, Thomas Hopoo, and J. Honoree and others have now gone on this errand and we wait with anxious expectation for the first intelligence.
> (7 o'clock p.m.). The boat has returned, having fallen in with a number of fishermen near the shore who readily answered their inquiries and the messengers have

astonished and overjoyed our minds by reporting...that the aged King Tamaha-maha is dead; that Rehoreho, his son, succeeds him, that the images of his gods are burned, that the men are all Ai-noa, that is, they eat with women in all the islands, that one of the chiefs only was killed in settling the affairs of government, and he for refusing to destroy his god; that Rehoreho (Liholiho), the king, and Crymokoo (Kalanimoku), often called Billy Pitt, resides at Kawaihae. These are interesting facts. They seem to show that Christ is overturning in order to take possession and that their souls are waiting for His law, while the old and decaying pillars of idolatry are falling to the ground.

More encouraging news arrived on Friday, March 31, Loomis noted:

The interesting intelligence of yesterday is confirmed today by a visit of Brother Ruggles, Thomas Hopoo, and William Tenui, to the residence of Crymokoo (Kalanimoku) where they were received kindly and entertained with unexpected civility. By them the widow of Kamehameha sent us a present of fresh fish, cocoanuts, sweet potatoes, bananas, sugar cane, breadfruit, etc., expressing much satisfaction that we had come to bring them good things. Today a number of the natives came off to the brig in their canoes, with vegetables, shells, etc., for the purpose of traffic and to gratify their curiosity. The sight of these children of nature drew tears from eyes that did not intend to weep. Of them we inquired whether they had learned anything about Jehovah, who made Hawaii and all things. They replied that Rehoreho, the king, had heard of the great God of white men and had spoken of Him, and that all the chiefs, but one, had agreed to destroy their gods and idols, because they were convinced that they could do no good, since they could not even serve their king. Idol worship is therefore prohibited and the priesthood entirely abolished. Sing, O Heavens, for the Lord hath done it.

Bingham, looking back over twenty years later from his desk in Connecticut, recalled the day as a shocking one for the mission party. The *Thaddeus* rounded 'Upolu Point in the Kohala District, passing the site of Kamehameha's birthplace and Pā'ao's ancient Mo'okini Heiau. Coming out to trade, outrigger canoes came alongside, paddled by the Native Hawaiians they had prayed for and believed that God had sent them to save. Now the idealism of "disinterested benevolence" took a back seat; the challenge was not fending off an attack, or being torn away from the *Thaddeus* and sacrificed on a pagan altar, but to overcome their own prejudices towards the people they had so many times in New England promised to lay down their lives for. Loomis continued his narrative:

...Their manoeuvres in their canoes, some being propelled by short paddles, and some by small sails, attracted the attention of our little group, and for a moment, gratified curiosity; but the appearance of destitution, degradation, and barbarism, among the chattering, and almost naked savages, whose heads and feet, and much of their sunburnt swarthy skins, were bare, was appalling. Some of our number, with gushing tears, turned away from the spectacle. Others with firmer nerve continued their gaze, but were ready to exclaim, "Can these be human beings! How dark and comfortless their state of mind and heart! How imminent the danger to the immortal soul, shrouded in this deep pagan gloom! Can such beings be civilized? Can they be Christianized? Can we throw ourselves upon these rude shores, and take up our abode, for life, among such a people, for the purpose of training them for heaven? Yes. Though faith had to struggle for the victory, these interrogatories could all be answered decidedly in the affirmative. At sunset they returned to their dark cabins, and we passed along a little further south."

On April 1, the *Thaddeus* sailed into the light-wind waters off the northwest coast of Hawai'i Island, "abreast of Kawaihae." Pu'ukoholā Heiau overshadowed the pocket bay. English sailor John Young built his compound at the base of the heiau. Young served as governor and the port official of Hawai'i Island. Bingham wrote:

...Kalanimoku and his wives, and Kalakua and her sister Namahana, two of the widows of the late king, came off to us with their loquacious attendants, in their double canoe. It was propelled with spirit, by eighteen or twenty athletic men. Having over their heads a huge Chinese umbrella, and the nodding kahilis or plumed rods of the nobility, they made a novel and imposing appearance as they drew near our becalmed Mission Barque, while we fixed on them, and their movements, our scrutinizing gaze. As they were welcomed on board, the felicitous native compliment, aloha, with shaking hands, passed between them, and each member of the mission family, Captain Blanchard and others. Their tall, portly, ponderous appearance seemed to indicate a different race from those who had visited the vessel before, or a decided superiority of the nobility over the peasantry.

A Tour of Pu'ukoholā

On Sunday morning, April 2 Hiram Bingham rowed to shore with Captain Blanchard to tour monumental Pu'ukoholā (Hill of the Whale) heiau. Stepping onto the white sand beach Bingham unknowingly followed the path of Keoua, the Ka'ū rebel chief and rival of Kamehameha, who landed there in 1791. Keoua stepped into a trap, and was ritually murdered by warriors of Kamehameha, and was sacrificed during the dedication of this luakini class heiau .

Kamehameha's building up of Pu'ukoholā was a significant landmark in the chain of events preceding the arrival of the Sandwich Islands Mission. According to John Papa I'i, a respected historian writing in Hawaiian-language newspapers in the mid-nineteenth century, Pu'ukoholā was built upon advice given to Kamehameha by a *kahuna kaula* (prophet) from Kaua'i named Kapoukahi. In the time of Kamehameha, Kaua'i was considered the island possessing the highest mana in its royal bloodlines, the premier source of spiritual power in all Hawai'i. Kapoukahi then lived in Waikīkī, where he was approached by an aunt of Kamehameha. Pu'ukoholā is to be dedicated to honor Kūkā'ilimoku, the war god bestowed to Kamehameha, the prophet told the woman, and then Kamehameha shall conquer and unite all Hawai'i.

By defeating all the warrior chiefs across the Islands, Kamehameha did bring peace to all Hawai'i.

Thus the first significant landing of the Sandwich Islands Mission in Hawai'i was made at the site key to the unification of the Islands and the end of centuries of warfare. The Roman Empire conquered nations from the British Isles across Europe to Israel; this led to peace and safe passage for the evangelists of the Bible and the spread of Christianity across the empire. So did Kamehameha's conquest allow the Sandwich Islands Mission to find safety and peace when they arrived to spread the Gospel across Hawai'i.

During Bingham's first hours ashore in Hawai'i he was joined by Kalanimoku, the prime minister and general known as the "Iron Chain of Hawai'i." Led by Kalanimoku, Bingham walked desolate, abandoned Pu'ukohola. (Two generations later, his grandson Hiram Bingham III hiked the ancient trails of Machu Piccuh in Peru, opening up that majestic site to the western world). Loomis described Bingham's tour:

> This monument of idolatry, I surveyed with mingled emotions of grief, horror, pity, regret, gratitude, and hope ;—of grief and horror at the enormities which men and devils had perpetrated there before high heaven;—of pity and regret that the victims and many of the builders and worshippers, had gone to their account without the knowledge of the Gospel, which ought to have been conveyed to them; of gratitude, that this strong-hold of Satan had been demolished and the spell around it broken; and of hope, that soon temples to the Living God would take the place of these altars of heathen abomination.

Sabbath Day Spent With the Ali'i

Bingham returned to the *Thaddeus* sunburnt. Following a Sunday service, Kamehameha's widowed queen Kalakua firmly explained she desired to wear without delay her own New England-style dress. The missionary wives promised they would sew for the queens, but only after the Sabbath, on Monday. Bingham commented:

> Kalakua...shrewdly aiming to see what the white women could do for her temporal benefit asked them to make a gown for her in fashion like their own...they cheerfully plied scissors and needle the next day, and soon fitted out the rude giantess with a white cambric (light cotton) dress.

Concert of Prayer in the Lee of Hualālai

Continuing south after the Sunday break the *Thaddeus* sailed into the lee of the Mount Hualālai volcanic crater on Monday, April 3. Streams of ebony-black lava flows cover fishponds and villages for miles along this coast, remnants of an 1801 eruption. A legend claims Kamehameha halted the eruption by cutting off locks of his hair, wrapping them in ti leaves and throwing them into the lava flow, making an offering to the volcano goddess Pele.

The monthly Concert of Prayer fell that day. The Sandwich Island Mission party gathered on deck as the *Thaddeus* sailed at a slow pace in the leeward wind shadow of the 9,000-foot-high Hualālai. Back home their churches and families gathered earlier that day joining a network of prayer that now ringed the globe from New England to Hawai'i, to Burma and Ceylon, and to Levi Parsons and Pliny Fisk in Turkey preparing to head for Jerusalem. Bingham and Thurston led the prayer meeting, praising God for opening wide the door to Hawai'i and singing hymns of thanks. Kamehameha's Prime Minister Kalanimoku sat enthralled. Prayers for finding favor with Liholiho were added; the mission party was still unsure if permission for them to stay in Hawai'i would be granted by the young king and Ka'ahumanu, his *kuhina nui* (coruler).

Arrival in Kona

The *Thaddeus* arrived off Kailua Bay on the morning of Tuesday, April 4. The mission party had arrived at a time when the people of Hawai'i faced immense changes. Their ancient Polynesian religion had collapsed following the 'Ai Noa, free eating, of men and women replacing the 'Ai Kapu, the restrictions of the kapu system. The ali'i nui, led by Ka'ahumanu and Hewahewa, ordered the destruction of wooden and stone images of their gods, and the old ways of the kāhuna went underground. Their powerful and wise veteran ruler Kamehameha died and his throne went to his young son, alcohol drinking, undisciplined Liholiho, Kamehameha II. Tahitians had arrived, bringing word of Christianity coming to the South Pacific. The coming of the whalers beginning in late 1819 increased the number of ships making rest and reprovisioning stops. With the arrival of fleets of whaling ships, the party spirit of the ports escalated, resulting in more drunkenness, and an expansion of prostitution bringing a wider spread of disease and infertility. Waves of epidemic diseases became more frequent, brought ashore by sailors and spread shoreward from brackish ship holds. The monopoly of Kamehameha over sandalwood trading ended at his death, from then on ali'i from all islands could order workers into the hills, deeper and deeper into the forests to collect the wood needed to pay off debts to foreign traders. A rise in the number of haole-Hawaiian children meant more orphans fathered by departed sailors needed to be cared for; the children were sometime cast out. The Kingdom of Hawai'i lay open to easy conquest by a western warship. Hundreds, if not thousands, of able bodied Hawaiian men sailed away aboard western ships; the lack of fathers and husbands helped decimate the birth rate, weakening traditional planting and fishing practices; some died at sea, many settled in the Pacific Northwest and elsewhere, and those returning told tales of adventures in faraway places thus drawing more and more men away.

Captain Blanchard ordered his crew to lower anchors to hold the brig about a quarter mile offshore of Kamehameha's former residence at Kamakahonu along Kaiakeakua (sea of the god) Bay. Blanchard and Bingham were rowed ashore. The bright Kona sun lit up this typical day in coastal Hawai'i. Fishermen, surfers, workers tending gardens went about their business, the excitement of greeting an arriving trading ship now old-hat. Bingham noted:

> As we proceeded to the shore, the multitudinous shouting and almost naked natives, of every age, sex, and rank, swimming, floating on surf-boards, sailing in canoes,—or, on shore, sitting lounging, standing, running like sheep, dancing, or laboring,—attracted our earnest attention.

Bingham, and later all the missionary party, stepped ashore upon an outcrop of lava rock at Kamakahonu. This was site of the compound where Kamehameha died and where he had worshipped at the 'Ahu'ena Heiau. In later years, a tradition grew and the landing became known as the Plymouth Rock of Hawai'i. Today the landing is buried beneath Kona Pier.

Bingham failed in his efforts to meet with Liholiho. He hoped to receive "...permission to settle in his country, for the purpose of teaching the nation Christianity, literature and the arts."

The next day at dawn Bingham returned ashore with printer Elisha Loomis and first mate James Hunnewell. Hunnewell spoke a dockside-style of conversational Hawaiian, a language essential to him during his trading sojourn taken in Honolulu in 1817-1818. Loomis noted in his journal:

> ...as we passed near shore, several chiefs were spending their idle hours in gambling, we were favored with an interview with Hewahewa, the late High Priest. He received us kindly and on his introduction to Brother Bingham he expressed much satisfaction in meeting with a brother priest from America, still pleasantly claiming that distinction for himself. He assures us that he will be our friend.

Hewahewa's Prophecy

Months earlier, Hewahewa the high priest of Kamehameha's kingdom, walked miles down the hot, dry trail paved with pebbles that ran from Kawaihae to Kailua. Hewahewa descended directly from the Tahitian kahuna Pā'ao who brought the kapu system from Tahiti six-hundred years earlier. At the landing at Kamakahonu, Hewahewa declared word of a new god who would soon be received at that spot.

James Jackson Jarves, noted art collector in New England in the late 1870s, and the editor of the *Polynesian* newspaper in Honolulu from 1840-48, quoted Hewahewa telling of the overthrow of the Hawaiian kapu system:

> I knew that the wooden images of our deities carved by our own hands were incapable of supplying our wants, but worshipped them because it was the custom of our fathers; they made not the kalo to grow, nor sent us rain; neither did they bestow life or health. My thought has always been, "Akahi waleno Akua-nui iloko o ka-lani"— there is "one only Great God dwelling in the heavens."

Missionary son Joseph Emerson's paper "Selections from a Kahuna's Book of Prayer," read before the Hawaiian Historical Society in 1917, reveals more about Hewahewa's actions prior to the arrival of the Sandwich Islands Missions.

> ...Hewahewa was a great favorite with the high chiefs and the royal family. A few days before the missionaries landed at Kailua he foresaw their coming and instructed his awachewer to run in front of the house, near the shore where the royal family were living, and call out, "E ka lani e, ina aku ke akua a pae mai. O King, the god will soon land yonder," pointing, as he spoke, to the very spot on the sandy beach where, a few days later, April 4th, 1820, the little band of missionaries landed from the brig Thaddeus, bringing with them the new god. In commemoration of this incident the spot received the name, "Kai-o-ke-akua," the sea of the god, by which name it has ever since been called. During the next few days the missionaries had audience with royalty and earnestly presented the claims of their god for the worship of the people. Their pleading made such an impression on the high chiefess, Kapiolani nui, that she told Hewahewa that the god had really landed, and expressed her willingness to accept the new religion...."

Hawai'i's Bible Prophecy

Bingham and Thurston returned the next day to present to Liholiho his father's copy of the gilt-edged English-language Bible sent out by the American Bible Society. The big, black book was embossed on its cover with his father's name, spelled in gold leaf as "Tamehameha." Also presented were smaller Bibles for Kamehameha's daughters, and "a good optical instrument," perhaps a spyglass, as a gift sent by the American Board of Commissioners for Foreign Missions.

The delivery of the royal Bible embodied a spiritual significance for Hewahewa and the ali'i nui, according to an account written by Martha Beckwith, the grand-niece of missionary wife Lucy Thurston. Yale University Press in 1940 published Beckwith's book *Hawaiian Mythology*, a book critics hailed as a monumental study on the subject. Source material for *Hawaiian Mythology* came from rare manuscripts and texts accessed through Beckwith's contacts in Hawai'i. One of her main infor-mants was Hawaiiana scholar Mary Kawena Pukui, a linguist at the Bishop Museum, and the leading authority on the Hawaiian language in the twentieth-century.

Mrs. Pukui was cited as the source for a passage in Beckwith's book that tells of a prophecy predicting the coming of the Bible to Hawai'i. This prophecy might have been inspired by Kamehameha and other ali'i nui seeing the use of the Bible and Anglican Book of Common Prayer aboard ship by Captains Cook and Vancouver.

> Some saw their old gods in printed words (palapala). They say that in ancient times the gods came to Hawaii from overseas with their families and followers and peo-pled the group. Up to that time only spirits dwelt here. For a long time they lived with their people as visible, personal gods, but when they became disgusted with their evil ways they left them and went elsewhere. But they left a promise that someday they would return in diminutive size and speaking strange tongues so that the people would not recognize them. When the white men came with their strange language and their art of printing, the tradition was recalled to the minds of some: 'E ho'i mai ana makou mai ka aina e mai, e olelo ana i na olelo malihini, a iloko o na hua makali'i, a e ho'oewahewa no kekahi o oukou i ko oukou akua (We shall return from a foreign country speaking a strange language and in little forms, and some of you will not recognize your gods). The Hawaiians hence felt that their gods had returned in the Bible. The size of the type used in its printing caused them to think that their gods had come in that shape.

An account similar to this prophecy spoke of this *palapala*, the written word, coming in a black box, a reference perhaps to either the wooden case commonly used to protect a Bible aboard a ship at sea, or just to the black box-looking Bible.

To Do All That Obookiah Wanted To Do

Liholiho did eventually decide to grant the mission company a one-year stay in Hawai'i, with Dr. Holman and his wife Lucia Holman to reside at Kailua Bay, along with Hopu. Hopu, as he was known at home in Hawai'i, wrote of his arrival in Hawai'i as a continuation of the vision of Obookiah.

Lord, now lettest thou thy servant depart in peace, for mine eyes have seen thy salvation. May you and I remember the prayer of Henry Obookiah, and his sweet words;—he who, I hope, knows what you and I are doing now. If my life is spared, and my health preserved, I must try to do all that Henry Obookiah wanted to do, to make known Christ and his great salvation to my countrymen. I hope you will pray to God for me, that I may still be supported by grace, until Christ shall commence his universal reign upon the Sandwich Islands.

By late July, 1820 Sybil Bingham had set up a makeshift school in Honolulu to teach Bible lessons to adults and children. Her words were repeated in Hawaiian by a translator, including her own simplified rendition of the *Memoirs of Obookiah*.

In the afternoon, about 20 were collected, when I read to them in the memoir of Obookiah, having it interpreted by J. Honooree and Sally J....I thought of a remark in a letter from our friend S. Taylor, soon after the death of Obookiah, to this effect, after speaking of the darkness of the providence, which snatched him away :—"but how much good may be done by his memoirs, should they be written, in the hands of missionaries among his countrymen." Little did I then think that I should be the first to read a page of these memoirs to them. But so, the mysterious providence of God, it was ordered.

Samuel Whitney looked upon the palapala schools that branched out of the missionary station at Waimea, Kaua'i as extensions of the Foreign Mission School in Cornwall.

God's mercies are still continued; and though it falls not to the missionary to drink of an unmingled cup, we have cause for eternal thanksgiving. Our little school still continues to prosper. The youth, I think, are becoming more and more interested in learning. We often look upon them as Obookiahs, Hopoos, and Honoorees in miniature.

In the journal written collectively and sent to the American Board in Boston, the Sandwich Islands Mission company looked back on 1820 as a tumultuous year:

...a year marked with vicissitudes and crowned with goodness, and whose history, as it respects us, is a history of mercies. We have been brought from the deeps of the stormy Atlantic, through the swelling dangers of la Maire and Cape Horn, and conducted in safety over the more peaceful waters of the Pacific, and allowed to take up a quiet residence in these isles of the Gentiles, and to commence the great work of enlightening and redeeming, by the power of the everlasting Gospel, this long lost race of men.

CHAPTER TWENTY
TAHITIAN CONNECTION

Ellis' *Polynesian Researches*

Auna and Aunawahine, the Rev. William Ellis of the London Missionary Society and company departed for the Marquesas and Hawai'i in 1822 aboard the British colonial ship *Mermaid*, departing from Fare Bay, Huahine in the Society Islands.

LIKE THE SOUND OF A THOUSAND FOREST SONG BIRDS lured to the coast, melodious hymns sung in the Tahitian language flowed out over the calm, clear waters of Kealakekua Bay in early April 1822. Obookiah's hope of bringing the Gospel to his uncle's home was being fulfilled by Christians from a place and people least expected: Polynesians from islands far to the south of Hawai'i, from Kahiki, from the Society Islands, an archipelago located half a world away from the Foreign Mission School in Cornwall.

The small 61-ton British colonial schooner *Mermaid* anchored about a quarter-mile offshore of Hikiau Heiau. Dozens of outrigger canoes surrounded the schooner. The *Mermaid* departed from hour-glass shaped Huahine, an idyllic island located about 100 miles north of Tahiti island in the archipelago then known as Otahiete. Traditionally, Otahiete was given the name Kahiki in Hawai'i; Kahiki was also the general term for lands beyond the horizon of Hawai'i.

The Hawai'i-Tahiti sail crosses over 2,600 miles of open ocean. Southeast trades blow steadily below the equator and the northeast trades above the equator. A slow mid-way passage through the equatorial doldrums adds days to the voyaging time, which takes in total about four to five weeks, depending on seasonal wind conditions.

In Kealakekua Bay aboard the *Mermaid* Auna, the son of a Raiatean chief, led the party in singing a hymn in the Tahitian language. Auna and his party had been sent out from the London Missionary Society's church in Huahine on a mission to

Courtesy Pastor Roy "Rocky" Sasaki

The ancient Taputapuātea (Temple of Sacrifices from Abroad) *marae* (Tahitian term for temple, heiau) is located on the island of Raiatea, used as the central navigators' temple for all of the Pacific Islands and established by AD 1000. Here knowledge of long-distance canoe voyaging navigation was shared and taught, and the Polynesian god 'Oro, the god of fertility and war was worshipped. The priest Pā'ao, who brought the kapu system and human sacrifice to Hawai'i, is said to have sailed on that voyage from this island. In 1995 Taputapuātea was rededicated at a gathering of Polynesian voyaging canoe crews sailing in from Hawai'i and South Pacific islands.

the Marquesas Islands. A detour due to contrary winds brought them to Hawai'i. Deacon Auna presented a "tall commanding figure" accompanied by his stately wife, Aunawahine, who took the biblical name Naiomi. Singing alongside the couple were the Huahine deacon Matatore, and his wife Matatorewahine. Accompanying them were the Rev. William Ellis of the London Missionary Society, and five Tahitian missionary assistants.

The London Missionary Society assigned Ellis to the Society Islands in 1817. He oversaw the printing of the Tahitian Bible along with other Christian publications translated into the Tahitian language. Once in Tahiti Ellis adapted himself to the needs he found, serving as "a minister, carpenter, botanist, printer, bookbinder, agriculturists, sugar manufacturer, boat builder and linguist."

Ellis possessed an innate sense of seeing beneath the surface of Tahitian culture and society. He systematically recorded what he learned: religious practices, the ways of daily life, of combat and politics. He compiled Tahitian word lists later used in dictionaries. The tall, detail-oriented missionary was soon fluent in the Tahitian language, able to teach and preach across the island chain.

"They all behaved very quietly, and listened with attention," George Bennet of

Ellis' *Polynesian Researches*

The High Priest of Tahiti ceding land in the District of Matavai to Captain James Wilson of the *Duff* for the use of missionaries sent by the London Missionary Society.

the London Missionary Society wrote in his account of the song service held in Kealakekua Bay. Bennet and the Rev. Daniel Tyreman, both aboard the *Mermaid*, were on a deputation, sent to inspect the widely spread foreign mission stations supported by the London Missionary Society. Inspections of stations in Asia were to follow the South Seas missionary station inspection. Detailed reports written by Bennet and Tyreman were posted to London and published in evangelical missions publications.

Bennet applauded the reception the Tahitians received in Hawai'i, he wrote, "The singing of our Tahitians appeared to interest them very much."

The Hawaiians who listened to the concert at Kealakekua Bay had often heard the beat of the shanties, sung by sailors repairing and cleaning ships in the bay. They had heard the loud, martial sound of drummers and pipers playing aboard visiting naval ships. But new to the people of Kealakekua Bay was this sweet, smooth sound, the harmony of hymn singing. The hymns were sung in a sister Polynesian language by people from Kahiki, a place their legends, genealogies and chants pointed to as a homeland of their ancestors. And the homeland of their departed god Lono.

Tahiti-Hawai'i Connection Renewed

Visions of Tahiti evoke clear blue waters, coconut palm-lined beaches and languor. Ironically, a revival from the rainy, foggy land of Great Britain spread across warm Tahiti. The British revivals dated back over a half century to the open-air preaching of George Whitefield, the Wesley Brothers, and to the missionary vision for the South Pacific seeded by the reading of descriptions of the islands published in Captain Cook's journals.

The first sparks of Tahitian revival to reach Hawai'i spread in the years prior to the landing of the Sandwich Islands Mission. The source: Hawaiians who had returned home after residing in Tahiti, there studying the Tahitian Bible translation printed by the London Missionary Society. Christian Tahitians settling in Hawai'i also came alongside influential ali'i with word of the surge of Christian conversions in their ancient homeland. This caused Kamehameha to take notice and inquire about how the introduction of Christianity had affected the South Pacific island group.

The Rev. W. P. Crook, a London Missionary Society Otahiete missionary, wrote a letter, published in Malacca in Southeast Asia in 1818. Crook described the change the arrival of Christianity brought to the religion and politics of Tahitian society:

> The whole of this group of islands is now professedly Christian...Theft is almost unknown among them. Family prayer is set up in every house, and private prayer is almost universally attended to. Women restored to their rank in society.

Crook's letter went the long way round to Malacca for it was first posted to the Sandwich Islands. As a salutation, Crook wrote of Hawaiians studying the Bible in Tahiti prior to returning home: "I have also some hopes of the Sandwich Islands, as the American brig *Clarion*, by whom I send this, is bound thither and takes passengers, some natives of these (Sandwich) islands who have been learning the word of God here." The 149-ton ship *Clarion*, Captain Gyzelar, sailed from Boston in 1817 and rounded the Cape of Good Hope, arriving in Tahiti via Tasmania in June 1818 before sailing north to Hawai'i.

Some of the Hawaiians mentioned by Crook may have been met by British ship's officer John Turnbull. Turnbull, aboard the ship *Margaret*, arrived in the Hawaiian Islands in late 1802 following a stay in Tahiti. Turnbull disclosed that "a number of Sandwich Islanders have at different periods passed to Otahiete, where they find every encouragement to settle from the young king Otoo, who, from their superior skill and warlike disposition, generally prefers them as attendants on his person."

The voyage by the *Margaret*, and of the *Clarion*, exemplified the reestablishment of communication between Tahiti and Hawai'i that began in the 1780s following Captain Cook's arrival at Waimea, Kaua'i in 1778. The ancient Tahiti-Hawai'i voyaging connection had gradually ceased about twenty generations earlier, leaving the Hawaiian Islands isolated from Kahiki (Tahiti) and the world outside. Memories of the Kahiki homeland in the South Pacific grew legendary. The accounts were preserved in *oli* (chants), memorized and handed down to generation after generation of chanters. The chanting of the lengthy genealogies underscored the power of ali'i nui; commoners were forbidden to record their genealogies.

Captain Cook renews Tahiti-Hawai'i ties

Captain Cook in sailing north to Hawai'i from Tahiti in 1778 undertook the first known voyage between the two island groups since the last voyagers from the South Pacific arrived in Hawai'i centuries earlier. About a decade after Cook, captains of western trading vessels, mostly on Northwest Coast-China trade voyages, began providing passage to Tahiti for Hawaiians, and passage to Hawai'i for Tahitians.

Captain Cook held the first Christian service in Hawai'i, a joint Christian-Polynesian burial of elderly gunner's mate William Watman at the Hikiau Heiau. Watman died of a stroke on February 1, 1779. The sailor's remains were interred in an opening in the rock wall of the heiau. Following Cook's reading of the British Navy burial service from the Anglican Book of Common Prayer, kāhuna at Hikiau Heiau requested permission to complete the burial. The flock of priests, possibly including Obookiah's uncle Pahua, placed in the grave of Watman a baked pig, coconuts, and bananas. The complex ritual lasted three days.

There is no mention in the extensive accounts compiled in Cook's journals of his comparing the cross of Christ to the wooden Lono Makua (a cross draped with a cloth that appeared to symbolize a sail which served as the main symbol of the god Lono during the Makahiki.). Cook led his life on his voyages to the tenets of Enlightenment philosophers and scientists, rather than to the orthodox Christian beliefs of the English church. The great navigator held no hope for the evangelizing of the Polynesian people. In his journal he criticized an earlier attempt made by Catholic priests in Tahiti: "It is very unlikely that any measure of this kind should ever be seriously thought of, as it can neither serve the purpose of public ambition nor private avarice; and without such enducements, I may pronounce that it will never be undertaken."

Huahine Mission

Earlier in 1822 Auna and his wife, along with the Matatores, stood up during a church service held in Huahine and committed to becoming missionaries to the Marquesas, a Polynesian island group then best known as Nu'uhiwa, in reference to its northern main port, Nuku Hiva. That island chain is located nine hundred miles to the northeast of Huahine. An assignment with the mission company was avidly sought in Huahine.

The surge of Tahitians joining the London Missionary Society church came following a drastic decline in the population of the Society Islands. Raging waves of diseases took many lives from windward Tahiti to Borabora, 'Eimeo (Moorea) to perhaps the hardest hit island of all, leeward Huahine. The Tahitians sought a new way, a new direction that would preserve their people.

Rev. William Ellis of the London Missionary Society's Otahite Mission co-wrote with the Rev. Hiram Bingham the first hymns written in the Hawaiian language.

Deaths continued to mount from an epidemic of contagious diseases brought aboard trading vessels, mostly from British and French ships. Venereal infections multiplied across their islands through Tahitian women infected by western sailors, bringing infertility and sometimes death. The plague surpassed by far the number of warriors killed in battle within the Society Islands, from natural deaths, from marae (heiau-temple) sacrifices, and from the practice of infanticide.

Providence lent a hand to the Nu'uhiwa mission with the arrival of Captain John Rodolphus Kent, a Colonial Service sea captain based in Port Jackson (Sydney Harbor), Australia. Captain Kent made an unscheduled stop at Huahine. He was sailing from Port Jackson to Honolulu to present a royal gift to Liholiho, Kamehameha II: the *Prince Regent*, a 71-ton schooner built at Port Jackson by order of King George IV of Great Britain. Presenting the schooner to Liholiho would fulfill a long-standing promise made to Kamehameha. This pledge dated back to explorer George Vancouver, who visited Hawai'i in the early 1790s. Vancouver promised to deliver a ship to Kamehameha in hopes of persuading him to cede Hawai'i to Great Britain. Kent's orders commanded him to present the *Prince Regent* in a ceremony at Honolulu, then take her crew aboard the *Mermaid* and sail back to Australia.

At Huahine, Kent crossed paths with William Ellis, who told him of the need for passage to the Marquesas for the Tahitian missionary party. The sea captain offered to stop at Nu'uhiwa as a side trip on his voyage north to Hawai'i, providing free passage. Ellis, Bennet and Tyreman, and the Huahine deacons, gladly accepted the offer, feeling it was a divine intervention of God, a blessing of their mission.

The Tahitians were to remain in the Marquesas in an attempt to relaunch a failed London Missionary Society mission. Ellis decided he and the Society deputation would temporarily stay in Nu'uhiwa, then sail back to the Society Islands. Bennet and Tyreman's next stop on their circumnavigation would be Macao and Canton.

On the voyage north the unfavorable winds kept Kent to the west of Nu'uhiwa, so he instead continued north to Hawai'i. The captain promised to sail to the Marquesas on his return trip south following the presentation in Honolulu of the *Prince Regent*.

Tahitian Christians Precede Sandwich Islands Mission

The Tahitian missionary couples, well dressed in European clothing and discipled as Christians, found the scene at Kealakekua noisy and unruly, as would have 'Ōpūkaha'ia. Auna and company noted a preponderance of crass trading practices. Dozens of whaling ships now stopped in Hawai'i on the way to the bountiful whaling grounds of the North Pacific. There were no whaling ships in Hawai'i when the *Triumph* provisioned there in 1808. Bennet wrote of "flagrant cheating in barter, &c." and compared the Yankee trading practices to the peace and tranquility found in the harbor of Fare in Christian Huahine. At Fare, a ban prohibited prostitution of Tahitian women to visiting sailors, a trade still practiced blatantly at Kealakekua to the profit of the ali'i. Contrasting Kealakekua with Huahine "deeply affected them," he added.

The Huahine contingent rowed ashore to bathe in fresh water and to inspect Hikiau Heiau. They noted seeing the coconut trees 'Ōpūkaha'ia planted at the Helehelekalani temple. They found the monumental lava rock walls of Hikiau in disarray. Ellis, speaking in Tahitian, confirmed that this abandonment was due to the overthrow of the kapu system. The mission party met an older man, carrying a wood wand with a feathery tip, a symbol of the priesthood of Lono. This kupuna may have been 'Ōpūkaha'ia's uncle Pahua, still clinging to his role as a kahuna.

Auna traveled north to Kailua to meet a Christian Tahitian named Toketa. Toketa sailed to Hawai'i from the island of 'Eimeo (Moorea) near Tahiti. He arrived in Hawai'i about two years prior to the Sandwich Islands Mission and was in the service of Ka'ahumanu's brother, Kuakini, the district governor at Kailua. Ka'ahumanu was now the kuhina nui, the coregent with Liholiho, Kamehameha II. Her consort was Kaumuali'i, now deposed as king of Kaua'i by Liholiho and brought to O'ahu.

Kahikona, another Tahitian Christian, arrived in Hawai'i in 1819. Kahikona trained as a teacher of the palapala in Hawai'i following the arrival of the Sandwich Islands Mission. He lived with Kuakini in Kailua, coming to Hawai'i after visiting the Pacific Northwest in 1818. Kahikona read and wrote Tahitian, skills taught him by the London Missionary Society missionaries. These skills adapted easily to the speaking of the Hawaiian language. Kahikona became an important native teacher, assisting the Sandwich Islands Mission. For his help he received grants of land from the ali'i nui.

On April 9, the *Mermaid* sailed from Hawai'i Island to O'ahu. The ship's arrival at Honolulu Harbor on April 16, 1822 came as a surprise to the Rev. Hiram Bingham and the Sandwich Islands Mission company. Bingham had corresponded with the London Missionary stations in the Society Islands, requesting copies of their Bible materials as translated into the Tahitian language, but didn't expect a visit.

Polynesian Gospel Perspective

In spring 1822, the New England missionaries faced a serious cross-cultural impasse. Two years into their pioneering mission, Liholiho and Ka'ahumanu still kept a safe distance between themselves and the missionaries. The ali'i nui stalled in giving full support. The early departure from the mission of Dr. Holman and his wife had hurt the mission's credibility. Meanwhile, the ali'i nui socialized with opponents of the missionaries among the traders and whaling captains in port in Honolulu. The traders arrived in larger numbers each year at the anchorage in Honolulu Harbor, many patronized the grog shops, imported cargoes of liquor, and allowed prostitutes to sleep aboard with their crew.

Polynesian input and perspective were needed if the American Board missionaries were to reach the ali'i nui and their people with the Gospel.

Christianity replaced the ancient Tahitian religion in 1815 through the conversion of the Tahitian chief Pomare II. This remarkable shift followed a civil war fought against rivals from the south end of Tahiti Island. In the years leading up to the sailing of the *Thaddeus*, reports from the London Missionary Society on the Christianizing of the Society Islands appeared in the pages of the *Missionary Herald* published in Boston. The South Seas missionary accounts were printed alongside news of the progress of Obookiah and Hopoo studying at the Foreign Mission School.

While the American Board of Commissioners for Foreign Missions and the London Missionary Society traded news of missions and revivals across the Atlantic, each agency retained its own culture and traditions. To avoid conflicts in the Pacific Islands, it was later agreed that Americans send out missions only to stations founded north of the equator in the Pacific Islands, and that the English limit themselves to missions south of the equator.

The mission party upon sailing from Huahine knew little of the work in Hawai'i led by Bingham and Thurston. In 1821 Bingham had hoped to create a working relationship with the Otahiete mission by sailing to Tahiti with Kaumuali'i aboard the Kaua'i chief's schooner. In Tahiti he was to observe and confer with the London Missionary Society's Bible translators, and go on a shopping spree for Ka'ahumanu. Along with mother of pearl crafts, the queen fancied a Tahitian surfboard. Samples collected from the Tahitian mission press were to be used as models in the process of translating Bible scriptures into the Hawaiian language and printed at the Sandwich Islands Mission's press in Honolulu. The plans for a royal voyage to Tahiti came to a sudden halt in the summer of 1821. Liholiho then forced Kaumuali'i into exile in Honolulu, taking him away from Waimea, Kaua'i aboard the royal yacht *Ha'aheo o Hawai'i*. (A son of the wealthy Crowninshield family of Salem, Massachusetts, had built the grand pleasure vessel in 1816 and christened her *Cleopatra's Barge*.)

"At Kou Harbor off Hanarooroo," Ellis wrote, paddlers aboard outrigger canoes pulled tow ropes to warp the *Mermaid* into the inner harbor. Bingham rode offshore in an outrigger canoe to greet Ellis, who proclaimed in Tahitian to Bingham, "He Akua hemolele," (God is good), to which Bingham exclaimed in Hawaiian, "Ke Akua no kaki," (He is our God)." Their greetings became the basis for one of the first hymns composed in the Hawaiian language.

The Sandwich Islands missionaries warmly greeted the Tahitian mission party, but were perplexed over why Ellis and the Tahitians had sailed north to Hawai'i.

The ali'i nui were apprehensive at first over Tahitians landing in Honolulu. They questioned Ellis, repeating rumors passed along by traders and foreigners residing in Hawai'i that accused the English missionaries of undermining the rulers of Tahiti. They had been told the missionaries damaged the Polynesian society of Tahiti through bringing the Bible and instituting Christian laws. Ellis responded:

> Shortly after our arrival, a public council of the king and chiefs of Hawaii had been held at Oahu. Auna and his companion, from Huahine, were invited to attend, and had an opportunity of answering the inquiries of the king and chiefs relative to the events which had transpired in the Society Islands, and of testifying to the feelings of friendship and esteem entertained by Pomare, and the rulers of those islands, much to the satisfaction of the latter; who were convinced that the reports which had been circulated among them respecting the hostile intentions of the southern Islanders, and the dangerous influence of Christian Missions there, were totally groundless. The complete removal of those prejudices which had been excited and nurtured by these means, was one great advantage of our visit.

The Sandwich Islands Mission invited Ellis and the Tahitians to stay as their guests. Auna and his wife Aunawahine joined the household of Kaumuali'i and Ka'ahumanu, whom the Tahitians knew as the "King and Queen of Atoowai (Kaua'i)."

At a formal ceremony staged at the Honolulu waterfront, Captain Kent presented the *Prince Regent* schooner to Liholiho, on May 1. Liholiho responded to the gift by writing a note to King George IV, requesting the king's protection for his kingdom. He noted, "The former idolatrous system has been abolished in these islands, as we wish the Protestant religion of your Majesty's dominions to be practiced here."

To everyone's surprise, Captain Kent announced a plan to sail the *Mermaid* on a trading trip south, a voyage needed to finance the upcoming trip to Nu'uhiwa. A proposal made to him by a Honolulu trader called for a sail to Fanning's Island, nine hundred miles to the south. There laborers would comb the reef to collect *beech de mer*, the sea slug, a delicacy to the Chinese, a cargo sought by merchants in Canton.

This unexpected sailing meant Auna, Ellis and their party would be stranded in Honolulu for weeks, perhaps months, delaying the launch of the mission to Nu'uhiwa.

A scandal erupted when Matatorewahine departed from the mission party, leaving her husband for Captain Kent. In the accounts of Bennet and Ellis there is mention of "unspeakable" and "unbelievable" behavior by the Huahine woman who joined Kent in his cabin aboard the *Mermaid* and sailed with him to Fanning's Island.

With the mission-planting voyage to Nu'uhiwa delayed, Ellis and his party felt stranded and uncertain of their next move. Resolution came through the English missionary's ability to speak Tahitian. This allowed him to preach in the Hawaiian language, a skill much needed by the Sandwich Islands Mission party. Bingham and Thurston still lacked the fluency in the language needed to preach a sermon, let alone translate the Bible into the Hawaiian language.

Life of Auna

The ali'i nui were provided a Polynesian viewpoint on Christianity from the words spoken by Auna, who held a noble Tahitian heritage, and by his wife Aunawahine. The father of Auna, a high chief on Raiatea, an island central to the Polynesian religion throughout the South Pacific, raised Auna as a priest, a relationship similar to the ties of 'Ōpūkaha'ia and his uncle Pahua. Auna was the first Tahitian chief known to convert to Christianity. Auna became a Christian while fighting as a warrior for the Tahitian king Pomare II when the king reconquered Tahiti in 1815 at the battle of Feipi. He attended a mission school in Moorea and in 1818 aided the London Missionary Society in establishing a mission station at Huahine. Like Pili, the Tahitian ali'i nui brought by Pā'ao to Hawai'i to bring chiefly order, Auna, also a Tahitian ali'i nui, arrived at a time of chaos in the spiritual state of Hawai'i following the collapse of the kapu system.

Tall, muscular and handsome, Auna left the Tahitian cult of the Arioi (or Areoi as Bennet spelt the name), to become a Christian. The Arioi wandered from island to island, like a traveling troupe of actors merged with a hula halau school. The brightest and most beautiful young men and women in the Society Islands were chosen as Arioi. Taking on the roll of an Arioi freed them from the toil of the commoners. The Arioi chose to remain childless so as not to hinder their lifestyle and looks, and practiced infanticide when a woman in the troupe bore a child. The arrival of the Arioi merrymakers broke up the routine of island life. Work stopped, allowing for days of feasting and entertainment. The Arioi mocked island rulers as court jesters do, danced, often performing with lewd gestures, partied. A sacrifice to the god 'Oro opened the festivities.

The arrival of the Arioi taxed village resources; the singers and dancers demanded extortionate payments of hogs from the chiefs of villages they wandered into. The arrival of Christianity brought an end to the old ways. By 1822, almost all leading Arioi had converted to Christianity after being inspired to use their talents to spread the Gospel and follow Christian ways.

Sunday Service Tahitian Style

In Honolulu, missionary wife Lucy Thurston observed with wonder a church service run by Society Islands Christians.

During this time Mr. Ellis has from the pulpit, twice a week addressed his little flock of nine Christian Tahitians in their own language. To see the group repairing to the house of God, clustering before the pulpit, all carrying with them their Bible and hymn book, all engaging in the exercise of singing, all looking out the text and the portion of Scripture read, all so much interested in the services in which they were engaged, and with so much apparent devotion–oh! it was a scene most interesting to witness! The heathen looked on and wondered and were convinced that it was missionaries—that it was the Bible that elevated them above a level with themselves.

Ellis accompanied the Tahitian couple at the pulpit in the thatched roof chapel of the missionaries, located makai of today's Kawaiahaʻo Church.

The king and three of his queens, and a great number of people filled the place and crowded around the doors and windows to see and hear what they could. The scene was strange to us, and might have seemed ludicrous, but for the affecting thought that this was an heathen audience to whom an unknown God was about to be declared (to Paul's audience on Mars Hill)....Rihoriho sat upon a chair in the middle of the chapel; the queens reclined on the floor at this feet; and each of these members of the royal family had servants in attendance with fly-flaps and fans of peacock's feathers to cool their faces and drive away the troublesome insects. The king seemed greatly surprised at the singing of our Tahitian friends; the sweetness, compass, and variety of their notes being new and almost marvelous to ears like his, accustomed only to the wretched music, vocal and instrumental, of his country,... To the sermon also he listened with apparently pleased attention; once of twice he smiled, and it was evident that he understood (from the similarity of dialects) the greater part of what was said.

Nothing more attracts the minds, of all ranks of people here, than the appearance, dress and conversation of our Tahitian friends; for all can perceive that, while the latter are of a kindred race with themselves, they are far superior in manners and intelligence. When they are told, therefore, that the gospel, "the good word," has made the difference, they feel a reverence for it, and express a desire to be instructed in it....

...This evening a messenger came from Keaumoku (Keʻeaumoku, brother of Kaʻahumanu), the governor of Maui, to request two of the missionaries to visit him. He had been greatly alarmed by a dream, in which he saw the whole island on fire, and all the water in the surrounding sea could not quench the flames. He had sought for safety, but in vain; he could find no shelter. Awakening in horror, therefore, he grasped at the hope set before him in the gospel. This, Mr. Ellis and Mr. Bingham faithfully unfolded to the dreamer, and to the persons assembled round him. These consisted of a goodly number of chiefs, many of whom were lying on the floor learning to spell or read, and some to write. Thomas Hopoo, the native convert, offered a fervent prayer for the salvation of his countrymen, and Mr. Ellis delivered a suitable discourse on the name of Jesus.

Hopu, seeing Auna treated as a full-fledged missionary, was emboldened and requested a higher status in the Sandwich Islands Mission. Hopu was still only a native assistant and translator for Bingham and the mission party after his years of training at Cornwall. For the mission he had faced the dangers of sailing around Cape Horn, and once home in Hawaiʻi proved loyal to the Sandwich Islands Mission leaders amongst his countrymen.

With the support of Ellis, Hopu requested permission to preach the Gospel. Bennet commented, "We strongly advised our missionary friends to admit him on trial, and send him forth into the villages round about, to instruct the people. He appears to have sound piety, correct views of divine truth, and ardent zeal for the salvation of sinners; at the same time maintaining a consistent walk and conversation."

Plight of Sandalwood Collectors

Ellis and his party observed first-hand the life and struggles of the maka'āinana. During a stop at Kawaihae, on a tour of Hawai'i Island led by Ka'ahumanu, a major source of the wealth of the ali'i nui came into view. A line of 2,000 men, women and children carried on their backs bundles of logs of fragrant *'iliahi* (sandalwood; the Hawaiian word *ahi* references the red color of the sandalwood tree leaves in bloom). Kāhuna used sandalwood as a medicine; kapa makers powdered their cloth with ground sandalwood to hide the smell given off by freshly-pounded *wauke* tree bark.

Ellis noted the porters used shinny, green ti leaves woven into a rope to hold on their backs the sandalwood they had collected in the Kohala hills. For some, delivering their quota of sandalwood took weeks. Deaths of sandalwood collectors were reported from exposure in the chilly mauka highland interior. Others died from exhaustion, crippled on the trail through carrying great weights on their backs.

The collectors measured the loads of sandalwood into cords of 133⅓ pounds. These cords were known by the Chinese term *picul*. The sandalwood logs measured from three to six feet in length. Before hauling, the bark and sap were removed using stone adzes. Sandalwood was used by the ali'i to pay off debts to sea captains, and to ship to Canton to raise money for the Kingdom of Hawai'i treasury. Upon the death of Kamehameha, the king's monopoly on all sandalwood sales ended, and ali'i of each island were allowed to collect and sell the valuable wood. This forced the maka'āinana to go deeper into the forest, and for longer lengths of time. Crops and fishing grounds were neglected and famine broke out in some districts.

Hewahewa

On the North Shore of O'ahu the party encountered Hewahewa, the high priest of Kamehameha's kingdom. He then lived in Waimea Valley, in an ahupua'a dedicated as a refuge for elderly kāhuna. Bennet commented:

(Hewahewa) asked whether Jehovah could understand if they prayed to him in Hawaiian, or whether they must all learn English? When he had received answers which appeared to satisfy him, he said it was maikai (good), and he was ready to receive instruction and to worship Jehovah as soon as Rihoriho should order it.

All seems to hang on the word of the king! The government of these islands is an absolute monarchy; there is no law but the king's will. The king says to the Missionaries and to us, that by and by he will tell his people that they must all learn the good word, and worship Jehovah; but that the Missionaries must teach him first, and themselves get well acquainted with Hawaiian.

Hewahewa had moved away from his home at the Pu'ukoholā Heiau in the years following his abolition of the kapu system at Kamakahonu. This bold move ended the priesthood that ran in his bloodlines through his direct descent from Pā'ao. The Polynesian priest and voyager had brought from Kahiki a god foreign to Hawai'i, a god who sought human sacrifice as worship, and ruled through a system of generally oppressive laws that became ever more complex and controlling.

The Christian Tahitians brought from Kahiki what they termed the "Word of the True God"–the Bible–translated into the Tahitian language. They now followed a faith based upon the sacrifice of the son of the Christian God. They were taught that the sacrifice of this divine person made human was the final sacrifice for all time for all people. No more sacrifices of animals and humans on heiau altars were needed to make their lives pono, nor was the merciless kapu system needed to appease their ancient gods and to guide their lives. Now those who believed and confessed their sins to the true God were pono. And mercy and grace was found in the printed book the Tahitians brought with them from Kahiki, the Bible written in the Tahitian language.

Brother Moe Bridges the Gap

Back in Honolulu, Aunawahine stared down in amazement from her ship. She had spotted Moe, a Tahitian who immigrated to Hawai'i in the early 1790s. Known in Hawai'i as Jack, in 1789 Moe sailed as a boy with the mutineers aboard the HMS *Bounty*. Aboard the *Bounty*, the prayers and hymn singing of the rebellious crew led him in becoming a Christian, a belief he carried with him to Hawai'i.

Jack turned out to be her long-lost brother, absent from Tahiti for thirty years, presumed dead or gone forever. Bennet detailed in his report the reunion of Moe and Aunawahine, and how that relationship swung the favor and personal interest of the ali'i nui towards the Sandwich Islands Mission. This providential moment in time turned the tide for the acceptance of Christianity in Hawai'i.

> Her (Ka'ahumanu) principal officer is a native of Tahiti, who, when we first landed, finding that our companions were from his country, entered into eager questioning-conversations with them, when, to the surprise and delight of all, he discovered that Auna's wife was his own sister, from whom he had been separated when a child, and brought hither, where he had resided many years without ever having had any intercourse with his family. He immediately introduced them to his royal mistress, who insisted on their taking up their abode with her. To this they consented one express condition that they should be allowed to have family prayer under the roof, morning and evening, and in every other respect be allowed to deport themselves as Christians. Kaahumanu graciously complied; and now she is so charmed with her visitors, that she may be said to employ herself all day long in making inquiries (of Auna's wife especially) respecting the South Sea islands, their new religions, politics, manners, dress and occupations, all of which she finds have been so wonderfully changed since "the good word" came to them. Auna spends most of his time with the king, who makes similar inquiries; and, from this admirable and intelligent convert to the gospel, Rihoriho will learn more readily and effectually what has been done among his countrymen, than any foreign missionary could in a much longer time communicate.

Soon William Ellis and the Tahitian Christians were warmly invited by the ali'i nui to stay in Hawai'i. The Sandwich Island Mission voted unanimously to seek their help, recognizing the benefits of Ellis' grasp of the Polynesian languages.

Your missionaries were laboring under great difficulties in acquiring the language of this people—difficulties which, we perceived, would not be surmounted for a considerable period. Mr. Ellis being intimately acquainted with the Tahitian language, which is radially the same with this, we were convinced that he would render essential service to your missionaries in this particular, and thus accelerate the period when they will be able to declare to these islanders, in their own tongue, the wonderful works of God—which is essential to their extensive usefulness....

Tahitian Hymns

The beautiful Hawaiian language hymn singing tradition was birthed through this Tahitian connection. Bingham noted that by early August "hymns prepared by Mr. Ellis were introduced into public worship with manifest advantage."

William Ellis composed the first four hymns written in the Hawaiian language, writing verses based on the Tahitian language version of the hymns. The Tahitians entranced the ali'i nui with their singing in harmony. Bennet noted:

The king seemed greatly surprised at the singing of our Tahitian friends; the sweetness, compass, and variety of their notes being new and almost marvelous to ears... You will hardly be able to conceive the delight we had in hearing these people for the first time uniting to sing the praises of Jehovah in their own tongue! A scene of great usefulness appears to be opening here. One, indeed, of greater interest and importance than that which is presented by the Sandwich Islands could scarcely be found.

The early Hawaiian hymns were printed by the Mission Press in a slim book titled *Na Himeni Hawaii* (*The Hymns of Hawai'i*). The hymns were kept short and simple on purpose, and not given titles except for noting the passage in the Bible they were based upon.

Auna's Journal

In mid-May, Ka'ahumanu and Kaumuali'i invited Auna and Aunawahine to join them on a tax collecting tour around the coasts of Maui and Hawai'i Island. Gifts were presented to the royalty, a practice known as *ho'okupu*, including abundant supplies of foods like taro, and crafts like woven *lau hala* mats.

Auna kept a journal of the trip, written in the Tahitian language, which Bennet later translated. Being fellow Polynesians eased the acceptance of Auna and Aunawahine among the ali'i rulers of the various ahupua'a visited during the tour. The chain of visits kept to no set schedule. The western ways of the New England and English missionaries followed a schedule based on the tick-tock of their Connecticut clocks, to a delineated time schedule. The Polynesian way of Hawai'i, and of their new Tahitian friends, let the natural timing of an event dictate when it might start and end. This trait bucked at times against the plans of the Sandwich Islands Mission. Bennet kept a diary of daily events on tour:

May 12—At Lahaina. A Sunday. A great many chiefs and people gather to greet the ship of Taumualii and Kaahumanu, with Keeaumoku into his house. Read a portion of Gospel of Matthew in Tahitian, prayed for their salvation. After meeting sat down under shade of a large kou tree, with many gathered around them, and taught them letters from Hawaiian spelling book.

May 17—wrote letters for Ellis to take back to Huahine, and boarded ship to sail to Hawaii Island.

May 28—Anchored off Hilo. Went ashore with Kaahumanu. Went into a small house owned by Liholiho for family worship. Singing, dancing to the beating of the huru (*pahu*-drum) till midnight.

June 1—(Lord's Day) We had public worship in Opiia's house, who, with her husband and family, attended. But so great was the disturbance with the companies of dancers, singing, and the beating upon the huru, that we could only have one service.

June 3—The people of the land brought many presents to Taumualii and Kaahumanu. There were twelve baked dogs, five hundred and ninety pieces of cloth, thirty-five calabashes of poi, and two large canoes.

June 4—Kaahumanu having commanded some of her people to go for the idol of Tamehameha, namely, Teraipahoa (the much-feared poison god), it was brought to-day, with nine smaller idols, and they were all publicly burnt.

June 19—At Kairua (Kailua), the residence of Kaakini (Kuakini), nephew of Kaahumanu, the chiefs brought us two hundred and twenty-nine fishes, twenty dogs, three calabashes of poi, and forty pieces of cloth...afterwards a grand huru (hula). Thirty-three men played on sticks, there were twenty-five dancers, and five great drums were beaten all the while.

June 20—...The feasting continued...Forty-one men danced in four rows; behind them were thirty-one musicians beating time on sticks, besides five great drums. The people drank very much of an intoxicating liquor made from the juice of sugar-cane. They often brought us some, and entreated us to taste, but we always refused, saying—Once we were as fond of it as your are, but now we know it to be a bad thing, and therefore do not wish to drink it, and we advise you to let it alone also....

June 23—Lord's Day, The chiefs were all gone to sport in the surf (surfing and swimming) this morning. At noon they returned, and then we had public worship. I read a chapter in one of the Gospels, and afterwards prayed with them. Aore, Kuakini, and several others, attended. Many more came to our family worship in the evening.

June 24—In the morning Miomio, a man belonging to the queen, was sent on board of the vessels to fetch eight of the idols which had been brought from the other side of the island, and were intended to have been carried to the king at Oahu. The reason why they sent for them now was–the man who had been left on board to take care of the goods, was seized with illness in the night, and removed from the ship to the shore. The chiefs immediately said, "It is the spirits of the idols which are trying to kill the man; let us therefore, send for them and burn them." In the afternoon the messenger returned with Teraipahoa, Tetonemotu, Paparahaamau, Hatuahia, Kauanruura, Maiora, and Akuahanai. These were all soon after devoured by the fire, at which my heart rejoiced.

June 26—Early this morning Kaakini's men, who had been sent on board of all the vessels to search for idols, returned. The chief man then ordered his people to make a large fire, and he himself set to work to help them. So he and his people burnt one hundred and two idols on the spot. Then I thought of what I had witnessed in Tahiti and Moorea, when our idols were thrown into the flames, particularly those that were consumed at Papetoai and Patii; and with my heart I praised Jehovah, the true God, that I now saw these people following our example. Taumualii and Kaahumanu talked a great deal with me this day about our destruction of the idols at Tahiti, and seemed very glad indeed that they had burnt theirs, though not all yet, for the people, they said, had hid some among the rocks.

Tahitian Reinforcements

By August, it was clear the Tahitian missionaries Auna and Aunawahine should stay in Hawai'i as aides to the Sandwich Islands Mission, and as companions of Ka'ahumanu and Kaumuali'i. The ali'i nui encouraged Ellis to go back to Tahiti, but to return accompanied by his wife and children. The ali'i nui and the Sandwich Islands Mission extended an invitation for Ellis to assist in Bible translating and helping the New England missionaries in mastering the Hawaiian language. Ellis replied:

> The chiefs prohibited their people from working on the Lord's day; and Keeaumoku, Karaimoku, Kauikeouli, the young prince, Kaahumanu, Taumuarill, Piia, Naihe, and almost every chief of rank and influence, were numbered among our pupils, or regular worshippers of the true God. Astonished and gratified by the wonderful change we had been permitted to witness during the period of our detention, and having received every expression of attachment, and desire for our return, from the Missionaries and chiefs...

Ellis was entrusted with a packet of friendly letters from the rulers of Hawai'i addressed to the Christian rulers of the Society Islands.

During this time–on Sunday, August 11–Hopu married his love Delia in the first Christian wedding performed for a Native Hawaiian couple in Hawai'i:

> A peculiarly interesting day. Mr. Ellis preached in the morning to a very full house, the king and queen being present. At the opening of the service, the marriage of Thomas Hopu to Delia...was publicly solemnized, the ceremony being conducted in the Hawaiian language. Agreeably to the practice in the Society Islands, the parties subscribed their names to the following note, in a blank book, provided for the purpose, together with the witnesses as follows: 'Married by the Rev. H. Bingham, Aug. 11, 1822. THOMAS HOPOO, Witness, DELIA.'...this is, doubtless, the first marriage ever celebrated in these islands agreeably to the customs of Christians...Mr. Ellis prayed (in the Hawaiian language).

Auna and Aunawahine sailed for Kaua'i and Ni'ihau with Kaumuali'i and Ka'ahumanu on August 13 aboard the *Ha'aheo o Hawai'i*. Joining them were Kalanimōkū, and Ke'eaumoku, "and their retinue of chiefs and servants, consisting of nearly twelve-hundred persons." In a joint letter, missionaries Samuel Ruggles, Samuel Whitney and Daniel Chamberlain wrote of the royal visit to Waimea, Kaua'i:

> On the 14th of Aug. Taumuarii and his new wife Kaahumanu, with several of the windward chiefs, came to this Island. We were happily surprised to see them all anxious to learn to read, and as everything passes for good which is practised by the chiefs, the desire to learn quickly spread through the common people in every direction....Auna and his wife, natives of the Society Isles, of whom you have doubtless heard, are valuable helpers. Their knowledge of the language gives them an access to the hearts of the people, which in a measure, is yet denied us.

On August 22 Ellis, Bennet and Tyreman sailed with Captain Kent aboard the *Mermaid* for the Society Islands.

On the sail home she died in her cabin in dishonor, according to an account in the English missionary press.

The Rev. Artemis Bishop arrived from New Haven in 1822 with the second missionary party, aboard the whaling ship *Thames*. Bishop confirmed the breakthrough for the Sandwich Island Mission brought about by Ellis' connection with the ali'i nui and commoners.

> His intimate knowledge of the Tahitian dialect enabled him, after a few weeks' residence, to preach in Hawaiian to the chiefs and people. He entered at once into the missionary work, preaching almost daily, assisting the stammering American brethren, new in the field, to settle the Hawaiian alphabet, to study the language, and to compose a few hymns for the use of public worship. He so interested the king and chiefs by his winning manner towards them, that they invited him to come with his family and reside here.

Auna, inspired by Hiram Bingham, began leading Tahitian-Hawaiian Concerts of Prayers in Honolulu. A report in the mission journal told of a Concert held on Monday, Feb. 3, 1823 inside the Sandwich Islands Mission's thatched church:

> At four a meeting with the natives in our place of worship. Not less than 200 attended. Two prayers were offered, the first by John Honoru, and the last by Auna, the Tahitian chief with much ability and fervency. Between the prayers, Mr. B. addressed the people on the design of the meeting. They were told that the good people of England and of America, and of other lands were praying to the great Jehovah for them, that He would open their ears to hear and give them hearts to love and obey the Gospel; and that He would send his ministers, with his holy word, to all the dark places of the earth, that the whole world might be filled with the knowledge and glory of his name.

In his book *Memoirs of Keopuolani*, Second Company missionary William Richards wrote of the effect of the Tahitian Christians on the ali'i nui: "The natural consequence was a great increase of confidence, on the part of the rulers of the islands, in the American missionaries." Richards' brother James took part in the Haystack Meeting with Samuel Mills and later sailed to Ceylon as an American Board missionary.

Bennet perceived a providential side to the stranding of the London Missionary Society group in Hawai'i.

> We left these shores, where a new era has assuredly commenced, with feelings very much exalted above those which had sunk our hearts on our first arrival, when we beheld their inhabitants wholly given up to the power of darkness....
>
> To ourselves, now, the reasons began to be manifested why we had been providentially diverted from our course to the Marquesas, brought hither, as it were by mischance, and detained here, contrary to our will, by perverse circumstances, which had grievously disconcerted us, though, being of a private nature.

As a reinforcement to Auna and Aunawahine, the Tahitian Christians Tau'ā and Tau'āwahine sailed with William Ellis when the English missionary returned to Hawai'i in 1823. Ellis was joined by his ailing wife and three Tahiti-raised children.

Stephen Popohe, a Tahitian who studied at the Foreign Mission School in Cornwall, also arrived in 1823 with the Second Company aboard the whaling ship *Thames*, departing from New Haven in November, 1822.

Tau'ā became a teacher and companion of Keōpūolani (the Gathering of the Clouds of Heaven), the sacred wife of Kamehameha, his wife who possessed a rank of mana far above the other rulers of Hawai'i. She was the mother of his heirs to power, Liholiho (Kamehameha II) and Kauikeaouli (Kamehameha III).

Keōpūolani took a leading role in the overthrow of the kapu system. She ate out in the open foods forbidden to women ('Ai Noa, "free eating") with Liholiho and Ka'ahumanu at Kamehameha's 'Ahuena Heiau complex at Kailua. Practicing human sacrifice at the heiau ended, and the ki'i images of wood and stone ordered destroyed. Many of the kapu laws giving power to the ali'i nui and kāhuna were abolished, gone forever, freeing the maka'āinana in many ways. Overall, this brought about the end of the ancient Polynesian religion brought to Hawai'i by the Tahitian priest Pā'ao.

The site of the 'Ai Noa ceremony is located on the grounds of the King Kamehameha hotel located at 'Ahuena on the Kailua-Kona waterfront.

Keōpūolani and Loyal Tau'ā

"The person of Keōpūolani had ever been counted particularly sacred," Richards wrote of this queen to whom he became a close friend at the Lāhaina mission station. "At certain seasons no persons must see her. In early life, she never walked abroad except at evening, and all who saw her walking at that hour, prostrated themselves to the earth."

Following the death of Kamehameha, Keōpūolani became the wife of Hoapili. In February 1823 the couple sought a personal teacher of the palapala (the written word; the Bible and Christian materials translated into the Hawaiian language). They requested that Tau'ā and his wife become their companions.

Keōpūolani suffered from a lingering disease. A relapse of the illness brought fears she would die. The queen sent for Tau'ā. He faced opposition from ali'i in her court who wanted him kept away from her death bed due to his Christian beliefs. William Richards described the incident:

When about to enter, some of the chiefs stopped him at the door, and told him he must not go in, for there was no room. They then went to Keopuolani, and told her it would not be well to admit him, for he was a bad man, and would tell her many lies. She said,"My teacher is not bad; he tells me no lies;—let him come in, for I greatly desire to see him." They replied. "The house is full, there is no room." She said, "Then you must make room." They said, "What do you want of this Tahitian?" She answered, "He is my good Christian teacher, and now while I am sick, I desire that he may come and speak to me, and pray with me." They said again, "The house is full, he cannot come in." She said to them, "Why do you say there is no room? There is room enough. I have done praying to my old gods, to stones and wood, and my desire now is, that while I lie here, my Christian teacher should come and pray with me to Jesus Christ."

Much conversation followed, during which some of the people, encouraged by a few of the chiefs, threatened Taua's life. But he still remained at the door, with the Gospels in his hand.

At length Keopuolani said, "Taua come into the house and pray with me." Some of the chiefs were still intent on stopping him, when the king approached saying, "Let him go in, and let all the chiefs and people be perfectly quiet while the good teacher of my mother prays to Jehovah."

Opposition to Keōpūolani's acceptance of Christianity continued:

So decided was her stand in favor of Christianity, that she thereby incurred the displeasure of many of the people, and of some of the chiefs. But their opposition, instead of driving her from the ground she had taken, only gave her an opportunity of showing more fully the firmness of her principles, and the strength of her attachment to the Christian cause.

On September 16, 1823 As Keōpūolani lay on her death bed Tauʻā witnessed her baptism by a sprinkling of water, the first baptism given in Hawaiʻi by the Sandwich Islands Mission.

In her first interview with Karaimoku, after he came to Lahaina, she said, "Great is my love to the word of God, by which I hope my mind has been enlightened. The word of God is a true word, a good word. Jehovah is a good God. I love him, and love Jesus Christ. I have no desire for the former gods of Hawaii. They are all false. But I love Jesus Christ. I have given myself to him to be his. When I die, let none of the evil customs of this country be practised at my death. Let not my body be disturbed. Let not my bones be separated and the flesh taken off, as in the days of dark hearts: but let my body be put in a coffin. Let the teachers attend and speak to the people at my interment. Let me be buried in the ground and let my burial be after the manner of Christ's people. I think very much of my grandfather Taraniopu, my father Kauikeaouli. My husband Tamehameha, and all my deceased relations. They lived not to see these good times, and to hear of Jesus Christ. They died without knowing Jehovah the true God. They died depending on false gods. I exceedingly mourn and lament on account of them, for they saw not these good times."

CHAPTER TWENTY-ONE
POSTSCRIPT

New Haven - August 21, 1824

"WELCOME LAFAYETTE" READ THE CANVAS BANNER strung above the entrance to Morse's, the grandest hotel in New Haven.

In advance of the fiftieth anniversary of the American colonies entering war with England, President James Monroe invited the Revolutionary War hero Marquis de Lafayette to return from France for a grand tour of the United States. Though near seventy years of age, impeccably-dressed Lafayette stood tall. The European-elegant nobleman ranked high in the pantheon of patriot heroes who rose to acclaim during the War.

Though a foreigner, the French royal remained cherished by Americans as a wartime compatriot of Washington, as a patriot; as the man who made the difference in turning the tide against the British ending years of conflict and giving freedom to the former colonies.

Now Lafayette served America once more. Monroe invited the much-loved Frenchman to sail across the Atlantic to again stir up patriotism.

Entering the Elm City about 10 a.m. the French general rode with his son George Washington Lafayette, sitting vis-à-vis in an open-air barouche carriage pulled by a team of prize horses. With waves and nods all around, Lafayette halted his entourage of mounted troops nearby Morse's. He threw a salute to a section of seats along Church Street reserved for the surviving Revolutionary War veterans of New Haven. Several of the men he recognized despite their aged faces. Full of joy, Lafayette embraced them, astounded to find still alive the companions in arms he encamped with in New Haven almost a lifetime earlier.

Intertwined French and American flags hung from the front windows of the Morse hotel. A parade review of New Haven's Iron Grays and Foot Guard military corps marched down Church Street, followed by a procession of Yale College scholars.

With the pageantry over, the general stepped down from his elegant carriage. Escorts opened a path through the crowd. He entered the grand hotel, heading for a ballroom set for a late breakfast with silver and crystal atop white linen tablecloths, a breakfast to be shared with one-hundred of the prominent men of New Haven.

Caleb Brintnall ranked among these New Haven dignitaries. He had earned and banked a China trade "old money" fortune. In 1824 Brintnall's name was golden in New Haven for his past heroics and fortune-making as New Haven's premiere sealing captain. Now his interests were in banking, investing and local politics; he had found a new life away from the sea in the Land of Steady Habits.

The final voyage undertaken by Captain Brintnall ended at Providence in 1821. The venture proved to be a lucrative one, one that took him and his crew to Peru. The death of Kamehameha in 1819 stalled his quest to be paid in full in sandalwood for his year of patrolling Hawaiian waters. He kept trying to collect through diplomatic and commercial channels, and through his sea-going son Charles.

At Providence, Brintnall auctioned off his prize possession, the sleek black-hulled *Zephyr*. Back in New Haven he remarried, to Content Mix, the younger sister of his late wife Lois. Content was the widow of ship master Francis Bulkeley Jr., who she married in 1811. Bulkeley died at sea in 1817, age 29, off Cape Trafalgar in southwest Spain aboard the American brig *Regent*.

After breakfast the Marquis de Lafayette and his entourage toured Yale College. By late afternoon they were on the road to Boston.

Across the street from the Morse Hotel a wax museum gallery opened under the banner Storer & Moulthrop. The gallery's name promoted its ties to the renowned New Haven self-taught portrait painter and bees-wax sculptor Reuben Moulthrop. He exhibited his traveling waxworks museum in cities and towns, even in the West Indies. Moutlhrop died in 1814, likely of typhus complications.

In Federal Era America the lure of the wax museum (a Storer & Moulthrop ticket cost twenty-five cents, half-price for children) offered the rare sensation of placing viewers in the presence of life-size images of famous historic figures. The life-like poses of the wax figures served as key elements in a tableau of a historical scene, often staged as a morality lesson. An air of eeriness emitted from the skeletal and musculature details done up in wax and detailed with oil paints. Exhibitors garbed the figures in authentic costumes tailored to fit the era of the character. To such a figure, a carefully crafted wax head and hands, glass eyes and human-hair wig added realism.

Stepping inside the Storer & Moulthrop gallery in 1824, the curious were greeted by kilted Scotsman William Wallace, posed fighting for independence from England in 1300. There Baptist Missionary Society Bible translator to India William Carey stood stiffly in a Subcontinent scene. Deer-skin-clad Pocahontas knelt at Jamestown pleading with her father for the life of Captain John Smith. Voltaire lay dying in his Paris bed, portrayed as an "infidel in agonies of death."

The morning of the *fete* for Lafayette, Caleb Brintnall might have lingered afterwards, crossing at the corner of Church and Crown streets to pay a visit to Storer & Moulthrop's. For in the gallery–in wax and wool and linen–lay Obookiah on his death bed. Here was an effigy of the young kanaka sailor the captain recruited at Kealakekua Bay in 1808 and brought home; the young heathen scholar grown into a Second Great Awakening celebrity at Litchfield; and here the pious saint dying in hope in a mock-up of the Stones' bedroom at Cornwall, a smile on his face. Alongside Obookiah, also in brown-skin wax, stood his sidekick, Hopoo, comforting his best friend, loyal to the end.

A Storer & Moulthrop advertisement highlighted the attraction of this New Haven-related addition to the collection of worldwide-known historical personages.

Henry Obookiah, the Owhyhean youth, who died at the Foreign Mission School, Cornwall Ct. represented as peacefully resigning his breath into the hands of the Savior he had so confidentially trusted for salvation–Thomas Hooppo his countryman and fellow-student, weeping at his bedside.

Kealakekua Bay, Hawai'i Island - June 13, 1824

Elijah Loomis, the young man sent as the Sandwich Islands Mission printer, accompanied by his wife Maria Sartwell Loomis aboard the *Thaddeus*, paid a visit to Pahua, the uncle of 'Ōpūkaha'ia during a mission trip from Honolulu to Hawai'i Island. Elijah's reading of the *Memoirs of Henry Obookiah* at his home in New York State inspired him to enroll at the Foreign Mission School in Cornwall to prepare for his work in Hawai'i. Months earlier in 1824, Chiefs Kapi'olani, Naihe and Kamakau sponsored the building of a thatched church at the village of Ka'awaloa, near the entrance to Kealakekua Bay where Captain Cook was killed atop a lava rock outcrop. The Rev. Asa Thurston traveled from Kona to dedicate the church in March, 1824. Elijah's description of his visit to Kealakekua Bay appeared in the *Missionary Herald*, in the September, 1825 issue.

Mr. Ely (the minister of the Ka'awaloa Church) preached twice in the native language. The congregation was numerous. After the morning service I crossed the bay in a canoe, with Thos. Hopu and collected about 70 persons to whom we each made an address. We also sung and prayed with them....I went with Thomas to see the place where Opukahaia formerly dwelt. As we approached the house, Thomas pointed out to me a number of coconut trees which were planted by Opukahaia. On entering the house, I was introduced to the uncle of Opukahaia, who now resides on the premises (only a few rods distant from the Heiau). He was formerly a priest and the remains of the Heiau where he and Opukahaia worshipped are still visible. I was introduced to him as a friend of Obookiah. When informed that we had held a religious meeting, he seemed to regret very much that he had not known it in season to attend.

We conversed with him respecting the true God, the immortality of the soul and the necessity of repentance. On all these subjects, I found he had previously been instructed by Thomas Hopu, but he appeared much interested in what we now said....He related several remarkable dreams which he had had of late, in which Opukahaia appeared to him and told him if he would be happy here-after he must attend to the instructions of the Missionaries and pray to Jehovah.

As he designed to visit Oahu soon, I gave him an invitation to call at our house. I would not but be interested in what I had seen and heard. This thought I, is the spot where Opukahaia dwelt. Here is the man who instructed devils, but from this Opukahaia was led by an unseen hand to a foreign land where first the light of Science and religion were opened to his view. In that Christian land, he became acquainted with Him of whom Moses and the Prophets did write and his whole soul, as it were, is drawn out in love and gratitude. He longs for an opportunity to return and make known the blessings of the gospel to his benighted countrymen. But such is not the will of God. Opukahaia is seized by the messenger of death and departs to the unseen world, resigned indeed to the will of his Saviour but with his latest breath imploring salvation for his countrymen. Happy Opukahaia! Though thou wast not permitted to preach to the people of Hawaii, yet thou hast preached to multitudes in Christian lands and thou hast been a means of gathering this Mission by whose instrumentality thy countrymen have proclaimed unto them the gospel of Jesus Christ.

Letter from Artemas Bishop, Kairu, Nov. 30th 1826 -
"Visit of Kaahumanu to Hawaii"

American Board of Commissioners' missionary Rev. Artemas Bishop accompanied Queen Kaʻahumanu on a visit to the abandoned Puʻukoholā Heiau at Kawaihae.
Kaʻahumanu then dwelt away from her former home in Kailua where she had once lived
with her late husband Kamehameha. Several years earlier Kaʻahumanu began her study of
Bible scriptures, learning to read and write the palapala, the written word. The influences
that led her to faith in Christ included the legacy of ʻŌpūkahaʻia that drew the American
missionaries to Hawaiʻi, by the Christian teachings brought by the Sandwich Islands Mission parties, by the Polynesian form of Christianity introduced to Hawaiʻi by Auna and
Aunawahine and other Tahitian Christians, and by the spirit of Kamehameha's high priest
Hewahewa who prophesied of the coming to the Islands of a new faith. Kaʻahumanu and
her prime minister Kalanimoku turned to Christian prayer in times of conflict. Kalanimoku, serving as a general in a battle against Humehume and his Kauaʻi warriors, in 1824
led his troops in Christian prayer for the first time prior to attacking.

Belief in the ancient Polynesian religion brought to Hawaiʻi by the high priest
Pāʻao still remained among some of Hawaiʻi's people. Wooden and stone kiʻi images
were hidden away and the beliefs of old went underground. Some people took part
in Christian services and Bible teachings while holding onto beliefs in Hawaiian
gods and pre-ʻAi Noa practices.

The Queen attended church services and sought to rule her kingdom according to Christian principles, influenced by Christians from New England, Tahiti and
Great Britain. The queen had taken on the biblical name Elizabeth.

A year earlier the body of Liholiho arrived back in Hawaiʻi accompanied by Lord
Bryon aboard the British frigate HBM *Blonde*; the young king had succumbed in
London to a bout of measles during his royal tour of England. On his death bed
Liholiho, knowing he was dying, said, "This is my death in the time of my youth;
great love to my country." During his reign of just over five years, the ancient Hawaiian religion, embodied in the kapu system, collapsed and had begun to be replaced
by Christianity. Word of Liholiho's death reached Honolulu in March 1825. It was
feared news of his untimely passing would bring chaos among the people of Hawaiʻi;
now a return to the reckless mourning that followed the death of aliʻi nui of the
past could now bring foreign intervention. To ward this threat off, Kaʻahumanu and
Kalanimoku concurred on holding a memorial service in the thatched missionary
church in Honolulu. Kalanimoku proclaimed twelve days of contrite prayer "offered
to God morning and evening, that he might pardon and save the nation."

Kaʻahumanu now controlled the Kingdom of Hawaiʻi. Kamehameha III, Kauikeaouli, was just an adolescent upon attaining the throne in 1825.

Artemas Bishop sailed from New Haven in 1822 with the Second Company
of missionaries to Hawaiʻi, aboard the whaleship *Thames*. Bishop's letter describing
Kaʻahumanu's tour of Puʻukoholā in late 1826 appeared in the *Missionary Herald*.

She... made an excursion... along the western shore to Kohala, in which I accompanied her.... the people every where giving their queen the most cordial reception; but nothing extravagant or improper was witnessed. The first thing was to
assemble them in the school ranai to give them an address.... The principal object

of Kaahumanu, was to enforce the observance of the decalogue, and to recommend a regard to the precepts and doctrines of Christianity. In addition to this she enumerated all their heathenish practices, as well as their vices contracted by an intercourse with foreigners, and in the most earnest manner forbad the practice of any of them. Almost every object, as we passed from place to place, called tender and melancholy recollections of former scenes to her mind. Her reflections upon these were truly affecting, and evinced the liveliest exercise of religious feeling. At one place, a battle had been fought; another, was once beautiful and populous, but now it was desolate, and without inhabitants. She corroborated a fact, of which we have long been convinced, that the present population of this island has diminished at least three-fourths, since Capt. Cook first landed here.

When we arrived at Towaihae, she ordered the canoe to put ashore about twenty rods this side of the usual landing place. It was the place of her husband's former residence. The walls of his house were standing, while every thing within and without was going to decay. She took a melancholy satisfaction in contemplating these ruins, and in pointing out to me the very places where Tamehameha used to sit, and where he slept. Directing my attention to the crumbling walls of a large heiau, on an eminence, she said, "There is the spot where my husband used to worship his gods, and where many a human victim has been sacrificed. Let us ascend and see the place." "But," said I, "did you never go there?" "No," she replied, "it would have been death for any woman to approach its sacred precincts." So we ascended together, and when we had reached the top, and had taken a full view of the whole place she stopped short lifted up her hands, and looking upwards, said, "I thank God for what my eyes now see; *ua pau ke kii i Hawaii nei*—Hawai'i's gods are no more." She then showed me holes in the wall, where the carved images of Tamehameha's gods once stood, and gave me their several names as we passed along. She then pointed out the altar where human and other sacrifices were offered. We looked for the human bones, that were formerly strewn about; but to the honor of the people residing here, we learned, that they all had been buried. She also described the dimensions of the buildings, which formerly stood in this immense enclosure, and added,—"But they were all destroyed in one day."

Christian R. Cook photos

The Memorial Arch and 'Ōpūkaha'ia plaque dedicated at the Mokuaikaua Church in Kailua-Kona in 1910.

Appendix

Centennial Cross Memorial at Bradford, Mass., placed by the American Board of Commissioners for Foreign Missions in 1910 to mark the centenniel of its founding in that town as requested by the Brethren.

ANTI-SLAVERY CONNECTION

Library of Congress

Josiah Wedgwood of Wedgwood China fame placed the slogan of the Society for the Abolition of Slavery in England – "Am I Not A Man And A Brother" – on medallions he created. Wedgwood designed and manufactured porcelain broaches of the seal. Funds raised went to support the anti-slavery cause in Great Britain. In the abolitionist era of antebellum New England the seal was frequently reprinted on anti-slavery broadsides.

THE LASTING LEGACY OF OBOOKIAH AND HOPOO in New England went beyond the sending of the Sandwich Islands Mission to Hawai'i.

Henry and Thomas met and influenced the lives of key young sons and daughters from New England, Yankee children and teenagers who later in life played leading roles in abolishing slavery in the United States.

In the 1810s, federal and state laws still permitted the owning of slaves in Connecticut. People of color–African-American, Polynesians, Native American, Asian–ranked low in the white society of New England.

But Henry and Thomas were able to breach this cultural barrier through their Hawaiian aloha, wit and wisdom combined with their providential connection to Captain Brintnall and prominent evangelical Christians in New England. As Polynesian sailors landed in New England, Obookiah and Hopoo roamed freely, sailors from exotic islands, curiosities to the general populace. How different their reception would have been if brought to America in chains aboard a Middle Passage slave ship out of a West African slave-trading port.

The arrival of Henry and Hopoo in New Haven in September, 1809 came eighteen months after a federal act went into effect banning the importation of African slaves to the United States.

In 1810, there were around 300 freed blacks residing in New Haven. Many of the blacks were drawn from the countryside to the city lured by wage-paying, non-farming jobs, mostly working in the trades. Though usually not well paid, the New Haven blacks earned enough to live in their own homes and neighborhoods. They lacked this sense of community when in the countryside on farms where they received temporary quarters, and dwelt in field hand or domestic servant housing, just one step up from slavery.

The urban freedom available in New Haven drew escaped slaves and freed blacks from the South. Black sailors, including the cook aboard the *Triumph*, made a good living as crew aboard coasting ships and in the West Indies trade.

If Obookiah and Hopoo landed at the Long Wharf in New Haven unaccompanied, they might have been seated in segregated, walled-off balconies in Congregational churches. They could attend the service, but not be seen by the white congregation. Fortunately in New Haven, Caleb Brintnall and his family insisted that Obookiah join their family in a prominent pew of the Brick Church, a church home to the elite of New Haven society.

Yale President Timothy Dwight, the leader of the evangelical church in Connecticut, and grandson of Calvinist theologian Jonathan Edwards, wrote a prejudiced view of the African-Americans in New Haven. In his *Statistical Account of the City of New-Haven*, published in 1811, Dwight opined:

> Uneducated to principles of morality, or to habits of industry and economy, they labour only to acquire the means of expense, and expend, only to gratify gross and vulgar appetite. Accordingly, many of them are thieves, liars, profane, drunkards, sabbath-breakers, quarrelsome, idle, and prodigal, the last in the extreme. Their ruling passion seems very generally to be a desire of being fashionable. Their ambition in dressing is not so much to be dressed richly, gaily, or splendidly as to be dressed fashionably....There are, however, exceptions to this character; and a greater number among the females, than among the males. Almost all, who acquire an attachment to property, appear to assume better principles; or, at least, better practices. Several of the men have in this manner become good members of society. A number of the females are well behaved.

A Providential Berth

Unlike many of the dozens of sailors from Hawai'i and the South Pacific then roaming in New England, Obookiah and Hopoo chanced to be picked up in Hawai'i by a Christian sea captain. This providential hiring led them beyond the docks and wharves once in the United States. They were welcomed into a genteel Christian society, hosted in the homes of prominent citizens in New Haven.

Thanks to this Christian connection, Obookiah and Hopoo avoided dwelling in the rowdy quarters of port towns where most Polynesian sailors landed. The Pacific Islands sailors usually congregated in seafaring taverns, rooming in cheap lodgings until finding a berth on an outgoing ship. Their lot was pictured by Herman Melville in his novel *Moby Dick*; his protagonist Ishmael, a New England sailor, rooms with Queequeg, the heavily-tattooed son of a South Seas chief.

Overcoming Stereotypes

Despite the advantages of their New Haven connections, as people of color Obookiah and Hopoo surely at times faced prejudice in Connecticut. Within Obookiah's home church at Torringford, in missions-supporting Litchfield County, some of the congregation were upset with Father Mills when he seated Obookiah

CONNECTICUT.   349

1756	{ 128,218 whites 3,587 blacks }	131,805		1790	{ 232,374 whites 2,764 slaves 2,808 free bl. }	237,946
1762	{ 141,076 whites 4,590 blacks }	145,666			{ 244,721 whites	
1774	{ 191,392 whites 6,464 blacks }	197,856		1800	951 slaves 5,330 free bl. }	251,002
1782	{ 202,597 whites 6,273 blacks }	208,870		1810	{ 255,179 whites 310 slaves 6,453 free bl. }	261,942

A Compendious and Complete System of Modern Geography
Connecticut's population included slaves in this 1756-1810 compilation by Jedidiah Morse.

---

with the Mills family in their front row pew. At the Morris Academy, a deacon of the local church criticized James Morris for allowing brown-skinned students, such as Obookiah and his 'ohana, to attend church services.

Samuel Mills feared Obookiah would be mistaken as a slave in New Haven. He asked Yale President Dwight to release Henry from his employment as a servant in Dwight's home, a student job that allowed Henry to continue his tutoring by Yale students. Mills persuaded Henry to move away from the city, to the rural, lightly-populated farming village of Torringford.

Edwin Dwight commented on how Obookiah helped reform the then-common stereotypes of people of color in Connecticut. Henry shattered the viewpoint that there were limits on their intelligence and ability to be educated. He proved the "heathen" were as much children of God as any New England-er. Church-by-church he opened eyes while on his American Board-promoting preaching tours in 1816-1817. Edwin wrote:

> Obookiah's visit to this part of the country was essential service to the cause of Foreign Missions. It has silenced the weak but common objection against attempting to enlighten the heathen, that they are too ignorant to be taught. This senti-ment has prevented much exertion. It had a wicked origin. We have first enslaved our fellow-beings, then degraded them by every menial service, deprived them of the means of mental improvement, and almost of human intercourse; and because, under these circumstances, people of colour are devoid of knowledge, we have has-tened to the irrational conclusion, that all the Heathen are a race of idiots. Adopt-ing this conclusion multitudes are utterly opposed to making any attempt to turn them from darkness to light. Influenced by this opinion, groundless as it is, no reasonings, or arguments, or motives which can be offered, are of any avail. But the appearance of Obookiah has done much in this region, to wipe off this disgrace thrown upon the Heathen, and to remove the objection so often made. The proof he gave of talents as well as of piety carried conviction to many that the Heathen had souls as well as we, and were capable of being enlightened and Christianized.

Acknowledgments to this effect have frequently been made to me; and now in the circle of his travels, there is no occasion to combat this objection.

Disinterested Benevolence

The openness of the Mills family in bringing Obookiah into their home, and treating him like a son, reflected Father Mills' support for treating all races as equals in the eyes of God. As early as 1791 Father Mills was active in anti-slavery societies. In that year he represented Torrington, joining lexicographer Noah Webster of Webster's Dictionary fame, at a meeting of the Society for the Abolition of Slavery held in Hartford. This society was one of the first anti-slavery organizations gathered in the United States.

Father Mills' stand against racial prejudice, especially towards Hawaiian students, and a look at how blacks were treated in Litchfield County churches, is described in Samuel Orcutt's history of Torrington published in 1878.

> ...pews were located in the gallery over the stairs, boarded up so high, that when the colored people sat in them, they could see no part of the congregation, and could be seen by no one in the assembly. Jacob Prince, after being made a freeman by his master, Abijah Holbrook, joined the church in Goshen, and then being placed in such a seat, and treated in other ways by the same spirit, refused to go to church, because, as he said, he was not treated as a brother and thereafter held prayer meetings in his own house on the Sabbath....
>
> ...Two such pews were in the old church in Torringford, but the Rev. Samuel J. Mills (whether as a rebuke to the spirit of cast or not is not known) always seated Henry Obookiah, Thomas Hooppo, and other tawny brethren of the Sandwich Islands, when they visited him from the Cornwall Mission school, in his own pew, in the front of the congregation, quite to the dissatisfaction of some even of that congregation.

The theology behind Father Mills' anti-slavery sentiment aligned with the "New Divinity" theology of the Rev. Samuel Hopkins. Hopkins, like the Torringford minister, graduated from Yale prior to the Revolutionary War. Hopkins was a star pupil when he trained for the ministry under Jonathan Edwards, and was noted for coining the theological catch phrase "disinterested benevolence" (a Christian acting for good in a totally selfless manner). This attitude became the expected mindset of students taking part in domestic and foreign missions, and social works inspired by the Second Great Awakening.

Father Mills conferred with, and corresponded with Hopkins. Hopkins ministered in Great Barrington, Massachusetts, in the Berkshire Mountains, about a day's ride from Torringford. The anti-slavery minister practiced what he preached when he freed his slaves prior to the Revolutionary War.

After the war, an effective anti-slavery movement in Connecticut began when representatives of evangelical churches organized meetings held in Hartford, the city that shared with New Haven the role of being Connecticut's capital. Hopkins mailed his anti-slavery essays to Torringford. One pamphlet kept on the Mills family's bookshelf presented Hopkins' "African Scheme" for civilizing and evangelizing Africa by immigration of Christian blacks from America freed from slavery.

Samuel Mills' early remarks on his drive for foreign missions appear to reference Hopkins' essays, such as *A Dialogue Concerning the Slavery of the Africans*. Mills, in an early Brethren statement on missions, exclaimed, "I long to have the time arrive, when the gospel shall be preached to the poor Africans, and likewise to all nations."

An anecdote collected in a memorial to Father Mills told of his acceptance of blacks in Torringford: A black man came "to his back door on an errand and Mr. Mills said to him, 'Why did you come to the back door? When you come to my house, come to the front door, for we shall all go into heaven by one door.'" The soul and spirit of his son Samuel Mills became burdened when Samuel came upon fields of oppressed slaves working on southern plantations during his Bible society tours in 1813, and in 1815.

By 1816, Samuel began to alleviate the plight of urban African-Americans facing a myriad of social problems and prejudices. Samuel assisted in creating a seminary training school near Newark, New Jersey for black ministers. He attempted to bring relief to the poverty of blacks in Manhattan while working in the slums of the city in 1816 with Ward Stafford's Female Missionary Society. Samuel led in organizing the American Colonization Society with hopes of ending slavery through mass emigration of freed slaves to West Africa, setting up a homeland governed by blacks, and as a missions base for the evangelization of Africa.

Through the Colonization Society, Samuel developed a close friendship with Native American-African American sea captain and trader Paul Cuffe from the Elizabeth Islands in Massachusetts. Cuffe, a Ye and Thee speaking Quaker, through much perseverance, boldness, wisdom and skill became the wealthiest black in New England. He used his wealth to sail freed slaves to settle in the British colony of Sierra Leone in West Africa. Upon hearing that Cuffe was suffering a grave illness, Samuel rushed to New Bedford. Before Cuffe died the prominent African-American blessed Samuel for his heartfelt commitment to Cuffe's cause.

Kauwā

The practice of slavery was known to Obookiah before he left Hawai'i. In his childhood he grew up in Nīnole, a village in the Ka'ū district located at the south tip of Hawai'i Island. There a camp of *kauwā*, or *kauā* (the untouchable, slave class of Kamehameha's kingdom) were kept on a kapu land section located mauka of Nīnole.

Today, discussing the role of kauwā in Native Hawaiian society in pre-missionary Hawai'i can be a contentious topic. There are a substantial number of credible references to kauwā in nineteenth-century and twentieth-century accounts written by Native Hawaiian historians.

The kauwā heritage and their role in Native Hawaiian society is quite different from that of African slaves in America who toiled in fields and as house servants under the control of their owners. In the same era, members of Pacific Northwest Indian tribes were captured by other tribes and enslaved.

Mary Kawena Pukui, a noted Hawaiiana scholar and Bishop Museum linguist who grew up in a traditional Native Hawaiian community in Ka'ū, identified the kauwā as descendants of the first migratory wave of settlers of the Hawaiian Islands: "...the outcasts known as Kauwa (later doomed to die as human sacrifices)...may have been descendants of some conquered local tribe who resisted the colonizing ali'i and their clansmen in the period of early Hawaiian settlement."

Native Hawaiian historian David Malo, writing from Lahainaluna school in Maui in the mid-nineteenth-century, drew drawings of the tattoos inked on the foreheads of kauwā, chevrons and dots that clearly marked them as outcasts for life. A gourd lei was draped over the neck of a kauwā to mark them as selected for human sacrifice.

Yale-based Hawaiian mythology chronicler Martha Beckwith claimed that the kauwā were outcasts because of their lack of bloodlines to the Tahitian conquerors from the South Pacific who arrived under Pā'ao. Beckwith wrote that this cut them off from the worship of the Polynesian gods and places of honor within Hawaiian society.

Freedom of the kauwā from their bondage was declared by Kamehameha III, Kauikeaouli, in his Declaration of Rights within the Kingdom of Hawaii issued in 1839. Kauikeaouli wrote, "God hath made of one blood all nations of men to dwell on the earth, in unity and blessedness. God has also bestowed certain rights alike on all men and all chiefs, and all people of all lands."

Kauiekaouli based Hawai'i's first constitution on biblical principles following the publication of the complete Hawaiian Bible in 1839. This constitution was made law during the peak years of the Great Revival that swept across the Islands and resulted in Hawai'i becoming more a Christian nation than one that held to the ancient beliefs of its people.

Obookiah's Anti-slavery Influence

During his New England odyssey Obookiah crossed paths with young Americans who would go on to become leaders in the anti-slavery movement of mid-nineteenth-century America. These boys and girls were attracted to him due to his friendliness and hopeful spirit of aloha, his intelligence and ingenuity both in what he said and did, and his American folk-hero celebrity as a heathen-turned-Christian. Obookiah proved to be an accessible person of color in a white-dominated society, a transitional figure for them in their growing awareness of the plight of African-Americans, both freed and slave.

Joshua Coffin, the boarder at Deacon Hasseltine's home in Bradford who Obookiah told about Captain Cook's death, went on to join forces in the 1830s with William Lloyd Garrison, the leading abolitionist in the United States. Coffin worked on the staff of Garrison's newspaper *The Liberator*. Coffin later became an exceptional school teacher; his first teaching assignment was at Bradford Academy. He risked his life one summer break while rescuing two freed blacks who had been kidnapped and taken to the South from Philadelphia. Returning to that city Obookiah's roommate chose to teach young black children.

In 1838, Coffin—who may have met Samuel Mills during Obookiah's schooling at Bradford or Andover—quoted Samuel in a call for the American churches to send missions to the blacks:

...remember the emphatic language of the Rev. Samuel J. Mills: "Facts will always produce an effect, at least on pious minds...facts must be proclaimed in the ears of the people, that they may be induced to send the hope of the gospel to the expiring and despairing slave, as well as to the debased and miserable free black."

In 1816, the Morris Academy founded its Heathen School with classes gathered in a parsonage located adjacent to its main academy building in South Farms, Connecticut. During several months of the 1816-1817 school year John Brown (later the famous abolitionist), then age 16, studied at the Morris Academy. Students enrolled in the two Morris Academy branches likely walked the short distance between the buildings to mingle after class, and in the evening in student boarding quarters.

Herman Vaill, Brown's tutor at the Morris Academy in 1816, wrote to the abolitionist just weeks before his former student was hanged. (Brown became famous—and was hanged—for leading of the Harper's Ferry abolitionist insurrection in 1859.): "I know you have not forgotten the winter of 1816-17, when yourself and your brother Salmon...were pupils in Morris Academy...and how we had meetings for religious conference and prayers, in which your own voice was often heard."

Owen Brown, John's father, left Torrington in 1800 after the birth of his son to settle his family in Hudson, Ohio. Owen knew the northeast corner of Ohio as New Connecticut. Following the Revolutionary War, Connecticut citizens who lost property to destruction by British troops were awarded homesteads known as Fire Lands in what became known as the Western Reserve of Ohio.

The family ties linking Father Mills and Owen Brown come through Mills' grandfather, Gideon Mills: Gideon's granddaughter Ruth Mills married Owen, a leather tanner by trade. The Brown family descended from Mayflower Compact signer Peter Browne.

Farm work was cut back in 1816 due to a summer blight caused by the Year Without A Summer. Owen saw this as an opportunity for his sons John and Salmon to study at an academy in New England. John sought to become a minister, inspired in-part by the Bible society surveying tours made by his kinsman Samuel Mills in Ohio and other frontier states in 1812 and 1814.

The Brown boys paid for their try at a New England education by selling the two horses they rode east. John Brown first enrolled at the academy in Plainfield, Massachusetts. There, under the Rev. Moses Hallock, he planned to prepare himself to enroll at Yale, to obtain a divinity degree. Chronic eye problems, and a lack of a New England-level primary education, held him back.

Unable to keep up with their classmates at Plainfield, John and Salmon moved to Litchfield County to study at the Morris Academy, enrolling in a lower grade level. At South Farms the Brown boys again struggled to learn, but one winter session at the school they gave up, returning to Hudson to settle down. John took up his father's trade, and studied the Bible on his own, eventually justifying with scriptures his militant actions. Salmon did find a bride at South Farms.

Heman Humphrey, the minister who preached the sermon at the ordination of missionaries Hiram Bingham and Asa Thurston, was a first cousin to John Brown.

Obookiah and Harriet Beecher Stowe

Uncle Tom's Cabin author Harriet Beecher Stowe, the writer Abraham Lincoln hailed as the little lady who started the Civil War, was born in Litchfield in 1811 to the Rev. Lyman Beecher and his wife Roxana Foote Stowe.

When Harriet was a young child Obookiah and Hopoo often stopped by her home for a break from the Foreign Mission School. The Beecher family lived in a spacious three-story parsonage located in the village of Litchfield. Roaming in the nearby woods and reading books pulled from an old wooden barrel found in her attic provided entertainment for Harriet.

Lyman Beecher led the First Congregational Church in Litchfield. Through his anointed preaching and intellect he came to the

Uncle Tom's Cabin author Harriet Beecher Stowe and her brother Henry Ward Beecher, one of America's best-known preachers in the late-nineteenth-century, are remembered and honored in Litchfield, Connecticut by this historic marker placed at the former location of their childhood home. Here Obookiah visited them.

forefront in New England Christendom during the Second Great Awakening.

Harriet and her older sisters, Catherine and Mary, attended the nearby Litchfield Female Academy, better known as Miss Sarah Pierce's Academy. Miss Pierce's was renowned for solely enrolling young ladies, an uncommon practice in those days. The high caliber of the education offered attracted female students from across the nation, from as far away as the West Indies. Margaret Mix, the daughter of Elihu and Nancy Mix, attended Miss Pierce's in 1818.

Obookiah and Hopoo paid visits to Miss Pierce's. Looking back decades later, a student recalled helping to provide for their education and welfare, likely by providing meals and baking pies.

Henry Ward Beecher, Harriet's younger brother, was born in Litchfield in 1813. Henry Ward became the most prominent, and controversial, preacher in America following the Civil War. On Sundays he drew a large congregation to his landmark Plymouth Church in Brooklyn, New York.

On Sunday, February 13, 1887, about a year prior to his death, the famous preacher told in his sermon of the influence during his impressionable early years

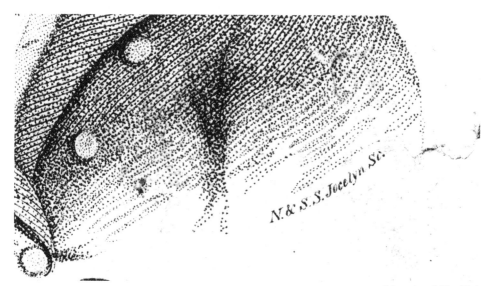

Memoirs of Obookiah

A close look at the frontispiece engraving credit in the Nathan Whiting edition of *Memoirs of Obookiah* reveals the trademark of anti-slavery New Haven brothers, bank note makers Simeon and Nathaniel Jocelyn.

---

of life at Litchfield by another Henry, a Henry who was perhaps his namesake:

> ...the whole world has been stirred up by the mission cause. I am what I am because Henry Obookiah, from the Sandwich Islands, was taught at the Cornwall School in Connecticut, and in my boyhood came down to my father's house, and produced an impression on me which has undulated, and propagated, and gone on influencing me. Some of the enthusiasm which I have felt for moral conditions came to me from seeing him.

The Jocelyns

The portrait of Obookiah found in the second New Haven edition of the *Memoirs of Henry Obookiah* offers another clue to Henry's influence on prominent figures in the anti-slavery movement. Tiny letters tucked away in the two-by-three inch frontispiece drawing of Obookiah credit "N. & S. S. Jocelyn Sc" as the engravers. This trademark identified the Jocelyn brothers of New Haven. Simeon and Nathaniel Jocelyn engraved bank notes as the mainstay of their business, with portrait painting as a sideline.

The Jocelyns also engraved and published "PRINT of four OWYHEAN YOUTHS" in 1822 as a fund-raiser for the Sandwich Islands Mission. The ten-inch by eight-inch print featured oval portraits of George Tamoree (Humehume) and John Honoree (Honoliʻi) Thomas Hoopoo (Hopu) and William Tenooe (Kanui). Samuel F. B. Morse painted the portraits prior to the Foreign Mission School students departures to return home to Hawaiʻi.

Simeon led abolition and temperance movements in New Haven. He boldly served as a pastor of the African-American Temple Street Congregational Church. Simeon attempted to open a "college for colored people" in New Haven in 1831. This resulted in a near-riot in downtown New Haven, with enraged citizens flinging stones at his home.

Nathaniel painted the famous portrait of Cinque, the leader of the West Africans who drifted into Long Island Sound aboard the slave ship *Amistad* in 1839. Joining him in defending the jailed *Amistad* slaves was Thomas Gallaudet of Hartford. Gallaudet employed his natural sign language to communicate with the West Africans in pretrial proceedings; this was prior to the abolitionists finding someone who spoke the native language of the Africans.

Sidney Moulthrop, son of renowned artist Reuben Moulthrop, who portrayed Obookiah's death bed scene in bees-wax, produced a life-like wax figure tableau of the *Amistad* Africans overthrowing the crew of the ship offshore of Cuba. Sidney took the *Amistad* scene on tour to Peale's Museum in Baltimore and to Barnum's American Museum on Broadway in Manhattan.

Andover Hebrew professor Moses Stuart, who indirectly helped teach the basics of that language to Obookiah, spoke out against the abolition movement. Stuart advocated against the militancy of John Brown and the abolitionists, seeking instead a more peaceful solution to ending slavery. His words caused students at Andover to stage a protest. The Rev. Ralph Emerson, Obookiah's connection in Hollis, New Hampshire, did sympathize with the anti-slavery movement. Emerson's home, today preserved on the campus of the Phillips Academy at Andover, served as a stop on the Underground Railroad. Emerson lived in the Andover house through 1853 while serving as a professor at the Seminary.

THE HOLY LAND & HAWAI'I

Sandwich Islands Mission station, Honolulu 1822

IN THE CHRISTMAS SEASON OF 1822, news of the death of Levi Parsons–of his "finding a sepulcher in the promised land" in Alexandria, Egypt–arrived from Boston at the Sandwich Islands Mission station in Honolulu.

The news drew the thoughts of Hiram and Sybil Bingham back to their departure from Boston in October, 1819. The couple then lived simply, in the Hawaiian style, in a dirt-floor, grass-thatched hale located mauka of Honolulu Harbor.

Three years earlier Levi, representing the American Board's Palestine Mission, stood with Hiram at the pulpit of Park Street Church. That day five hundred Bostonians took communion with the two foreign mission parties scheduled to leave for foreign shores within a week of each other. Hiram and Levi both had earned degrees at Middlebury College in Vermont.

As a youth, Hiram struggled with the wishes of his parents. They were farmers, and by tradition, as their eldest son, Hiram was obliged to stay at home to take care of them in their last years. He believed God led him to leave the farm for an education and a career in ministry. His departure from home was a difficult transition. Levi, the son of a minister,

Levi Parsons pictured about 1819.

found favor without reservation from his parents; they had dedicated him before birth to be used by God.

Bingham and Parsons were seen as being in the vanguard chosen to bring in the New Millennium through America. Parsons' dream was the conversion of Israel as a precursor to the coming return of Christ to the earth; Hiram's was taking the Gospel to the ends of the earth, to the Isles of the Sea in the Pacific Ocean, 18,000 miles away. Their signatures appear in the chronological list of Brethren enrollees kept in a ledger, below the names of Samuel Mills and his Haystack Meeting prayer partners.

Hiram and Sybil, comfortably settled in Honolulu, faced accepting the death of a close friend and fellow missionary. Levi had given his life up for the Brethren's idealistic foreign missions quest. In their hands lay a report of suffering and death half a world away. A dispatch sent from Boston spelled out the details of Parsons' demise. Sybil, soon to give birth to the couple's first son, looked back wistfully to her engagement with Levi made back in 1816. Then she held great hope for a future life with him on the mission field. But the next year the American Board of Commissioners placed a caveat in Levi's assignment to a foreign mission field: "You are not to marry" if you take up our charge of the mission to Palestine. The Turkish caliphate's rule of the Levant was under siege–taking along a young Christian wife to Jerusalem was a mission just for single men.

Mission to Jerusalem and the Jews of America

Instead of enjoying courtship and marriage and departing to a mission field with his bride, the American Board sent Levi out on a speaking tour of the southern states. Raising financial support came before heading for a mission field. The American Board wanted Levi, as Obookiah did at Amherst, to prove his worth before American congregations before heading off to lead a key foreign mission. Levi found favor speaking at gatherings of revival-stoked youth. Levi positioned himself as one of them: a young American spreading a tent peg of the New England Second Great Awakening to the gates of Jerusalem. He and his partner Pliny Fisk were on a holy mission to the lands of the Bible, "to the Jews, the Mohammedans, to ancient Egypt, Persia, and Syria."

Returning the Jews to their ancient homeland of Israel was a main tenet of Second Great Awakening end-times eschatology. Converting the Jews of America, Great Britain and Europe became a mission field. Study of the Hebrew language rekindled at Yale and other New England colleges.

Jewish-American population centers in 1810 were located in New York City, Philadelphia, and Newport, Rhode Island. Estimates of the Jewish population in the United States in 1820 ranged as high as 5,000 people. However, few if any of the Brethren had ever been inside a synagogue. Their vision of the role of Jews in God's plan for America was one made as an abstract concept. They aligned their theology with their New Millennium fervor, rather than through a personal connection and knowledge of the religion, customs, and society of the Jewish community of America.

Yale President Ezra Stiles did seek the friendship of Rabbi Isaac Cargill, the rabbi who led services at the Newport synagogue for six months in 1773. Stiles attended Purim and Passover services as a guest of Rabbi Cargill. Back at Yale, Stiles made Hebrew a required language class. He became a Hebrew scholar and in September, 1781 delivered his Yale commencement address in Hebrew, Aramaic and Arabic.

Just Parsons and Fisk

Unlike the Sandwich Island Mission family of over twenty souls, just Parsons and Fisk made up the Palestine Mission. As did the evangelist Paul, they were to travel light, explore. They were to be roving evangelists, unfettered and unmarried, foregoing a settled life on a mission station, expecting a youthful death. Their first step in heading to Jerusalem was to study the modern Greek language in preparation for distributing Greek Bibles and Christian tracts; Greek was then the common language of Palestine.

While the Sandwich Islands Mission was welcomed to hold their departure service in the sanctuary of the Park Street Church, Bingham and Thurston and party held no long-term attachments to that congregation. The church was handy due to its location near the Long Wharf in Boston.

However, the sending of a mission to Jerusalem had for years been prayed for by the Park Street Church. A fund for such a mission had been collected for almost a decade. The Rev. Edward Griffin planted the vision in sermons delivered as the first pastor at Park Street, a church built in Boston in 1809 as an evangelical stronghold in Unitarian-dominated Boston.

The Palestine Mission, the American Board of Commissioners claimed, was the

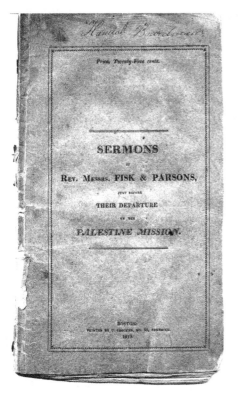

The sermons delivered on the eve of the departure of the Palestine Mission from Boston by Pliny Fisk and Levi Parsons closely connected the Palestine Mission with the Sandwich Islands Mission. An advertisement on the back cover of a print copy of the sermons lists for sale *Memoirs of Henry Obookiah*, the sermon delivered at the wedding of Hiram and Sybil Bingham in the Brick Church in Hartford, and the ordination sermon of Sandwich Islands Mission leaders Hiram Bingham and Asa Thurston delivered at Goshen. Printed sermons were used often to be read aloud on "Deacon Sunday," a Sabbath day when a pastor was unavailable and a lay preacher took to the pulpit.

first-ever Protestant mission to go out to evangelize in Palestine, in particular to Jerusalem. The Rev. Sereno Dwight, son of Timothy Dwight and in 1819 pastor of the Park Street Church, wrote:

> "It is to us an interesting fact that the first mission to Jerusalem and Palestine should have been established by the American Church. America is the only Christian nation, which has never persecuted the descendants of Israel. It was proper, therefore, that she should have the honor of leading the way in their ultimate restoration to the land of their fathers. That land is itself associated with all that is dear to our feelings, or animating to our hopes."

By October 31, Parsons and Fisk were ready to depart for the island of Malta, the

A side-note to the Brethren written by Pliny Fisk from Malta Harbor on December 27, 1819 to Isaac Bird at the Theological Seminary in Andover.

---

staging area in the Mediterranean for their mission. That evening Parsons preached a keynote sermon at Park Street Church: *The Dereliction and Restoration of the Jews.*

Parson and Fisk sailed from Boston Harbor on November 3 as America's "...first messengers of peace to the inhabitants of the Holy Land," taking a cabin in the ship *Sally Ann*, bound for British Gibraltar, the first scheduled landfall for the ship when it sailed from the Long Wharf in Boston. Eleven days earlier the Sandwich Islands Mission had departed for Hawai'i.

Palestine Mission reports excerpted from their travel journals appeared monthly in the *Missionary Herald*. Considered newsworthy, the reports were reprinted in newspapers up and down the East Coast. Accounts of the adventures of Parsons and Fisk drew an avid readership. Their serial travelogue told of evangelism, providential encounters, and exotic wanderings in biblical places. Parsons and Fisk wrote first-hand reports on current events, most notably of witnessing battles between Greeks and Turks. Evangelical readers followed closely the adventures the duo encountered touring the sites of the Seven Churches of the Book of Revelation.

From Jerusalem to Eternity

Early in 1821 Parsons sailed from Cyprus with Holy Land-bound pilgrims to the Palestine port of Joppa. From the sea coast he was to make his way up to the holy hills of Jerusalem. Parsons hung a leather pouch on his belt with a diplomatic passport tucked away inside. President James Monroe had signed his proof of American citizenship.

Parsons wrote in his mid-February, 1821 journal: "...we began to ascend a high mountain; and at twenty-five minutes past four o'clock my guide exclaimed (we were at the mount of Olives) and in just half an hour we entered, by Joppa gate, the holy city." His account, published in Boston in 1822, drew acclaim as the first published report sent back to the United States by an American entering Jerusalem.

After checking in with his connection in Jerusalem, Parsons joined the parade of Holy Land pilgrims he accompanied upland from the Mediterranean coast. "Without a moment's delay I hastened thither, to unite with the professed followers of Christ upon Mount Calvary, and to render thanks to God for the happy termination of my voyage to the holy city."

This moment of jubilation for the Brethren missionary is also counted as the first-ever entrance into Jerusalem by a Protestant missionary sent to establish a permanent presence in the Holy Land. The Palestine Mission of Parsons and Fisk is considered the seed for the young United State's connection to Israel. By the mid-nineteenth century a mania was in full swing for Americans to make pilgrimages to Jerusalem.

Parsons dwelt in Jerusalem for several months, distributing books of scripture printed in Greek, Arabic, Armenian, Persian, and Italian. He found an attentive audience amongst Holy Week pilgrims to Jerusalem.

After months of perilous traveling, in December, 1821 Parsons rejoined Fisk in Smyrna on the Aegean coast. The culmination of his travels in the Levant–eating local foods, drinking foul water and being exposed to strains of diseases uncommon to Americans–caught up with Parsons. His reunion with Fisk was bittersweet, one of joyful reunion saddened by the onset of a serious decline in Parson's health. As a cure, physicans advised Parsons to travel to Alexandria, Egypt for its warm climate. Fisk accompanied Parsons, and cared for his Brethren brother, staying alongside him until his fellow missionary died in the Egyptian city on February 10, 1822.

Levi Parsons Bingham

Back in Hawai'i, the Bingham's son was born on New Year's Eve 1822, Sybil giving birth inside their simple thatched hale in Honolulu. Just days later the infant took sick. On January 17, 1823 Hiram wrote, "The little L. Parsons Bingham, at the age of sixteen days, passed away suddenly, as did the dear missionary in Alexandria, whose name he was expected to bear..."

In a sketch of her mother's life, Lydia Bingham Coan, the wife of missionary Titus Coan, wrote of her parents acceptance of the infant's death and the baby's tie to the Palestine missionary.

> We gave him the name of our much-beloved deeply-lamented brother, Levi Parsons, and suffering our thoughts to run a few years down the vale of time, we said, "Perhaps, treading in the steps of him whose loved name he bears, he, too, shall lift up the standard for Israel's return." Our hearts rejoiced in this our pleasant child, while we desired to acknowledge God's superior claim. Sixteen days after he gave, he asked for the surrender of the precious gift. Our fond hearts clung to the darling treasure, but grace enabled us to say, "It is the Lord; let him do what seemeth to him good."

The ali'i nui took pity on the Binghams. Perhaps for the first time they saw the haole missionaries had soft hearts lying beneath their black waist coats and "long neck" bonnets, and stiff ways. The death of young Levi Parson Bingham opened the door wider to understanding by the ali'i nui on their own terms of the Christian message brought to Hawai'i from New England, and Tahiti.

Three days prior to the funeral of the Bingham's new born, a *punahele* (favored child) to Liholiho died. Liholiho requested the Binghams' assistance in holding a funeral similar to that of Levi Parsons Bingham. Hiram wrote:

> This morning the little half sister of the king and queen...died of the dropsy, and they propose to have funeral services at the internment, in the same manner as on last Sabbath. Kaahumanu requested one of us to pray, "that the soul of the child might go up to heaven."

Kaahumanu and Taumuarii, who have lately returned from Tauwai, and Kamamalu, and others called in a very friendly manner to sympathize with the bereaved parents. As strangers and sojourners with the people, we felt the affecting necessity of asking of the rulers of the land the possession of a burying place with them, that we might bury our dead out of our sight. At our request the king and queen and Kaahumanu granted us a place near the church as the burying ground of the mission.

The burying place was marked out, and the first grave opened in it for the remains of a tender infant. How affecting to look upon this spot...as the receptacle of the mission family. Here probably, many of us, and of our children, will slumber till the resurrection morning.

Bingham's prophetic words came true. A second infant son, Jeremiah Evarts Bingham, died in 1825 and was buried alongside his brother Levi. The Binghams placed a small gravestone in remembrance of their two sons. Around this tiny grave grew the Kawaiaha'o Church cemetery in downtown Honolulu. The gravestone is still standing today, no taller than a forearm. The stone marker is a symbol of the bond that connected the Brethren mission to the Holy Land half the world away, the birthplace of Christianity, with the Sandwich Islands Mission sent west to Hawai'i, to the ends of the earth from Jerusalem, in the far isles of the sea.

HANA HOU

'Ōpūkaha'ia - Henry Obookiah

Some say the name 'Ōpūkaha'ia (which translates as stomach cut open) was bestowed in the tradition of *inoa ho'o mana'o*–that is giving a name to a newborn tied to a significant event, or sign. His name might commemorate the death in battle of a high chief whose stomach was slashed open. Or, as other sources claim, the name cites a Caesarian birth. Hawaiiana scholar Mary Kawena Pukui gave Ka'ū lore as her source for the giving of the name. Pukui pointed to a time decades prior to 'Ōpūkaha'ia's birth, to an incident when a chiefess died in childbirth. Her husband immediately cut open her stomach delivering a living child, a surgical procedure unknown then in Ka'ū, and possibly all of Hawai'i. As with Hawaiian place names and significant words, the name 'Ōpūkaha'ia may be *kaona*, that is have several levels of meaning, a literal one, a pun-like meaning, and a spiritual meaning.

Following his death in 1818, the life of Henry Obookiah became known across the Protestant world as an inspirational, poignant story of a Native Hawaiian youth whose providential life led to the sending of a Protestant mission to the Sandwich Islands.

By the 1830s, the *Memoirs of Henry Obookiah* had become a popular book in Sunday schools across the United States. In 1830 the American Sunday School Union published a revised edition of the book and widely distributed it. In about 1840 the American Tract Society printed the *Memoirs*, crediting for the first time Edwin Welles Dwight as editor and author.

About 50,000 copies of the *Memoirs of Henry Obookiah* were printed between 1818 and the 1840s, making it a significant book in the history of American Christian publishing. The book is often credited with inspiring the sending of missionaries to Hawai'i, making it also a significant book for Hawai'i.

In 1865, into 1866, the Rev. S. W. Papaula, pastor of the Kahikolu Church at Napo'opo'o, Island of Hawai'i, serialized a Hawaiian-language version of the *Memoirs* he wrote and published in the Hawaiian-language newspaper *Kuokoa*.

After the *Memoirs* appeared in *Kuokoa*, the Rev. Papaula interviewed elderly kūpuna knowledgeable of Obookiah and his family and life at Kealakekua, likely some among his congregation at Kahikolu, a congregation once made up of 3,000 persons. The kūpuna provided more details on 'Ōpūkaha'ia's family and life, and set 1787 as Henry's birth year, moving it back from 1792.

The American Tract Society provided the printing plates for the Hawaiian edition of the *Memoirs*, printed to reach Hawaiian language readers. This edition included the new information gathered by the Rev. Papaula. The title of the Hawaiian translation is *Ka moolelo o Heneri Opukahaia, ua hanauia ma Hawaii, M. H. 1787, a ua make ma Amerika, Feberuari 17, 1818 : oia ka hua mua o Hawaii nei*, or *The History of Henry Opukahaia born in Hawai'i in 1787, and died in America, February 17, 1818. The first fruit of Hawaii*. About two-thousand copies were printed in a variety of binding colors, all with the title "Heneri Opukahaia" stamped in gold gilt on the spine.

In the early twentieth-century, great plans were made in New England and

Hawai'i to mark the one-hundredth anniversary of the formation of the American Board of Commissioners for Foreign Missions. In 1910 thousands of people gathered at Bradford, Massachusetts, in a park located in the same neighborhood where Henry attended Bradford Academy, to dedicate a memorial monument.

Coinciding with this celebration, the Moku'aikaua Church in Kailua-Kona erected a memorial arch, dedicated in July 1910 to commemorate the 90th anniversary of the arrival of the first missionaries. A bronze plaque placed on the arch reads: "The First Hawaiian Christian Henry Opukahaia Died at Cornwall, Conn., 1818." At the dedication service the Rev. S. L. Desha of Hilo, who wrote a definitive biography of Kamehameha in a Hawaiian language newspaper, spoke on "Opukahaia and His Christian Comrades, Hopu, Kanui, and Honolii."

At the conclusion of a long series of speeches Frank Damon (a great-grand nephew of Samuel Mills) spoke. A report in *The Friend* newspaper noted, "Mr. F. W. Damon displayed a letter written by 'Ōpūkaha'ia, probably the only autograph letter of 'Ōpūkaha'ia in Hawai'i. Mr. Damon spoke of him as the magnet that drew attention to Hawaii as a field of need, and that irresistibly led not only to the inauguration of mission work here, but to missionary undertakings elsewhere. Intense interest was aroused by these personal and historical reminiscences, which formed a fitting climax to a notable day's program."

'Ōpūkaha'ia was portrayed in "One Hundred Years of Christian Civilization in Hawaii," a pageant marking the centennial of the arrival of the Sandwich Islands Mission in Hawai'i. Samuel Mills' kin Ethel Moseley Damon wrote the pageant. An audience of 10,000 gathered to watch the play acted out on Rocky Hill at Punahou School in mid-April, 1920.

Making a pilgrimage from Hawai'i to the Obookiah grave site in Cornwall became popular soon after his death in 1818. Cloth lei, stones and shells carried from Hawai'i, along with other remembrances, began being left atop the inscribed stone set atop the raised grave. In 1940 a Ni'ihau shell lei was placed on the grave cover by Ben Alexander of Lihu'e, sent as a gift from the Waimea Congregational Church in Kaua'i.

In the 1920s, University of Hawai'i student Charles Kenn began research with plans for writing a biography of 'Ōpūkaha'ia. While Kenn never wrote that book, he did publish an English language translation of Rev. Papaula's book. The translation appeared as a magazine serial over several issues in 1944, in the popular *Paradise of the Pacific* monthly published in Honolulu. Kenn's translation was the first comprehensive sketch of the life of Obookiah published since the release of *Ka moolelo o Heneri Opukahaia*.

Clarice Bromley Taylor wrote the daily Hawaiiana column *Tales about Hawaii* for the *Honolulu Star-Bulletin*. In 1954 Clarice published a series of twenty-one short sketches from the life of Opu-ka-ha-ia, as she spelled his name; beyond the excerpts taken from the *Memoirs of Henry Obookiah*, her sources are uncredited.

Taylor was a Hawaiiana writer for the *Star-Bulletin*, leading to her being recruited as the main research assistant for author James Michener in the mid-1950s during the writing of his epic novel *Hawaii*. Michener's friend, University of Hawai'i professor and author A. Grove Day, also recommended Taylor. Michener based his character Keoki Kanakoa on 'Ōpūkaha'ia. Keoki was portrayed as young man stouter than Obookiah, a young man who was overly Calvinistic in

New England who returns to Hawai'i as the missionaries's go-between with the ali'i nui. Keoki falls away from the Sandwich Islands Mission over his forbidden love for his sister. He dies distraught taken down to a tragic death during an epidemic, ending his futile life torn between the ways of old Hawai'i and Christianity.

Michener gave Clarice a back-hand compliment in his book, using her middle name as the maiden name of his lovely missionary wife, Jerusha Bromley Hale.

The 'Ōpūkaha'ia Memorial Chapel is located mauka of Punalu'u Beach at Ka'ū in Hawai'i Island, just north of Nīnole, and dedicated in April 1957. The structure was erected by the Laymen's Fellowship of the Congregational Christian Churches of Hawai'i.

The United Church of Christ's Woman Board of Missions for the Pacific Islands, Hawaii Conference published in 1968 an edited version of *Memoirs of Henry Obookiah*. The book included notes on research into the life of Obookiah and pages of photographs to mark the 150th anniversary of the death of Obookiah. The Rev. Edith Wolfe served as editor, assisted by missionary descendant Albertine Loomis, the author of the Hawai'i missions book *Grapes of Canaan*. Loomis wrote in the book's introduction: "It is a tale of two cultures–Hawaiian and New England–It is the story of Aloha in a land which had not the word but had at least the spirit; the story of an island boy who never made it back to the islands–but whose life and death helped to make the islands what they are today." An updated edition of the book was published by the Woman's Board in 1990.

The Hawaiian Mission Children's Society presented the Honolulu premiere of the film *Island Boy* in 1969 at Punahou School. The 16mm documentary film was produced by the Hawaiian Mission Sesquicentennial Committee. The film pictures the events that took place on February 18, 1968 in commemoration of the 150th anniversary of the death of 'Ōpūkaha'ia. The film focuses on six "pilgrims" who traveled from Hawai'i to Cornwall, Connecticut in his honor. Scenes are included of the service at Kawaiaha'o Church honoring Henry. The Rev. Edith Wolfe wrote the script and described the production of the film at the premiere.

Cecily H. Kikukawa wrote *Ka Mea Hoala, the Awakener: the story of Henry Obookiah, once called Opukahaia*, published in 1982. The seventy-one page book dramatizes the life of Obookiah.

"He wants to come home," are the inspirational words that Deborah Li'ikapeka Lee of Hilo sensed God told her on October 11, 1992. Deborah was residing at the time near Seattle, but soon returned home to began her mission of returning the remains of 'Ōpūkaha'ia to Hawai'i.

Deborah and her family formed the non-profit organization *Ahahui O 'Ōpūkaha'ia* to fulfill her vision. Soon the family found support from churches, the local community, schools and businesses.

The United States Congressional Repatriation Act aided the Lee family in overcoming legal hurdles in requesting to return to Hawai'i the remains of their beloved family member who died in 1818. Deborah is a first cousin of 'Ōpūkaha'ia, seven times removed.

God's blessing on the project found the Lees on their way within ten months to Cornwall, Connecticut. The door had opened wide for Henry's return.

The project took on a life of its own. News of the return of the remains of 'Ōpūkaha'ia to Hawai'i became news in Connecticut and Hawai'i, and eventually nationwide. Ahahui O 'Ōpūkaha'ia found support in Connecticut from the United Church of Christ, the Cornwall Historical Society and a State of Connecticut archaeologist.

In Cornwall, local residents resigned themselves to having the remains of Obookiah returned from his hillside grave in Cornwall to another hillside gravesite, this one overlooking Kealakekua Bay where he departed from.

Connecticut State Archaeologist Nicholas Bellantoni exhumed the grave located on a hillside in the Cornwall Cemetery.

The remains of 'Ōpūkaha'ia were interred in a koa wood coffin. On August 6, 1993 Henry's remains arrived at Keahole Airport in Kona to begin a homecoming tour. Deborah Lee and her 'ohana organized services held at sites significant to his in life in Hawai'i, and sites important in the history of the Sandwich Islands Mission.

On August 15, at the City of Refuge at Honaunau Bay, the koa casket was blessed and placed on a platform joining two outrigger canoes. At the request of Deborah Lee, Henry was returned by water to Kealakekua Bay. There a young man from the Ho'omanawanui family, also family to 'Ōpūkaha'ia, dove into the bay from a rock at Napo'opo'o Beach to greet the canoe, reenacting the departure of 'Ōpūkaha'ia aboard the *Triumph*. As the canoe approached the shore, sunlight broke through a gloomy sky, and spinner dolphins began their dance nearby the canoe. The coffin was taken ashore and brought to the Kahikolu Church, located inland, on a rise above Kealakekua Bay. There a ceremony preceded the placing of his remains in a vault at a site on the church grounds looking out to Kealakekua Bay.

The words of *Ka Ohe Ola Hou*, the organization formed by the Lee family to perpetuate the Christian heritage of 'Ōpūkaha'ia, and to hold him up as a role model for Native Hawaiians, sum up his return to the Islands: "...as Hawaii Aloha and *Aloha Oe* are sung...the words 'He wants to come home,' are fulfilled. Henry 'Ōpūkaha'ia is Home."

Coinciding with the return of Henry, Christopher Cook released a pre-Internet web browser, eBook copy of the *Memoirs of Henry Obookiah* along with digitized accounts of 'Ōpūkaha'ia from other sources. In subsequent years, the files were turned into a website–www.obookiah.com–which is being updated to become an extension of *The Providential Life & Heritage of Henry Obookiah*.

In 2009, Maui-based filmmaker Jo Danieli released her six-hour historical documentary film *Native of Owhyhee*, a film which includes an overview of the life of 'Ōpūkaha'ia.

The Life and Legacy of Heneri Opukaha'ia Hawai'i's Prodigal Son was presented in December 2011 by Wayne H. Brumaghim as his thesis for his University of Hawai'i at Manoa Master of Arts in Hawaiian Studies degree. The thesis presents a biography of 'Ōpūkaha'ia from a Native Hawaiian perspective, and features a thorough account of the genealogy of 'Ōpūkaha'ia.

The Woman's Board of Missions released a third revised version of the *Memoirs of Henry Obookiah*, released in 2013. Deborah Lee's account of her fulfilled vision of returning 'Ōpūkaha'ia to Hawai'i appears in this edition.

Andover Theological Seminary

Andover Theological Seminary's connection to the American Board of Commissioners for Foreign Missions resulted in the sending out of 222 foreign missionaries over its 100 years of instruction on Academy Hill. The founders of the Seminary aimed at preserving Calvinistic Puritanism in the face of the expansion of the liberal wing of the Protestant church in America. Students studied the Bible, biblical languages, church history and evangelical theology.

By the mid-nineteenth-century students from across the globe began traveling to Andover to study at the Seminary including foreign students from Japan, China and India. The godly reputation of Andover spread around the world.

Local residents today refer to Andover as the "Center of the Universe" due to its global influence spread through students who studied at Andover and notable academics who taught in the town's prestigious schools: in the past at the Theological Seminary at Andover and the Abbot Academy, and from the eighteenth-century into the twenty-first century at the prestigious Phillips Academy at Andover preparatory school founded in 1778.

In 1908, the Andover seminary merged with Harvard Divinity School for eighteen years. Today, Andover Newton Theological School is located in Newton Centre, Massachusetts, a suburb of Boston. The Andover Newton Theological School's Trask Library is home to the Henry Obookiah Collection of Pacific-Asian Studies.

Baibala Hemolele

The seed of *Ka Baibala Hemolele*, the Hawaiian language version of the Bible, is the pioneering work of Henry Obookiah in translating the first chapter of Genesis into the Hawaiian language directly from the Hebrew language. Obookiah's Bible translation work began humbly. "In 1814 at Goshen, Connecticut, ...a tall, comely Hawaiian lad who worked as a farm hand part of the time was trying, he wrote, 'to translate a few of the verses of the Scriptures into my own language, and making a kind of spelling-book, taking the English alphabet and giving different names and different sounds.'"

In 1815, Henry wrote: "I have been translating a few chapters of the Bible into the Hawaiian language. I found I could do it very correctly...my countrymen have no Bible and no Sabbath...I long to see them."

By 1816, he completed a translation of the Book of Genesis into his own written version of the Hawaiian language. He did this by studying the Hebrew language, likely using Theological Seminary at Andover Hebrew class lessons hand written by biblical language professor Moses Stuart. Obookiah worked on the translation "of his own accord, without a regular instructor, acquired such knowledge of the Hebrew, that he had been able to read several chapters in the Hebrew Bible and had translated a few passages into his native language. He had a peculiar relish for the Hebrew language, and from its resemblance to his own, acquired it with great facility; and found it much less difficult to translate the Hebrew than the English into his native tongue."

Obookiah found a striking resemblance between the language of the Hebrews and the oral Hawaiian language. His translating work was noted by Jewish scholar Leon Nemoy, who named Henry a Christian Hebraist, a title denoting a

Christian who achieved an understanding of the ancient Hebrew language.

When the Sandwich Islands Mission arrived in Hawai'i in 1820 only a handful of Native Hawaiians could read or write. The missionaries with the help of Hawaiian scholars developed a Hawaiian alphabet, opened schools for children and adults, and began to translate and print selections from the Bible in the Hawaiian language.

The coral-stone walled Oahu Mission Press located adjacent to the Kawaiaha'o Church struck off its first pages in 1822. Millions of pages followed.

The work of translating the New Testament and the Old Testament into the Hawaiian language fell to eight members of the mission. The group decided to translate directly from the Greek and Hebrew languages into the Hawaiian language. The Rev. Hiram Bingham began translating the Book of Matthew at the Honolulu mission station in 1823. The Sandwich Islands Mission leader drew from Tahitian, Latin and English versions of scriptures, comparing them to ancient Greek versions. At the Maui mission station, William Richards worked with Hawaiian scholar David Malo and Tahitian Christian translator and missionary Tau'ā on Matthew. Asa Thurston and Artemas Bishop delved into Matthew with Governor Kuakini at the Kailua mission station on Hawai'i Island.

The American Board of Commissioners received a report in 1826 on the cross-cultural translation of the Book of Matthew. Richards passed his translation of the scripture from Greek into the Hawaiian language to David Malo, his instructor in the Hawaiian language. Tau'ā at the same time gave Malo his Tahitian language version of Matthew. Then Malo drew up his edited version, drawing on the translations provided by Richards and Tau'ā. The edited copy was then read to the ali'i and maka'āinana to check on the clarity of the translation, and if it would be accepted as a correct translation by the Hawaiian people. New words, Hawaiian language words based on biblical words, were part of the translation.

In 1827 Hiram Bingham sent to the Mission Press in Honolulu a section of the Gospel of Luke with enough copy to fill twelve pages. His translation of the Sermon on the Mount came out in 1828, in a printing of 25,000 copies. The ali'i nui Kalanimoku, Ka'ahumanu and Ke'eaumoku paid for the paper fed into the press.

The complete Gospel of Luke became the first book of the Bible completed and printed at the Oahu Mission Press. Sandwich Islands Mission printer Elisha Loomis departed Hawai'i in 1828, carrying to a press in Rochester, New York the manuscripts for the books of Matthew, Mark and John. These early books were printed as stand-alone publications.

Printers from the Oahu Mission Press, set up at the Lahainaluna school on the slopes of West Maui, printed several books of the Old Testament.

In 1832 the first copy of the complete New Testament, bound in a red morocco leather cover, was rushed from the Mission Press at Kawaiaha'o to the death bed of Christian ali'i nui Elizabeth Ka'ahumanu. The queen clutched the book, and proclaimed it *maika'i*, excellent. Her first copy was later sent by Kinau, Ka'ahumanu II, to the American Board of Commissioners in Boston as a gift given in thanks for providing the funds for printing the Hawaiian New Testament.

The American Bible Society and the Philadelphia Bible Society funded the early printing of *Ke Kauoha Hou*, the New Testament.

Eight scholars from the Sandwich Islands Mission along with Native Hawaiian scholars, spent over fifteen years in compiling the translation from original Greek and Hebrew languages into the *Palapala Hemolele* (the Holy Written Word), the first complete, Old Testament and New Testament, Hawaiian language Bible.

Work on *Palapala Hemolele* involved missionaries and Native Hawaiian translators. The work was passed around from the desk of the missionaries: One third by William Richards, one fourth by Asa Thurston, one fifth by Hiram Bingham, one seventh by Artemas Bishop. Small sections were completed by Sheldon Dibble, Jonathan Green, Lorrin Andrews, and Ephriam Clark.

The translation by Hiram Bingham of the last verse of the Book of Ezekiel completed the work. This came a few days prior to the nineteenth anniversary of the Sandwich Islands missionaries first spotting Hawai'i Island from the deck of the *Thaddeus* in 1820.

The first edition of the *Palapala Hemolele* encompassed a massive 2,331 pages. The thick book, nicknamed by its readers *Ka Buke Poepoe*, "The Fat Book," was printed and bound at the Mission Press.

The printing, distribution and widespread reading of the Hawaiian Bible is credited with sparking the great revivals Hawai'i experienced in the 1830s. Hiram Bingham Jr. commented in the 1880s, "The first edition of the entire Bible was published in the midst of one of the most remarkable revivals of religion since the days of Pentecost." By 1838, the Rev. Titus Coan ministered to a congregation of over 5,000 at Hilo; it was claimed the Hilo church gathered the largest congregation at that time of any Protestant church in the world.

Perhaps the outstanding literary achievement of *Palapala Hemolele* is found in the style of its Old Testament poetical sections–Deborah's song, Song of Solomon, sections of Job, Psalms. All are printed as lyrical poetry, as they appear in the ancient Hebrew scrolls. The seventeenth-century English scholars authoring the *King James Bible* translated these books of the Bible as straight text.

From January 7, 1822, when the first pages of scripture in Hawaiian came off the mission press, demand for the *palapala*, the printed word, never abated. In the 1880s a tally showed millions of pages in the Hawaiian language had been printed. A study of Bible printing in the Pacific Islands published in the 1880s reported on the Hawaiian Bible: "The publishing of the Bible at this time was most opportune, and soon there was scarcely a family in the kingdom where a copy was not to be found, and where it was not constantly read. The American Bible Society of New York furnished the means for the printing of tens of thousands of portions of Scripture, and also of the first three editions of the entire Bible."

As the pages of scripture came from the O'ahu and Maui presses shipments were sent to outlying mission stations. They were traded for poi, woven mats, even prized canoe paddles carved by residents of the remote Nā Pali coast of Kaua'i. Almost every home possessed pages of scripture in the Hawaiian language.

The desire to read drove the opening of palapala schools around each island. Native teachers were trained by missionaries. Their students went on to teach other students, and literacy took off. Within a few decades of the release of the *Palapala Hemolele* the Kingdom of Hawai'i ranked as one of the most literate nations in the world.

The legitimacy of the *Palapala Hemolele* within the Native Hawaiian culture came through the rhythmic language style employed, a style reminiscent of the Hawaiian chant. The Hawaiian scriptures are said to read like Hebrew.

By 1830 more than one-thousand palapala schools were being held. Mostly native teachers taught their pupils in the Hawaiian language, resulting in a literacy rate by that year for the Kingdom of Hawai'i of about 50 percent. Festive hō'ike, quarterly public exams, were held at the schools, a continuation of the practice started at the Foreign Mission School in Cornwall.

In the article "Our Hawaiian Bible," written in 1939, Hawaiian language teacher and folklorist, and missionary daughter, Laura C. Green delved into use of Hawaiian words and terms employed by translators. "Sometimes a word in Hawaiian conveys a fuller meaning than in English because the idea in original is closer to Hawaiian thought," she wrote in an article published in Honolulu in *The Friend* newspaper.

Laura Green's father was Sandwich Islands missionary the Rev. Jonathan Green. He translated sections of the Old Testament for the first printing of the *Palapala Hemolele*. In protest of the American Board accepting donations from Southern slaveholders, the Rev. Green in 1842 withdrew from the covering of the American Board and founded his own church in Makawao, Maui. Laura grew up in Makawao in a close relationship with the Hawaiian community. As an adult she served many years as a teacher of girls in Maui and in Honolulu. She became a gifted translator of the Hawaiian language into English, and assisted author Martha Beckwith in writing the book *Hawaiian Mythology*. Green became known by the name Mele Kaina.

In her *Friend* article, Green listed references to Hawaiian cultural practices and terms appearing in *Palapala Hemolele*. They include:

• Genesis 2:7, where the Hawaiian word *ha*, the breath of life, as in *aloha*, is used in the verse "breathed into his nostrils the breath of life." In John 20:22 *ha* is used when Jesus breathes upon his disciples, and says "Receive ye the Holy Ghost." Green notes that in the Hawaiian culture, the "master of any art passes his own skill to a favored pupil by breathing into or passing spittle into the pupil's mouth."

• In Psalm 61, where David speaks of "trusting in the cover" of God's wings, the Hawaiian word *kanoho* is used, meaning resting under the protection of.

• In John 14:27 "Peace I leave with you, peace I give to you, peace is translated as *aloha*, or love.

• Psalm 90:1 tells of a *pu'uhonua*, a place of refuge, in place of the English language biblical phrase dwelling place. In a Native Hawaiian sense, *pu'uhonua* is much closer in meaning to the original Hebrew phrase, which was also a walled enclosure where one could flee in times of trouble and persecution.

• A crossover from the Native Hawaiian religion based on the kapu system appears in II Corinthians 12:9. There "my strength is made perfect in weakness," is translated using the word "mana" for strength, mana being the Hawaiian word for power, a word that conveys the "indwelling of divine power."

In addition to Miss Green's insights, a careful reading of the Hawaiian Bible turns up even seafaring terms; the Hawaiian canoe sails in the Hawaiian Bible, too. In James 3:4, *ka hoeuli uuku loa, ma kahi e makemake ai o ke kahu moku*, the small rudder of a big ship becomes the steering paddle of a large canoe.

To read the Bible in the Hawaiian language go to www.baibala.org. Viewable online are page images and pages of text from the editions issued in 1839-1994.

In 2012, Mutual Publishing of Honolulu issued an updated edition of the *Ka Baibala Hemolele*, an version featuring modern diacritical marks. The Kamehameha Schools released a special Pauahi Edition of this version to commemorate the 125th anniversary of the school's founding. In 2014 Mutual released a Hawaiian-English, side-by-side, version of the New Testament.

Hiram Bingham

Hiram Bingham led the Sandwich Islands Mission station in Honolulu for twenty-one years. Hiram and his wife Sybil Moseley Bingham left Hawai'i for good in August 1840, stopping in Tahiti on the way home to New England.

The Binghams left behind a legacy of Bible translation into the Hawaiian language, of service to the people of Hawai'i, and a laying of the foundation of the Sandwich Islands Mission and the Protestant church in Hawai'i.

Less well known is the legacy of the land they donated on behalf of all the Sandwich Islands missionaries. The Bingham homestead in Honolulu, known as Ka Punahou for a legendary fresh water spring found on the land, was given by the family for the site of a school for missionary children. In 1859 the school was named Oahu College, and later renamed Punahou School.

Punahou came to the mission in 1829, the gift of Queen Ka'ahumanu. At a celebration in the 1870s, Bingham son Hiram II described his parent's reason for donating the Punahou land: "This land of Punahou...stretching from the summit of Round Top to King street, supplemented by fish-ponds, salt-beds, and coral flats, all more or less valuable....His gift is witness to his sincere gratitude that there had come to his people those who had labored faithfully to introduce and maintain Christian education and culture among them, and to do them good."

In October 1832 Hiram crossed the Kaua'i Channel in a small sailboat to assist Waimea, Kaua'i missionary Peter Gulick; fellow missionary Samuel Whitney was on a mission to the Marquesas Islands. The Honolulu-based missionary was met and warmly greeted by an elderly man who had been at Waimea when Captain Cook arrived in 1778, and another elderly Hawaiian, a warrior from O'ahu whom British Captain George Vancouver mentioned in his journal of 1792.

Each island in Hawai'i has its own personality, thus Christianity unfolded in a similar, yet in some ways in a unique manner, on each island. Hiram discovered the first major revival in all the Hawaiian Islands breaking out at Waimea, emanating in part from a sermon on the death of Queen Ka'ahumanu who had died in June 1832, and the release of *Ke Kauoha Hou*, the New Testament. Gulick sent a plea to Bingham for help in counseling, ministering, and teaching the Bible to the overwhelming number of people drawn to West Kaua'i by the revival. Bingham noted a Sunday service held along the coast at Waimea drew men, women and children from across Kaua'i who formed a congregation numbering over 2,000, about one-fifth of Kaua'i's people. The Waimea revival peaked in September, 1832.

Keeping his Calvinist, predestination-influenced theology in mind, Bingham viewed the revival with caution. Groups of Native Hawaiians, called by the sound of a conch shell, gathered at the thatched Waimea church at the sunset "golden hour," when the warm sun setting towards Ni'ihau gives a warm glow to the red-dirt West Kaua'i landscape. Among them he viewed spiritual manifestations similar to those described by theologian Jonathan Edwards in mid-eighteenth century Massachusetts: children hiding under large leafs in tears, adults trembling, others falling face-first on the ground weeping.

Bingham quoted missionary Peter Gulick, who described the revival scene.

"From the pagan priest, down to the humble devotee of superstition, all classes, and every age...have felt, as we are fully persuaded, the sacred influences of the Holy Spirit. There was a depth and pungency in their convictions which I had never before witnessed at the islands, except in a few cases."

Author Clifford Putney, in his book *Missionaries in Hawai'i: The Lives of Peter and Fanny Gulick, 1797-1883*, analyzes the legitimacy of the Waimea revival, which he terms the "first full-blown revival in Hawai'i." Putney wrote:

> Like revivals in America, the revival on Kaua'i included fervent outpourings of emotion, and for that reason it upset some theologically conservative missionaries on the islands. But the Gulicks strongly endorsed the revival, because they viewed it as proof that Christianity was not merely a religion that had been foisted on the Hawaiians by their chiefs.

The great outpouring on Kaua'i dissipated by spring 1833. This happened in part due to the strict rules of the missionaries regarding church membership set up to test the genuineness of the commitments pledged at the revivals.

Back in New England in the 1840s the Binghams departed from the busy lives they led in Honolulu, and the power in the Kingdom of Hawai'i Hiram held as leader of the mission. The couple fell upon "straitened circumstances" with Sybil in failing health and Hiram lacking an appointment in New England by the American Board. To help support his family, Hiram wrote his classic missionary account *A Residence of Twenty-One Years in the Sandwich Islands,* sold by subscription in 1847. Sybil died at age 56 in 1848 in Easthampton, Massachusetts where her family was aided by the Williston family, the prosperous button manufacturers.

In September, 1869 Hiram returned to Goshen from his home in New Haven to celebrate the semi-centenary of his ordination as a missionary to the Sandwich Islands. An account of the day reads, "...a survivor of the first missionary band of five, was present, and took part in the services, at eighty years of age still vigorous and active."

Hiram passed away on November 11, 1869. His grave is in the Grove Street Cemetery in New Haven. Years later Sybil's remains were disinterred by her family from an Easthampton cemetery and buried in a plot adjacent to her husband.

Brethren

The Brethren foreign mission society (birthed at Williams College c. 1806-1808) is the seed of the student mission movements subsequently organized in America. By 1809 the covert Brethren moved on to the Theological Seminary at Andover, recruiting missions-minded students. Successful candidates were referred to the American Board of Commissioners for assignment. Many of the

American Board Missionaries were enrolled in the Brethren, into at least the 1860s. The overt face of the Brethren, the Society of Inquiry, publicly raised interest in foreign missions among college students for decades, founding libraries, holding seminars. The Brethren also quietly prepared programs for numerous missions-focused Concert of Prayer meetings.

A Brethren member recruited in the 1830s recalled that the group, "...moved in a sphere of its own, silent, gentle, and unknown, but operating powerfully and producing important and lasting effect."

Key Christian organizations birthed during the Second Great Awakening originated from within the Brethren, and had significant influence in evangelizing the United States, in Hawai'i, and nations around the world, "...it lived long enough to have its influence felt to the remotest corner of this ruined world." The list includes: the American Board of Commissioners for Foreign Missions, the United Foreign Missionary Society, the African School Society, the American Tract Society, and the American Temperance Society.

The Rev. Melville Horne of the London Missionary Society, a mission to the British freed-slave colony of Sierra Leone in West Africa in the first decade of the eighteenth-century, influenced the Brethren. The Brethren looked to the Society as informed leaders in all aspects of foreign missions. After facing the dangers and diseases of the West African coast Horne wrote a series of letters of advice to fellow missionaries. He advised foregoing marriage and child rearing if going out into such dangerous foreign fields. Horne later recanted his statement. Mills wrote a letter describing how, based on Horne's advice, he had faced temptation to waiver from his Brethren pledge of total commitment to missions and bachelorhood.

> I have not found many acquaintances in town among the fair. I know but three or four. These are eminently pious, and have much of that unaffected loveliness and simplicity of manner so truly captivating. Don't be alarmed. I am not yet caught up in an evil net. But in truth our hearts need steeling to give up all hopes of domestic happiness, the one bliss (as says the poet) which has survived the fall. But let us remember what Mr. Horne says. "That man is not fit for a missionary who sighs for the delights of a lady's lap."

In the Brethren roll book, the signature of James Neeshima of Japan appears, making him a spiritual descendant of Samuel Mills. His name appears third from last in a long list of Brethren members. The ruled, hand-written list runs for page after page in an oversized journal. Samuel Mills and cohorts appear at the head of the list. With Neeshima, the first foreign student enrolled in the Brethren, the missions society came full-circle just prior to closing its book, mission accomplished.

Neeshima was the first Japanese man with Protestant Christian ties to become a well-known public figure in his homeland. Neeshima's life story portrays him as a Japanese Obookiah. As a student, he sailed to Boston in 1865 after fleeing under threat of arrest and death for leaving the confines of Japan without royal permission. He sought to learn more about Christianity and America, and found a berth in Hong Kong as a cabin boy on an American ship.

Neeshima was drawn into his Christian life by reading a summary of Christianity and scriptures bordering a map, and by reading books by missionaries written in Chinese. On the long voyage to America, the captain of the ship taught him English. In Boston ship owner Alpheus Hardy met Neeshima and saw him as the fulfillment of his own youthful dream of going out in Christian service. Poor health kept Hardy back and he went into business. He carefully checked out the sincerity of Neeshima, giving him the name Joseph. Hardy paid Joseph's way through Phillips Academy at Andover, Amherst College, and then the Theological Seminary at Andover. Neeshima honored his mentor by taking on the American name Joseph Hardy Neeshima. Neeshima went on to be a leading Christian educator back in Japan.

Caleb Brintnall

New Haven sealing captain Caleb Brintnall, the man who brought Obookiah from Kealakekua to New York City, retired from the sea in 1821 following a voyage to Peru aboard the *Zephyr*. Brintnall is acclaimed as the most successful sea captain in the post-Revolutionary War era of New Haven's lucrative China Trade sealing ship voyages.

About a month following his return from Peru, widower Brintnall married his late wife's younger sister, Content Mix Bulkeley. The couple lived in a two-story white frame home in New Haven. Their house later became the third home of Mory's, the landmark New Haven tavern immortalized in the Yale glee club's *Whiffenpoof Song*.

Caleb and his family faced a tragedy in 1828 when his son Charles Brintnall, 26, died at sea during a return trading voyage from China. Charles was seven years old when Obookiah roomed in the family's New Haven home.

Caleb Brintnall became a prominent citizen in New Haven, serving as director of the Hartford branch of the United States Bank, and as a New Haven alderman. He died in 1850, in New Haven, and is buried alongside his wives, the Mix sisters of New Haven, in the Grove Street Cemetery.

Cornwall

Today the history of the Foreign Mission School is online thanks to the Cornwall Historical Society at www.cornwallhistoricalsociety.org/exhibits/foreign_mission_school.html. *Visions and Contradictions - The Foreign Mission School 1817-1826* was an exhibit presented by the Cornwall Historical Society in 2010. A virtual tour of the exhibit is online at the Society's Foreign Mission School webpage. The Obookiah gravesite is located about one-third mile from the Cornwall Historical Society, just outside the village in Cornwall, at 7 Pine Street, just off Route 4. Check the Society's web page for information on current exhibits and a list of Society publications. The village of Cornwall remains as picturesque as ever, more similar than changed from the days when Obookiah studied there.

Damon Family

Jeremiah Mills, Samuel Mills' brother who patiently tutored Obookiah at the Mills' family home in Torringford, sent off his daughter Julia Mills Damon (born in Torringford in 1817) on a mission to Honolulu. Julia departed in 1842 with her husband the Rev. Samuel Chenery Damon. The Damons shipped to Hawai'i the mahogany writing desk upon which Samuel Mills penned his many letters and reports. Samuel Damon used the desk of Julia's uncle for over forty years, writing, editing and publishing in Honolulu the Congregational church newspaper *The Friend*. Samuel Damon concurrently served as pastor of the Seamen's Bethel Church on the Honolulu waterfront. He reached out to the Chinese community in Honolulu and assisted in organizing in 1877 the first Chinese church in Hawai'i.

The Seamen's Bethel Church evolved into the Central Union Church. Frank Damon, the son of Samuel and Julia, great-nephew of Samuel Mills and great-grandson of Father Mills, was born in Honolulu in 1852. Frank became an activist in bettering conditions for Chinese sugar plantation workers. He helped to found in 1892 the Mills Institute for Boys, a boarding school for the sons of Chinese immigrant workers. Frank named the school in honor of Samuel Mills.

The Kawaiaha'o Seminary for Girls, and the Mills Institute, merged in 1908 to become Mid-Pacific Institute. The roots of the First Hawaiian Bank trace back to Samuel Mills Damon, also a son of Samuel and Julia, who purchased Bishop & Co., from its founder Charles Bishop.

William Dodge

William Dodge, the young boy who sold potatoes to support Obookiah's studies at the Foreign Mission School, co-founded the Phelps-Dodge corporation, one of America's largest mining companies. His tie to Obookiah continued in Hawai'i from afar with his support of Oahu College, now Punahou School. At his funeral, William was remembered for his generosity to many Christian causes including missions, as an early supporter of American Indian civil rights and the abolition of slavery. He joined in founding the Young Men's Christian Association.

A statue of the prominent New York City businessman stands today in Bryant Park in Manhattan. His wife, Melissa Phelps Dodge, remembered her husband's belief that his kind act in support of Obookiah was the seed for his tremendous success in business. In 1868 she donated the bell for the Kahikolu Church, which is today the home for Henry's gravesite. After the fall of the kapu system, large stones from the Hikiau Heiau were used in building the Kahikolu Church. In her youth Mrs. Dodge was a friend of Mary Paris, the wife of Kona-area missionary John D. Paris, who oversaw the building of the Kahikolu Church. *The Friend* newspaper reported the bell "was afterwards hung on a wooden tower, where it calls the people to prayer, from Ke'ei to Ka'awaloa. The tower itself is a landmark for thirty miles down the coast."

Edwin Welles Dwight

The family of Edwin Welles Dwight took great pride in his connection to Obookiah and the Brethren. Leaving the Foreign Mission School, Dwight was called to be pastor of the Congregational Church in Richmond, Massachusetts, a rural town located in the Berkshire Mountains about 40 miles north of Cornwall. Richmond is near Stockbridge, Massachusetts, the birthplace of Edwin. Lyman

Beecher preached his installation sermon. Edwin died in Stockbridge in 1841 at age 52. His papers, including letters written from Hawai'i to him by his Foreign Mission School students, are today located in the archives of the Norman Rockwell Museum in Stockbridge.

William Ellis

London Missionary Society Bible translator William Ellis assisted the Rev. Hiram Bingham in preparing the forty-six hymns printed in the first Hawaiian language hymnal. The original of some of the hymns can be found in the Tahitian hymnal brought to Hawai'i by Ellis.

A report in the March 1889 issue of *The Friend* tells the story of one of Ellis's hymns. *He Akua Hemolele (The Holy God)*, written in 1823, is one of the earliest, and most popular, sacred hymns written in the Hawaiian language. Kapiolani sang the hymn with her followers on the rim of Kīlauea Crater during their defiance of the volcano goddess Pele in 1824. Ellis is noted as the first foreigner to visit the Kīlauea volcano.

The words of *He Akua Hemolele* resonated back to Ellis on January 21, 1857. The English missionary was aboard a ship sailing in the Indian Ocean, on a voyage from the island of Mauritius to England. His ship came upon the shipwreck of the American whaler *Henry Crappo*. *The Friend* report continues: "Only two survivors were found, the Captain and a Sandwich Islander. They were nearly exhausted. Mr. Ellis addressed the native in his own language, but received no reply. He then repeated the first two lines of his own hymn. The man's countenance brightened, and when Mr. Ellis ceased speaking, he took up the strain, repeating the remaining lines of the verse. He also added the remaining verses of the hymn, with evident satisfaction. So did the bread cast upon the waters by the Lord's servant, return to him after many days."

Ralph Emerson

Ralph Emerson left his post as a tutor at Yale to serve as pastor of the Congregational Church in Norfolk, Connecticut, a village located fifteen miles northeast of Cornwall. Ralph ministered there beginning in 1816 during an era of revival and church growth within his congregation. In 1826 Emerson was called upon to join the committee tasked with closing down the Foreign Mission School.

In 1830 he became professor of Ecclesiastical History at the Theological Seminary at Andover. Ralph remained a life-long friend of his Yale roommate and fellow choir singer Sidney Morse, and Sidney's younger brother and Yale student Samuel F. B. Morse, the inventor of the telegraph.

Foreign Mission School

The Foreign Mission School succeeded in its inaugural goal of launching a mission to the Sandwich Islands. Students Thomas Hopu, William Kanui, George Prince Kaumuali'i, George Sandwich, and other young Hawaiian men sailed home to Hawai'i to assist the New England missionaries.

In 1826, racial problems erupted in Cornwall following the marriage of Harriet Gold of Cornwall to Buck Oo Waitie of the Cherokee tribe, a former Foreign Mission School student and Andover seminary scholar. Buck took on the name of Elias Boudinot in honor of the American Bible Society president who assisted him with funding his education. The marriage followed an earlier marriage of Cherokee student John Ridge to Sarah Northrup, the daughter of the Foreign Mission School steward. Elias and Harriet was burned in effigy in Cornwall.

In the autumn of 1826, the American Board of Commissioners announced the Foreign Mission School was closing, claiming this was due to a change in opinion on how best to educate mission candidates from non-western nations, as advised by the Rev. William Ellis of the London Missionary Society's Tahiti mission.

The American Board made a statement on the closing of the Foreign Mission School in its fiftieth anniversary volume. "By the year 1825, a considerable number of the youths educated at the Cornwall school had been returned, where there were missions, to their native lands, and the theories of the past were corrected by experience."

Paul H. Chamberlain, Jr. of the Cornwall Historical Society wrote in 1968, "It was a school dedicated to the teachings of Christ, but failed because these same teachings went ignored."

Foreign Mission School, Nantucket Island, Massachusetts
Left Behind at the Nantucket Foreign Mission School
(From the *Religious Intelligencer*, May 1822)

"This place has long been the resort of youth from pagan countries. Not many years since, there resided here twenty Society and Sandwich Islanders, who, on stated evenings when the sky was clear, assembled in the streets, erected the ensigns of idolatry, and in frantick orgies paid their worship to the host of heaven. No Barnabas nor Paul ran in among them, saying why do ye these things? a kind of school has recently been instituted into which 15 natives of Owhyhee and other islands of the Pacific, have been received. Of these, 7 are still here where are mostly between 14 and 17 years of age and generally remarkable for mildness of disposition, cleanliness of person, and symetry and activity of body. They are anxious to learn, but as yet, ignorant of the true God and eternal life, and more or less addicted to idolatry. One who had known Obookiah in Owhyhee and merely heard of his having obtained 'a good deal of learning' in this country, used to weep bitterly when here, because he could not read the good book. Others have discovered emotion at religious truth. Could one of the pious youth in Cornwall School be placed in our academy, he would enjoy the instruction of an able and devoted preceptor, late of the Theological Seminary in Andover, and perhaps render at his leisure as great service to his countrymen, as though he was stationed in Owhyhee. Many more will probably arrive and sojourn here during the current year. We lamented to hear of the lack of means for the support of a greater number at Cornwall, since it has frustrated our hopes of introducing a very promising candidate from Chili, and another from the Sandwich Islands. Such as might be given up by their master to receive an education, will if permitted to remain here, be sent to sea. Could they therefore be taken into the pious families of pious mechanics in the country, they might earn qualifications for future and extensive usefulness in connexion with some foreign mission."

Thomas Gallaudet

Thomas Gallaudet, the pioneer educator of deaf students in America, was honored in 1894 when Gallaudet College for the deaf and hard of hearing opened in Washington D.C. A statue of Gallaudet and Alice Cogswell, the deaf student he married, today stands at its entrance. Working with Laurent Clerc, a deaf French student who was the first sign language teacher in America, Gallaudet discovered a "natural language" of key signing phrases used by the deaf in America, in part with the help of Thomas Hopoo. Gallaudet and Clerc developed this "natural language," a first, foundational, step in creating the American Sign Language.

Hewahewa

Hewahewa, the high priest of the Kingdom of Hawai'i, later moved to the valley of the kāhuna at Waimea on the North Shore of O'ahu. Hewahewa attended the missionary church in the Hale'iwa section of Waialua, and is buried in a secluded grave in Waimea Valley. A visit by Hewahewa to the Waialua Mission is recalled in a journal entry for May 21, 1833, written by its *kahu*, the Rev. John S. Emerson: "He expressed his affection for us, his confidence in us as leaders, and the wish to unite himself with the people of God and spend the remainder of his days in His service. To see an aged man, who had spent his youth in the service of the Prince of Darkness, wishing now in his last years to learn of his newly-discovered Saviour, is touching beyond words." Among the descendants of Hewahewa is the late Eddie Aikau, the legendary North Shore of O'ahu big wave surfer and lifeguard.

Honolulu Harbor - location of Kou

The entire shoreline of Honolulu Harbor-Kou in the days when Captain Caleb Brintnall anchored in the harbor is now developed, and man-made. The fort built by Kamehameha at Kou partly lies under the foot of Fort Street.

Hopu - Thomas Hopoo

Thomas Hopu, returning to Hawai'i aboard the *Thaddeus*, served as a key translator and assistant to the missionaries and the ali'i nui. Thomas translated the *Memoirs of Henry Obookiah* into Hawaiian in retelling the account in the early 1820s while teaching the *palapala* during the first years of the Sandwich Islands Mission in Hawai'i. He read the book out loud, chapter by chapter, using a copy brought aboard the ship. On Sabbath morning, August 11, 1822, Hopu married Delia, "doubtless, the first Christian marriage ever celebrated in these Islands." Hiram Bingham led the marriage ceremony held at the close of a Sunday service attended by Liholiho, Kamehameha II and foreign residents of the growing city. In a practice instituted by the London Missionary Society in Tahiti, the native Hawaiian couple signed their names in a record book to record and solemnize their marriage. Hopu joyfully reunited with his father soon after his return home to Hawai'i.

Thirty years later, the Rev. Henry Cheever wrote of Hopu, whom he met in Maui in the early 1850s: "This same Thomas Hopu is now bronzed and wrinkled beyond his years, and his lamp of life must soon go out. Though his conduct as a Christian since his return is said to have been by no means always exemplary, nor his influence upon his countrymen what was to have been looked for from his advantages, we must lean to the side of charity in our judgements both of him and his fellows." Where Hopu is buried is uncertain. His grave may be in Wailuku, Maui, near the historic Bailey Mission House.

Isla Guadalupe

Isla Guadalupe became a nature conservancy area in 1928, one of the first established by Mexican government. Thousands of goats were rounded up and evacuated. The goats were first brought to the island as a food stock in the early nineteenth-century by Russian whalers and sealers. The animals denuded rare species of plants and birds native to the island. The loss of high forests, which collected fog, ruined the main water supply. Northern elephant seal and Guadalupe fur seal populations are returning. Divers consider Isla Guadalupe a prime island for observing the great white shark, which are attracted to the island due to its abundant population of seals and other marine mammals.

James Hunnewell

James Hunnewell and Andrew Blanchard sailed to the Northwest Coast aboard the *Thaddeus* in 1820. Hunnewell, under the employ of Boston firm Bryant & Sturgis, remained in Honolulu after the ship was sold, attempting to recoup sandalwood payments owed the firm. On January 7, 1822 he struck off the third impression made on the missionary press brought aboard the *Thaddeus*.

In 1826 Hunnewell sailed the vessel *Missionary Packet* from Salem, Massachusetts, around the Horn to deliver the small sail boat to the Sandwich Islands Mission, a voyage of over nine months. He remained in Honolulu until 1830, establishing the firm that became C. Brewer & Co. He arrived home in Charlestown, Massachusetts and lived there the remainder of his life. He continued to be a philanthropist for Christian causes in Hawai'i, sending donations on numerous occasions.

Ka'ahumanu

Queen Ka'ahumanu professed her conversion to Christianity in 1824, about five years after she led in the 'Ai Noa, free-eating, that overthrew the kapu system. As kuhina nui (coruler) of Hawai'i, she introduced laws based on the Ten Commandments and other biblical scriptures. She was baptized in December, 1825 in Honolulu, taking the Old Testament name Elisabeta (Elizabeth). She openly encouraged her people to follow the way of the Christian God. In 1832 the Rev. Hiram Bingham presented her a red morocco leather-bound copy of one of the first copies from the Mission Press of the Hawaiian language version of the New Testament. She died on June 5, 1832 in Manoa Valley. Just before her passing she uttered a Hawaiian hymn: "Now will I go to Jesus, My Lord who pitied me, And at his feet lie prostrate, For there I cannot die...." Hiram Bingham presided at her funeral held at the Kawaiaha'o Church.

Mark Twain

Author Samuel Clemens returned to San Francisco from Hawai'i in 1866. There as Mark Twain, Clemens took to the stage and delivered to much acclaim a talk he titled *Our Fellow Savages of the Sandwich Islands*; some literary critics see the talk as the launch of his career as a speaker and author. Late in Clemens' career, the American humorist wrote his time-travel novel *A Connecticut Yankee in King Arthur's*

Court. The setting of the novel in sixth-century Britain is a veneer overlaying a tale by Twain about Hawai'i, according to literary critic Fred W. Lorch of Iowa State College. Lorch is convinced that the foundation of Twain's critique of feudal society came from his observations of life in Hawai'i. Twain wrote the first chapters of a novel about Hawai'i in the winter and spring of 1883-1884 "...immediately prior to the time he came upon Malory's Morte d' Arthur." Lorch sees Twain's version of Malory's wizard Merlin as a character based on a kahuna, King Arthur upon a composite of Hawaiian kings, and the feudal society of Britain a slice of rural Hawaiian life overlaid with the Union Jack.

Park Street Church

The Park Street Church in Boston remains an active Conservative Congregational Church with a congregation of two-thousand. The historic, landmark church is located on Brimstone Corner near the Boston Commons. Park Street Church has retained it ties to Hawai'i over the years.

Tahiti

In 1820, the church of Auna and Aunawahine on Huahine erected a sanctuary one-hundred feet long and sixty-feet wide. Lime made from burning blocks of coral was used to plaster walls. Chandeliers were hung with coconut shells for oil lamps. In the late 1830s a whaling ship captain commented that Tahiti was the most civilized place in the South Seas, with good laws, no liquor allowed to be brought ashore, and a Sunday service where the queen of Tahiti sat at the front of the church with thousands of her subjects around her. In the 1840s the French government took control of Tahiti, abolishing the missionary-inspired laws and allowing the importation of liquor, closing the Protestant mission schools. The London Missionary Society withdrew from the Society Islands, but the Protestant churches held fast with a strong core of members. In the 1890s sixteen Protestant churches remained open on the island of Tahiti.

Brig Thaddeus

In May, 1820 Captain Blanchard and First Officer James Hunnewell sailed the *Thaddeus* to the Northwest Coast, where they anchored off the Russian American Company's headquarters at Sitka, Alaska and dined with Governor Alexander Baranov.

At Sitka, the ship's officers were approached by a coastal Indian tribe who had, "... heard of missionaries being sent to teach the Sandwich Islanders, inquired why were not sent to them. When they were told...perhaps that they had nothing for missionaries to eat, they replied–'We would give them such as we have.'"

The *Thaddeus* officers sailed Northwest Indians to the Sandwich Islands to free them from tribal slavery. The *Thaddeus* was sold by its Captain Andrew Blanchard, representing the fur trade and shipping company Bryant & Sturgis of Boston, in October 1820 to an ali'i nui who pledged to pay 4,000 piculs of sandalwood. Blanchard sailed on another ship for China and left James Hunnewell in Honolulu to collect the debt in sandalwood. A cargo of sandalwood was later shipped aboard the *Thaddeus* to Canton. In 1821, a shipboard fire at dockside in the Pearl River burnt the *Thaddeus* beyond repair. Registration papers from the ship were turned into the American Consulate at Canton. By autumn 1822, only 1,700 piculs of the *Thaddeus* debt had been paid.

GLOSSARY OF HAWAIIAN WORDS

AHUPUAʻA - island district land division that stretched from the sea up into the mountains; almost all resources needed for life were found within; overseen by a konokiki.

ʻĀINA - land

AKUA, AKUA - a word used both as a name for a Supreme Being (Akua), and (akua) for a god, goddess, spirit, ghost.

ALIʻI - member of the nobility, the chiefly class.

ALIʻI AKUA - highest ranking aliʻi, usually born of piʻo relationship, straightforward tranlation is "god-king."

ALIʻI NUI - highest-ranking chiefs and chiefesses.

ALOHA - love, affection.

ALOHA KE AKUA - God is love.

ʻANĀʻANĀ - practice of sorcery performed by kahuna including praying a victim to death.

ʻAUMAKUA - protective ancestorial god in non-human form, e.g. shark, sea turtle.

BAIBALA - Bible.

HALA - pandanus tree (*Pandanus tectorius*); leaves (lau hala) used to weave mats, sails, baskets.

HĀLAU - a long house used to shelter canoes; a shelter for hula instruction.

HALE - a house, a building.

HĀNAI - adoption of a child, giving of a child to another.

HAOLE - originally a foreigner, more commonly a white person.

HEIAU - a pre-Christian Hawaiian temple used in the pre-overthrow of the kapu days. Construction of a heiau ranged from complex structures built of lava rocks, to a simple rock platform with raised stones to mark ancesteral gods. A luakini heiau was a temple used by aliʻi to pray and for human sacrifices. also referred to as a poʻokanaka (skull) heiau.

HEMOLELE - holy, as in Baibala Hemolele (*Holy Bible*).

HOLOHOLO - wandering for fun. walking, going out for a sail.

HOʻOKUPU - ceremony of giving gifts to aliʻi, literally means to sprout.

HONI - touching of noses, sharing of breath of life, traditional greeting.

HULA - traditional dance.

KAHIKI - specifically, Tahiti, generally, any foreign place.

KAHU - a minister, a guardian, or keeper.

KAHUNA - a priest who served at a heiau, kahuna were also masters of skills like canoe building (kahuna waʻa). Plural form is kāhuna.

KAHUNA NUI - a high priest, especially of Kū priesthood, served a heiau for ruler.

KAHUNA PULE - a praying kahuna, a kahuna who led heiau ceremonies.

KĀLAIMOKU - advisor to king, in early nineteenth-century similar to a prime minister.

KALO - the taro plant (*Colocasia esculenta*).

KAMAʻĀINA - lit. "a child of the land," one who is tied to land through long-term relationship to certain place.

KANAKA MAOLI - a native of Hawaiʻi.

KAPA - bark of a softwood wauke tree (paper mulberry) pounded into cloth.

KAPU - laws dictated by ali'i that prohibited use of a forbidden thing, denied access to a place, dictated a behavior, declared an object or person as sacred.

KĀULA - prophet, kahuna who could read oracles and provide a prophecy.

KAUWĀ also KAUĀ - the lowest class in society, an outcast, the slave class, an untouchable, offered as human sacrifices.

KOA - warrior; treasured hardwood tree (Acacia koa).

KŌLEA - the Golden Plover migratory bird.

KONOHIKI - representative of ali'i konohiki who managed ahupua'a.

KŪ - god of war, one of four main gods of Hawai'i.

KŪKĀ'ILIMOKU - the manifestation of Kū who served as war god of Kamehameha.

KULA - dryland without irrigation, often used for cultivation 'ulua, the sweet potato.

KULEANA - a homesite; ones responsability.

KUPUNA - elder; an ancestor. Plural is kūpuna.

LAKA - the god of the hula.

LAU HALA - leaf of the Pandanus tree, used for weaving mats and other objects.

LO'I - irrigated kalo (taro) patch.

LOKO KUAPA - rock-walled fishpond built upon coastal reef.

LONO - one of four gods in Hawai'i said to have been brought from Tahiti, the god of the harvest, clouds, rain.

MAIKA'I - good.

MAKA - eyes.

MAKA'ĀINA'NA - the commoners.

MAKAI - towards the ocean.

MALO - garment worn as a loincloth by men.

MANA - divine power manifested in a person, object. to hold power.

MAUKA - towards the moutains, inland.

MENEHUNE - legendary people of small stature, builders at night of fishponds, heiau.

MOKU - an island.

MO'OLELO- telling of a history, a story, a tradition.

NŪPEPA - Hawaiian newspaper.

'OHANA - family, both blood relatives and an extended family, a group of close friends

'OPIHI - limpets found on coastal rocks.

PĀ'Ū - a skirt made of kapa cloth in ancient Hawai'i.

PALAPALA - in days of missionaries the sciptures of the Bible and learning, more commonly various types of written documents, a letter, a manuscript.

PI'O - marriage between brother-sister, or half-siblings, limited to marriges of highest-ranking ali'i.

PŌHAKU - rock or stone.

POI - the basic food of the Hawaiians, a pasty food made by pounding kalo (taro) corms and adding water.

PONO - righteous, good, done correctly.

PU'UHONUA - a place of refuge, lives spared within of kapu breakers or warriors defeated in battle.

PUNAHELE - a favorite, a favored child.

'UHANE - soul, spirt.

WAHINE - a woman.

ACKNOWLEDGMENTS

I am humbled by the fine work others have accomplished in bringing to light the life of 'Ōpūkaha'ia-Henry Obookiah. The Rev. Edwin Welles Dwight of Richmond and Stockbridge, Massachusetts was for Henry a mentor and teacher, close friend and memorialist. Deborah Li'ikapeka Lee and her family from the Haili Church in Hilo brought Henry's heritage into national prominence in 1993 with their efforts in returning his remains to Hawai'i, to a stately gravesite on the grounds of the Ka-hikolu Church in Napo'opo'o overlooking Kealakekua Bay. Accompanying the Lee 'ohana was Aletha Kaohi of Waimea, Kaua'i who has been a valuable guide to me as a reader, scholar and kupuna in the editing of this book. The Rev. Edith Wolfe, along with author and missionary descendant Albertine Loomis, brought the Memoirs of Henry Obookiah back into the mainstream of Hawaiian literature through an updated and edited version of the book the United Church of Christ in Hawai'i first published in 1968. I was fortunate in paying a visit to Ms. Loomis late in her life, her book Grapes of Canaan is an excellent fictionalize account of the early years of the Sandwich Islands Mission.

Two branches of the family of Captain Caleb Brintnall provided essential materials and kind support in my research: Peter Brintnall Cooper in New Haven, and James Dodds in Stockton, California. Peter Cooper graciously provided input on the China trade, and invited me into his home to view an incredible set of oil paintings brought home from China by Caleb Britnall. Sadly Jim Dodds passed away during the writing of this book. Jim was the most valiant writer I have ever met, overcoming a debilitating disease to daily write his quota for his well-written historical novels. Thanks also to his son Tony Dodds.

The Rev. S. W. Papaula in the mid-1860s translated the Memoirs into the Hawaiian language, in a book published in New York he titled Ka moolelo o Heneri Opukahaia; in doing so, the Rev. Papaula began the task of fleshing out the sometimes vague details found in the Memoirs of Henry Obookiah. Charles Kenn, master of the Hawaiian martial art known as lua, translated back into English the work of the Rev. Papaula, and had planned to write his own biography of Henry. More recently Wayne Brumaghim presented "The Life and Legacy of Heneri 'Opukaha'ia Hawai'i's Prodigal Son" as his Master of Arts thesis in the Hawaiian Studies Department at the University of Hawai'i; his work in collecting the genealogy of 'Ōpūkaha'ia is notable. And in 2014 Yale professor emeritus John Demos released his long-anticipated book on the Cornwall Foreign Mission School, The Heathen School, which includes a chapter on the life of Obookiah.

Each of these contributors added to the rich legacy of 'Ōpūkaha'ia through their own worldview. I hope my contribution through The Providential Life of Henry Obookiah will stand with their works. My worldview comes from the evangelical Christian church in Hawai'i; through my own New England heritage dating back to the Pilgrims; through my own missions experiences in Southeast Asia; through living and working and writing in the multi-cultural society of Hawai'i over a span of forty-five years; and from the surfing subculture in Hawai'i.

The descendants of the Native Hawaiian people of Obookiah's time today avidly seek a reconnection to, and reconciliation with, their past. A renewing of their culture can be seen across Hawai'i, in many ways and forms. This renaissance gained momentum during my time studying at the University of Hawai'i in the early 1970s. In the ensuing decades I have been fortunate to observe closely this reawakening. This Native Hawaiian renewal came after over a century of being marginalized as a people, and is ongoing. While I tell the story of Obookiah and his life and times from my own viewpoint (that of a Christian haole named Cook) I hope this work serves as a positive contribution to this cause. Throughout the creation of *The Providential Life & Heritage of Henry Obookiah* I have aimed at reflecting the good in all I have learned and experienced during my life in Hawai'i.

Roxanne Olson, Yolanda Olson, and David Ross in Kailua-Kona for their years of support and exchanges of information, Ann Schillinger and the Cornwall Historical Society, Edwin Chesney of Bay Village, Ohio, for the account written by Edward Townsend Mix, Hollis Historical Society, Congregational Church of Hollis, Mary Requilman and Kaua'i Historical Society, Jane Gray and 'ohana at Kaua'i Museum, New Haven Colony Historical Society, Sally Holm - Phillips Academy at Andover, Bennett Hymer of Mutual Publishing, Forks Library, Aletha Kaohi - Director of the West Kaua'i Visitors Center and Stanley Lum, Barbara Dunn and John Clark - Hawaiian Historical Society, Congregational Library at Boston, Susan Remoaldo - Waimea Library, Carolyn Larsen - Lihu'e Library, Bob Kajiwara - Kaua'i Community College Library, Dolores Blalock for Hewahewa materials, Rosalie Hunt for Adoniram and Ann Judson materials, Torringford United Church of Christ. Special thanks to Rick Bundschuh of Kaua'i Christian Fellowship who has provided opportunities for me to develop this book in the public arena, to Danny Lehmann, Hawai'i Director of Youth With A Mission for his long-time support, and to Adam Boyd of Wycliffe Bible Translators who provided wise and timely advice sent from Papua New Guinea where he works with the Enga people.

My family: parents Lee and Sunny Cook who first brought me to Cornwall, Davy and Christine Cook, Christian Cook and Tamiko Hobbs, Kathi and Rich Collette, and Chiara. Don and Barbara Tofte who early on inspired me in the Lord and in Obookiah. Dan and Linda Moriarty, who many years ago challenged me to "find something new, unknown" to write about Hawaiian history. Deborah Li'ikapeka Lee and family, and the Ho'omanawanui family. Pastor Matt Higa, Pastor Davida de Carvalho, Edwin Nakakura, Captain Rick Rogers and Paul Johnston from Cleopatra's Barge project, Peter Mills, Carlos Andrade, Doug and Margaret Peebles, Bruce and Ellen Columbe and family, Douglas Warne, Julia Neal, Rita De Silva and all my friends from *The Garden Island* days, my 'Ohana-In-Laws Steve and Carol Alvezios, Dave Walker for my Captain Cook sail, Christine Fayé, David and Sue Boynton, Ruth and Jim Cassel Sr., Katie and Jim Cassel Jr., Tom Cassel, Uncle Mel and Rick Harding, Pastor Olaf Hoeckmann-Percival, Pastor Darryl and Liz Kua, Pat and Liz Thompson and congregation of Westside Christian Center, Ed and Cynthia Justus of Talk Story Bookstore in Hanapepe, John and Nanci Connors, Bette O'Grady, Bill and Kitty Sperry, Elaine Wright Colvin-Writers Info Network, Scott and Sandi Tompkins, David Cunningham, Daniel Kikawa, Leon Siu, Roxanne Olson, Yolanda Olson, Fay Williams, "Hallelujah" Bill and Karen White, Pastor Bob Schwartz, the Ray Family, Kevan and JoAnn

Scott - Hale'iwa days, Ed and Maria Minkel - Kawela Bay days, Yossi and Ku'ulei Johnson, Tom Wolforth, Pastors Mike Wellman and Dain Spore from Kaua'i Christian Fellowship, Kalaheo Missionary Church, Lihu'e Missionary Church, Kapa'a Missionary Church, Joe Victorino, Karen Mendoza, Joe Henriques and family, Brad Cowan, Pastor Rennie Mau, Leonard Mahoe, Pastor Larry and Charlene Gillis, Pastor Stephen and Trish Thompson, Larry and Lori Dill and the Smith-Waterhouse family especially Uncle Bob Watts and Peter Dease, Michel and Jody Junod, Tom and Cheri Hamilton and family, David "Tiki" McLaren, Tom Burroughs, James and Jean Goodall and family, Pastor Butch and Aunty Jo Kahawai, Samson and Auntie Bernie Mahuiki, Chipper and Hauoli Wichman and family, Sue Kanoho, Tani Bova, Mike and Sally Durham, Pastor Pat and Lora Henderson and the family at Solid Rock, Nunzio and Elaine Lagattuta, Pastor Jesse and Marge Layaoen, Charlie Ortal, Pastor Larry Read, Dane and Donna Kirkpatrick, Robert Purdue and family, Mark and Marilyn Mohler, Jim and Cyrila Pycha and family, Ralph Young, Barnes Riznik, the Haraguchi Family, Mike Fitzgerald, Nick Beck and family, Pastor Robb and Nora Finberg, John Wehrheim, Kaua'i mayors Tony Kunimura, JoAnn Yukimura, Maryann Kusaka, Bryan Baptiste and Bernard Carvalho, Pastor David Rees-Thomas, Rudy Valle and Island Breeze Ohana, Pastor Kealoha and Taimane Kaopua, Pastor Cal Chinen, Steve and Cheryl Farrell, Eileen Widner and friends at Congregational Church of Hollis, Phil Jacksonand the Adoniram and Ann Judson bi-centennial project, Pastor Larry Matsuwaki, Toby and Mike Neal, Herb and Ruth Bockleman who believed in me from the start of this project, Tim Dela Vega, Ken Binder and family - Woodbridge to Kaua'i, Keath and Maria Hacker and boys, George and Bunny Baldwin, Ken and Mindy Blackburn, Doug and Kim Blackburn, Pat and Janet Durkin, Paul Fuller, Steve Glass, Sue Ellen Riseau, Brown McClatchy Maloney, all my crew at the *Forks Forum*, Glynda Schaad and the Peterson Family of Forks and the Hoh, the Quileute Tribe especially Russell Woodruff, Jay and Yvette Cline, Francis Kyle, Molly Ericson and Peter Breed, Erwin "Tiny" and Pat Aanderud, hearty handshake to Ted Lauder & Payton and Zina Hough and family, Rusty and Cathy Weaver, Cecily Weaver Campbell, Leroy and Cindy Metzger, Mark and Dorien Nakatsukasa and family, Jerry and Karen Terui, Clayton and Shelly Sui and family, Rev. "Rocky" and Daly Sasaki, Kerry and Annie Crain, Pastor Bruce and Janet Baumgartner, Paul Staples, Ian and Coral Miles and family, Ramon Rashkover, Mark Stroh, John and Kaipo Walsh, Jim Carney and family, Rev. Vil and Grace Galiza, Rev. Tom and D'Lissa Iannucci, Dondi and Tai Ho, Pastor Bob and Becky Hallman, Patty Ewing, Myles Ludwig, Berlin and John "Creature" Sadler (boar), Norman and Susie Heitman and family, Duane and Sammy Albano, Emery Kauanui Sr., Mark Savage, Stephen and Deanna Shaw and family, Pastor Art Moreland, Gordon Gracey, Mike Harmon and Carol Young, Duane and Florence Miles, Alan Drinen and Dr. Martha McLeod, John Scarkino, Carla and Makana Rowan, Ed Ka'ahea, Scott Johnson.

SELECT BIBLIOGRAPHY

Books

Alexander, James McKinney. 1895. *The islands of the Pacific. From the old to the new.* New York: American tract society.

Alexander, W. D. 1899. *A brief history of the Hawaiian people.* New York: American Book Co.

Andover Theological Seminary, and John L. Taylor. 1859. *A memorial of the semi-centennial celebration of the founding of the theological seminary at Andover.* Andover [Mass.]: W. F. Draper.

Bakke, Robert O. 1993. *The concert of prayer: back to the future?* Minneapolis, MN: Evangelical Free Church of America.

Bardwell, Horatio. 1834. *Memoir of Rev. Gordon Hall, A.M.: one of the first missionaries of the Amer. Board of Comm. for For. Missions, at Bombay.* Andover: Flagg, Gould and Newman.

Beckwith, Martha. 1940. *Hawaiian mythology: Pub. for the Folklore Foundation of Vassar College.* New Haven: Yale Univ. Press.

Bingham, Hiram. 1847. *A residence of twenty-one years in the Sandwich Islands.* Hartford [Conn.]: H. Huntington.

Blake, William. *History of the Town of Hamden Connecticut, with an account of the Centennial Celebration, June 15th 1886.* New Haven: Price, Lee & Co. January 1888.

Bryan, E. H. 1941. American Polynesia: coral islands of the central Pacific. Honolulu, Hawaii: Tongg Pub. Co.

Busch, Briton Cooper. 1985. *The war against the seals: a history of the North American seal fishery.* Kingston [Ont.]: McGill-Queen's University Press.

Cahill, Emmett, Herbert Kawainui Kane, and Virginia Wageman. 1999. *The life and times of John Young: confidant and advisor to Kamehameha the Great.* Aiea, Hawai'i: Island Heritage Pub.

Chamberlain, Paul H. 1968. *The Foreign Mission School.* Cornwall, Conn: Cornwall Historical Society.

Cheever, Henry T. 1851. *The island world of the Pacific; being ... travel through the Sandwich or Hawaiian islands and other parts of Polynesia.* New York: Harper & Bros.

Clark, John R. K. 1985. *Beaches of the Big Island.* Honolulu: University of Hawaii Press.

Crossman, Carl L. 1972. *The China trade; export paintings, furniture, silver & other objects.* Princeton [N.J.]: Pyne Press.

Cuningham, Charles E. 1942. *Timothy Dwight, 1752-1817, a biography.* New York: The Macmillan Company.

Damon, Ethel M., and Mary Dorothea Rice Isenberg. 1931. *Koamalu; a story of pioneers on Kauai, and of what they built in that island garden.* Honolulu: Priv. Print. [Honolulu star-bulletin Press].

Daws, Gavan. 1968. *Shoal of time; a history of the Hawaiian Islands.* New York: Macmillan.

Day, A. Grove. 1977. *Books about Hawaii: fifty basic authors.* Honolulu: University Press of Hawaii.

Demos, John. 2014. *The Heathen School: a story of hope and betrayal in the age of the early Republic.* New York: Alfred A. Knopf.

Desha, Stephen, and Frances N. Frazier. 2000. *Kamehameha and his warrior Kekūhaupi'o.* Honolulu: Kamehameha Schools Press.

Dwight, E. W. 1819. *Memoirs of Henry Obookiah a native of Owhyhee and a member of the Foreign Mission School : who died at Cornwall, Conn., Feb. 17, 1818, aged 26 years.* New-Haven [Conn.]: Nathan Whiting, agent of the Foreign Mission School.

Dwight, E. W., and S. W. Papaula. 1867. *Ka moolelo o Heneri Opukahaia, ua hanauia ma Hawaii, M.H. 1787, a ua make ma Amerika, Feberuari 17, 1818: oia ka hua mua o Hawaii nei.* Nu Ioka [New York]: Paiia e ko Amerika Ahahui Teraka.

Dwight, E. W. 1968. *Memoirs of Henry Obookiah: a native of Owhyhee and a member of the Foreign Mission School, who died at Cornwall, Connecticut, February 17, 1818, aged 26 years.*

Honolulu: [Woman's Board of Missions for the Pacific Islands].

Edwards, B. B. 1842. *Memoirs of Rev. Elias Cornelius.* New-York: Saxton & Miles.

Elsbree, Oliver Wendell. 1928. *The rise of the missionary spirit in America, 1790-1815.* Williamsport, Pa: Williamsport Print. and binding Co.

Englizian, H. Crosby. 1968. *Brimstone Corner; Park Street Church, Boston.* Chicago: Moody Press.

Fanning, Edmund. 1838. *Voyages to the South seas, Indian and Pacific oceans, China Sea, Northwest coast, Feejee Islands, South Shetlands, &c. ... with an account of the new discoveries made in the southern hemisphere, between the years 1830-1837.* New York: W.H. Vermilye.

Forbes, David W. 1999. *Hawaiian national bibliography Vol. 1, Vol. 1.* Honolulu: University of Hawai'i Press.

Foster, John, and Abijah Wyman Thayer. 1824. *A sketch of the tour of General Lafayette, on his late visit to the United States, 1824.* Portland [Me.]: Printed at the Statesman office, by A.W. Thayer.

French, Thomas. 1961. *The missionary whaleship.* New York: Vantage Press.

Gabriel, Ralph Henry. 1941. *Elias Boudinot, Cherokee, & his America.* Norman: University of Oklahoma Press.

Garrett, John. 1982. *To live among the stars: Christian origins in Oceania.* Geneva: World Council of Churches.

Goodell, William, and E. D. G. Prime. 1876. *Forty years in the Turkish empire; or, Memoirs of Rev. William Goodell.* New York: R. Carter and Bros.

Handy, Edward Smith Craighill, and Mary Wiggin Pukui. 1972. *The polynesian family system in Kau, Hawaii.*[New ed.]. Rutland, Verm: C.E. Tuttle.

Hawaiian Mission Children's Society. 1969. *Missionary album; portraits and biographical sketches of the American Protestant missionaries to the Hawaiian Islands.*

Hewitt, John Haskell. 1914. *Williams College and foreign missions: biographical sketches of Williams College men who have rendered special service to the cause of foreign missions.* Boston: Pilgrim Press.

Hiney, Tom. 2000. *On the missionary trail: a journey through Polynesia, Asia, and Africa with the London Missionary Society.* New York: Atlantic Monthly Press.

Hunt, Rosalie Hall. 2005. *Bless God and take courage: the Judson history and legacy.* Valley Forge, Pa: Judson Press.

Jackson, Susan E. 1914. *Reminiscences of Andover.* Andover, Mass: Andover Press.

Jarves, James Jackson. 1843. *History of the Hawaiian or Sandwich Islands.* Boston: Tappan and Dennet.

Joesting, Edward. 1984. *Kauai: The Separate Kingdom.* Honolulu, Hawaii: University of Hawaii Press.

Kamakau, Samuel Manaiakalani, and Samuel Manaiakalani Kamakau. 1992. *Ruling chiefs of Hawaii.* Honolulu: Kamehameha Schools Press.

Kaohi, Aletha. 2008. *Celebrating advocacy: past, present & future.* Honolulu, Hawaii: State Council of Hawaiian Congregational Churches.

Keller, Charles Roy. 1942. *The second great awakening in Connecticut.* New Haven: Yale University Press.

Kirch, Patrick Vinton. 2012. *A shark going inland is my chief the island civilization of ancient Hawai'i.* Berkeley: University of California Press.

Kienast, Evabeth Miller, and John Phillip Felt. 2009. *Lewis Coolidge and the voyage of the Amethyst, 1806-1811.* Columbia, S.C.: University of South Carolina Press.

Kikawa, Daniel, Leon Siu, and Tomas Watene Rosser. 1994. *Perpetuated in righteousness: the journey of the Hawaiian people from Eden (Kalana i Hauola) to present times.* [Hawaii]: D. Kikawa.

Kling, David William. 1993. *A field of divine wonders: the New Divinity and village revivals in northwestern Connecticut, 1792-1822*. University Park, Pa: Pennsylvania State University Press.

Kuykendall, Ralph S. 1968. *The Hawaiian kingdom*. Vol. 1. Honolulu: Univ. of Hawaii Pr.

Little, Henry Gilman. 1894. *Hollis, seventy years ago: personal recollections*. Grinnell, Iowa: Ray & MacDonald.

Marsden, George M. 2003. *Jonathan Edwards: a life*. New Haven: Yale University Press.

Marshall, Peter, and David Manuel. 1977. *The Light and the Glory*. Old Tappan, N.J.: Revell.

Mizrachi, Eli. 1995. *Two Americans withing the gates: the story of Levi Parsons and Pliny Fisk in Jerusalem*. Hagerstown, MD: McDougal Pub. Co.

Montgomery, James. 1832. *Journal of voyages and travels by the D. Tyerman and G. Bennet*.

Morris, James, and Robert Clark Morris. 1933. *Memoirs of James Morris of South Farms in Litchfield*. [New Haven]: Printed by the Yale university press for the Aline Brothier Morris fund.

Murray, A. W. 1888. *The Bible in the Pacific*. London: James Nisbet & Co.

Nolen, Barbara. 1976. *The Morris Academy: pioneer in coeducation*. S.l: 1976.

Obookiah, Henry, and E. W. Dwight. 1990. *Memoirs of Henry Obookiah: a native of Owhyhee and a member of the Foreign Mission School, who died at Cornwall, Connecticut, February 17, 1818, aged 26 years*. Honolulu, Hawai'i: Woman's Board of Missions for the Pacific Islands.

Orcutt, Samuel. 1878. *History of Torrington, Connecticut from its first settlement in 1737, with biographies and genealogies*. Albany: J. Munsell.

Osterweis, Rollin G. 1953. *Three centuries of New Haven, 1638-1938*. New Haven: Yale University Press.

Phipps, William E. 2003. *Mark Twain's Religion*. Macon GA: Mercer University Press.

Piercy, LaRue W. 1992. *Hawaii's missionary saga: sacrifice and godliness in paradise*. Honolulu: Mutual Pub.

Pukui, Mary Kawena, and Samuel H. Elbert. 1986. *Hawaiian dictionary: Hawaiian-English, English-Hawaiian*. Honolulu: University of Hawaii Press.

Pukui, Mary Kawena, E. W. Haertig, and Catherine A. Lee. 1972. *Nānā i ke kumu = Look to the source*. Honolulu: Hui Hanai.

Richards, Thomas C. 1906. *Samuel J. Mills, missionary pathfinder, pioneer and promoter*. Boston: The Pilgrim Press.

Richardson, Don. 1984. *Eternity in their hearts*. Ventura, CA: Regal Books.

Robbins, Sarah Stuart. 1908. *Old Andover days memories of a Puritan childhood*. Boston: Pilgrim Press.

Robinson, Keith. 2011. *Approach to Armageddon: one Christian's speculation about the end of the age*. Merrimac, Mass: Destiny Publishers.

Rosell, Garth. 2009. *Boston's historic Park Street Church: the story of an Evangelical landmark*. Grand Rapids, MI: Kregel Publications.

Silverman, Jane L. 1987. *Kaahumanu: molder of change*. Honolulu, Hawaii: Friends of the Judiciary History Center of Hawaii.

Spring, Gardiner. 1820. *Memoirs of The Rev. Samuel J. Mills, late missionary to the South Western Section of the United States and agent of the American Colonization Society, deputes to exlore the coast of Africa*. New-York: New-York evangelical missionary society, J. Seymour, printer.

Starr, Edward C. 1926. *A history of Cornwall, Connecticut, a typical New England town*. New Haven, Conn: Tuttle, Morehouse & Taylor.

Stokes, John F. G., and Tom Dye. 1991. *Heiau of the Island of Hawai'i: a historic survey of native Hawaiian temple sites*. Honolulu: Bishop Museum Press.

Thurston, Lucy Goodale. 1882. *Life and times of Mrs. Lucy G. Thurston, wife of Rev. Asa Thurston, pioneer missionary to the Sandwich Islands*. Ann Arbor, Mich: S.C. Andrews.Thurston,

Tracy, Joseph. 1842. *History of the American Board of Commissioners for Foreign Missions*. New York: Dodd.

Turner, Paul Venable. 2000. *Academy Hill: the Andover campus, 1778 to the present*. New York: Princeton Architectual Press.

Warne, Douglas, and Holly Kilinahe Coleman. 2008. *Humehume of Kauaʻi: a boy's journey to America, an aliʻiʻs return home*. Honolulu: Kamehameha Pub.

Withington, Antoinette. 1953. *The golden cloak; an informal history of Hawaiian royalty and of the development of the government during each reign under steadily increasing foreign influence*. Honolulu: Honolulu Star-Bulletin.

Wolfe, Edith. 1975. *The voyage of the brig Thaddeus from Boston to Hawaii 1819-1820*. Honolulu: Mission Press.

Wood, Gillen D'Arcy. 2013. *Tambora: the eruption that changed the world*. Princeton : Princeton University Press.

Articles, Monographs, Letters and Other Papers

American Board of Commissioners for Foreign Missions. 1816. *A Narrative of Five Youth from the Sandwich Islands, now receiving an education in this country*. New-York: Printed by J. Seymour.

Barrere, Dorothy and Marshall Sahlins. "*Tahitians in the early history of Hawaiian Christianity: the journal of Toketa*". 1979 Hawaiian Journal of History Vol. 13, Hawaiian Historical Society [Honolulu]

Brumaghim, Wayne H. *The Life and Legacy of Heneri ʻOpukahaʻia Hawaiʻiʻs Prodigal Son*. Honolulu: Master of Arts in Hawaiian Studies Thesis. December 2011.

"*Capt. Mix Dead - An able navigator of Sixty Years Ago*," June 7, 1882, New Haven Evening Register.

Christian history & biography: Spring 2006, Issue 90. 2006. Carol Stream, IL: Christianity Today International.

Cook, Chris. "*In search of Hawaiian lore in New England*". Lihuʻe, Kauaʻi: October 8, 1985, The Garden Island newspaper.

Damon, Ethel "*Ka Palapala Hemolele*". The Friend. Honolulu: May, 1939.

Damon, Samuel. "*The Last of the Cornwall Scholars*". The sailor's magazine.December 1863 Vol. 36 No. 4 New York: American Seamen's Friend Society.

Dwight, Timothy. 1811. *A statistical account of the city of New-Haven*. New-Haven: Printed and sold by Walter and Steele.

Dwight, Timothy. 1808. *Sermon preached at the opening of the Theological Institution in Andover and at the ordination of Rev. Eliphalet Pearson, L.L.D., September 28th, 1807*. Boston: Farrand, Mallory and Co.

Gallaudet, Thomas, "*The Language of Signs*". The Family magazine, or monthly abstract of general knowledge. 1835. New York: [Redfield & Lindsay].

Harvey, Joseph. 1815. *A sermon preached at Litchfield before the Foreign Mission Society of Litchfield County at their annual meeting February 15, 1815*. New-Haven [Conn.]: Hudson & Woodward, printers.

Hill, Mabel "*Bradford Academy: A Jubilee Sketch*". The New England magazine New Series, Volume 28. 1903. Boston: [New England Magazine Co.]

Hopoo, Thomas. *Memoirs of Thomas Hopoo*. Collection of Andover-Newton Theological Seminary. n.d.

Hunnewell, James Frothingham, William Tufts Brigham, and Sanford B. Dole. 1962. *Bibliography of the Hawaiian Islands*. New York: Kraus Reprint Corp.

Kenn, Charles W. *The History of Henry Opukahaia*. Honolulu: Paradise of the Pacific magazine. August 1942-January 1943 (except December 1942).

Lee, Rev. Chauncey. "*Letter from the Rev. C. Lee*" and "*Letter From Henry Obookiah, A Native of Owhyee To A Friend in Middlebury*". The Adviser or Vermont Evangelical Magazine, No. 11 November, 1814, Vol. VI.

Loomis, Albertine G. 1980. *By Faith*: Kawaiaha'o's Ali'i Founders. Honolulu: Offset Printing House.

Loomis, Elisha. 1937. *The journal of E. Loomis.*

"Mills and Obookiah at Andover". Good things selected from the Congregationalist and Boston Recorder, 1868-1870. 1870. Boston: W.L. Greene & Co.

Moore, William H. 1870. *Torringford: in connection with the centennial of the settlement of the first pastor, Rev. Samuel J. Mills.* Hartford: Case, Lockwood & Brainard.

Obookiah, Henry, and James Rumford. 1993. *A short elementary grammar of the Owhihe language.* Honolulu: Manoa Press.

"On Educating Heathen Youth in our Own Country". Missionary Herald July1816

Orr, J. Edwin. 1981. *The Re-Study of Revival and Revivalism* [Pasadena]: School of World Mission.

Phillips, Clifton Jackson. 1969. *Protestant America and The Pagan World: theFirst Half Century of the American Board of Commissioners for Foreign Missions, 1810-1860.* [Cambridge, Mass.]: East Asian Research Center, Harvard University; distributed by Harvard University Press.

Restarick, Henry B. *"Historic Kealakekua Bay".* 1928. Papers of the Hawaiian Historical Society. Number 15. [Honolulu]: Printed by Honolulu Star-Bulletin.

Spoehr, Anne Harding. *"George Prince Tamoree: Heir Apparent of Kauai and Niihau".* 1981 Hawaiian Journal of History Vol. 15, Hawaiian Historical Society [Honolulu]

Taylor, Clarice. Honolulu: *"Tales About Hawaii - Opu-ka-hai-a, Hawaii's Pioneer Linguist".* 22 part series, February 17-March 13, 1954. Honolulu Star-Bulletin.

Trowbridge, Thomas Rutherford. 1882. *History of the ancient maritime interests of New Haven.* New Haven: Tuttle, Morehouse & Taylor.

Periodicals

Damon, Samuel Chenery, and Sereno Edwards Bishop. 1845. *Friend.* Honolulu, Oahu, H.I.: S.C. Damon.

Panoplist, or The Christian's Armory Boston, 1806-1817

Missionary Herald, 1818-1824

The Religious Intelligencer. 1816-1827. New-Haven: [Published by Nathan Whiting].

Boston Recorder. 1817. Boston: [N. Willis. 1817-1824].

The Connecticut Magazine. 1899-1908. Hartford, Conn: [s.n.].

Web Sites

www.obookiah.com - Ongoing presentation and discussion of life and legacy of Henry Obookiah-Ōpūkaha'ia. Text version of first edition of Memoirs of Obookiah.

www.totakeresponsibility.blogspot.com - Ongoing presentation of notable events, places, persons from Hawai'i's history.

www.baibala.org - The Bible in the Hawaiian language. Searchable PDF from 1839 and 1868 editions.

www.hawaiianhistory.org - The Hawaiian Historical Society, specializes in nineteenth-century history of Hawai'i.

www.kauaihistoricalsociety.org - The Kaua'i Historical Society, many resources on history of Kaua'i.

www.facebook.com/chriscookauthor - Facebook page of author Christopher L. Cook.

Sources

A detailed overview of sources used in writing *The Providential Life of Henry Obookiah* is being posted as a series of articles at www.obookiah.com.

INDEX

Illustrations are in italics, SIM - Sandwich Islands Mission,
ABCFM - American Board of Commissioners for Foreign Missions

Special Pricing

SPECIAL PRICING is available for bulk orders of *The Providential Life & Heritage of Henry Obookiah*. Please contact author Christopher Cook - obookiah@gmail.com. Go to obookiah.com for more details.

Please Review

PLEASE ADD YOUR OWN REVIEW of *The Providential Life & Heritage of Henry Obookiah* on the book's page on Amazon.com and other websites. Commentors are invited. If you have a comment about this book, an account of Henry and his impact on your life, an anecdote to share, and especially a new detail from his life and times, please pay a visit and join the discussion. Go to www.obookiah.com to discuss this book with the author and other readers.

email updates

PLEASE SEND AN EMAIL TO obookiah@gmail.com to receive updates on *The Providential Life & Heritage of Henry Obookiah* and postings at obookiah.com.

Made in the USA
Las Vegas, NV
03 January 2022

39836744R10125